"The one thing that doesn't abide by majority rule is a person's conscience."

—spoken by Atticus Finch in Harper Lee's *To Kill a Mockingbird*

In memory of Judge Howard M. Holtzmann (1921–2013)

who, like Atticus Finch, was an honorable man.

Acknowledgments

Primary Writer: Daniel Sigward

Facing History and Ourselves is profoundly grateful to Jill Garling and Tom Wilson for their outstanding support, which will ensure that teachers, students, and communities globally may access this resource. Thanks to Jill and Tom's leadership, generations of readers will be encouraged to use this resource to draw the connection between the choices made by the characters in Harper Lee's classic novel and the moral and ethical choices each of us confronts throughout our lives.

Facing History also extends special gratitude to the Holtzmann/Richardson family for their generous support.

Developing this guide was a collaborative effort that required the expertise of numerous people, and many Facing History and Ourselves staff members made invaluable contributions. The guide would not be possible without the guidance of Adam Strom from start to finish. Laura Tavares played a critical role as a thought partner with Dan Sigward and reviewer of his early drafts. Margot Stern Strom, Marc Skvirsky, Marty Sleeper, and Dimitry Anselme were a thoughtful and supportive editorial team. Karen Barss, Denise Gelb, Michele Phillips, Steven Becton, Jocelyn Stanton, Stephanie Richardson, and Lisa Lefstein-Berusch also provided critical suggestions and feedback throughout the guide's development. Catherine O'Keefe, supported by Ariel Perry, Andrew Phillips, and additional editorial and design consultants, attended to many details that transformed the manuscript into this beautifully polished publication. Alexia Prichard, Wilkie Cook, and Liz Kelleher also require acknowledgment, as they developed the website and companion videos. Brooke Harvey, Anika Bachhuber, Lara Saavedra, and Samantha Landry also helped move the writing and production processes forward in countless ways. The project would not have been possible without the work of Lori Rogers-Stokes, Cyrisse Jaffee, and Rhonda Berkower, who drafted early versions of the guide. Many thanks to Facing History's communications and external affairs team for creating and implementing the outreach plan about this important initiative.

Table of Contents

Introduction

What Did You Learn in School Today?

Margot Stern Strom, Executive Director, Facing History and Ourselves

To Kill a Mockingbird is set in a small town in Alabama in the 1930s, a town much like the one in which author Harper Lee came of age. Although I grew up a generation later, I see much of myself in Scout, the young white girl who narrates the book. Like Alabama in the 1930s, Tennessee in the 1950s was a place where separate never meant equal. It was a place where "colored" water fountains did not spout brightly colored water as a child might expect, but stood as symbols of the dogmas of racism, which meant indignity, shame, and humiliation for some and indifference, false pride, and hate for others.

At school my teachers carefully avoided any mention of race, class, or gender. Like Scout, I learned those lessons from my family. When Scout comes to her father with questions about human behavior, he doesn't give her advice on what to say or do. Instead, he tells her that the "trick" to understanding another person is to consider things from his or her point of view. For nearly 40 years that has been the work of Facing History and Ourselves. We trust students to wrestle with complex choices in the past and present so that they will better understand the social mores of our time. We encourage them to think critically and independently in much the way that Atticus, Scout's father, engages his children.

Like my teachers, Scout's teacher misses an opportunity to trust her students with the complexities of history and human behavior. In one lesson, a child, Cecil, shares his current event: the fact that "old Adolf Hitler has been prosecutin' the Jews." Miss Gates stops him to correct his choice of words; it is "persecuting," not "prosecuting." Cecil shrugs off the correction and describes how Hitler's "puttin' 'em in prisons and he's taking away all their property and he won't let any of 'em out of the country."

Another child asks how Hitler can just lock up people without the government stopping him. Miss Gates replies, "Hitler is the government." And then, "seizing an opportunity to make education dynamic," she prints "DEMOCRACY" in large letters on the chalkboard and asks for a definition. Scout responds by reciting an old campaign slogan she learned from her father: "Equal rights for all, special privileges for none." Miss Gates smiles her approval and prints "WE ARE A" in front of the word "DEMOCRACY" on the chalkboard. She then tells the class that this is the difference between America and Germany: "We are a democracy and Germany is a dictatorship." She goes on to say, "Over here we don't believe in persecuting anybody. Persecution comes from people who are prejudiced." And she enunciates the word: *Pre-ju-dice*.

When a student asks why the Germans don't like Jews, Miss Gates says she doesn't know the answer but perhaps it's because they are a "deeply religious people" and "Hitler's trying to do away with religion." At this point, Cecil offers another explanation. He tells Miss Gates he doesn't know for certain, but the Jews are "supposed to change money or somethin', but that ain't no cause to persecute 'em. They're white, ain't they?"

Miss Gates responds by shutting down the discussion. Surely she knows, as most people did at the time, that Hitler was persecuting Jews because he claimed they belonged to an evil and inferior race; but race is a forbidden subject in a community where Jim Crow is part of the fabric of society. So Miss Gates decides to ignore Cecil's question and move on: "Time for arithmetic, children."

Scout spends the rest of the period looking out the window, convinced that school is irrelevant. It doesn't help her reckon with the prejudices that inflame the community during the trial of Tom Robinson, an African American her father defends in court after Robinson is falsely accused of raping a white girl.

It is at home that Scout and her older brother, Jem, begin to confront the injustice done to Robinson and begin to acknowledge the racism that defines their community and underpins its legal system. When Jem expresses his anger at the jury that convicted Robinson, Atticus tells Jem that if he and 11 other boys like him had been on that jury, Tom would be a free man. He goes on to say of the actual jurors:

> Those are twelve reasonable men in everyday life, Tom's jury, but you saw something come between them and reason . . . . There's something in our world that makes men lose their heads—they couldn't be fair if they tried. In our courts, when it's a white man's word against a black man's, the white man always wins. They're ugly, but those are the facts of life.

Jem mutters that those facts don't make things right; his father agrees. He reminds the boy that "the one place where a man ought to get a square deal is in a courtroom, be he any color of the rainbow, but people have a way of carrying their resentments into a jury box." Atticus tells Jem and Scout that someday there will be a "bill to pay" for the injustices, the violence, and the persecution.

That day has not yet come. As a result, Scout and Jem are attacked by a white man because their father defended a black man in court. In the end, the children are saved by Boo Radley, a neighbor who is a recluse. Scout and Jem have always imagined him as a monster who threatens small children. By the end of the book, they discover that he has been quietly protecting them at a time when their father could not. After saving their lives, "Mr. Arthur" (as Scout now thinks of Boo) allows the young girl to walk him home. As they reach his house, Scout realizes her father was right to tell her that "you never really know a man until you stand in his shoes and walk around in them." Later that evening, Scout decides that she and her brother would eventually "get grown," but as a result of their experiences with the trial and with Boo, "there wasn't much left" for them to learn at school, "except possibly algebra."

When Harper Lee's book was published in 1960, it became an overnight sensation. Courageous African Americans were bringing issues of race, fairness, and simple justice to the attention of the nation and the world by appealing to the conscience of all people everywhere. The discussions they inspired are at the heart of a democratic society—one that truly strives to provide "equal rights for all, special privileges for none," one that insists on "a square deal" for every individual in its courtrooms and every child in its classrooms. *To Kill a Mockingbird* is as relevant today as it was in 1960; there have been significant gains, but we still have a way to go. These issues are at the heart of a Facing History and Ourselves classroom.

Using This Resource

Teaching Mockingbird interweaves a literary analysis of the text with the exploration of relevant historical context, allowing students to engage in a richer, deeper exploration of the themes of growth, caring, justice, and democracy at the heart of the novel. This approach develops students' literacy skills, as well as their social-emotional skills and competencies. It closely aligns with the instructional shifts encouraged by the Common Core State Standards and is informed by Facing History's unique pedagogical approach, grounded in adolescent and moral development.

The resource is organized into seven sections, following the journey, or scope and sequence, that shapes every Facing History and Ourselves course of study. Students begin with an examination of the relationship between the individual and society; reflect on the way that humans divide themselves into "in" groups and "out" groups; dive deep into both the text of *To Kill a Mockingbird* and the history of the American South in the 1930s; and then explore the legacies of both this classic novel and the injustice it captures. This guide also includes resources to help students understand moral growth and development and apply those principles to both the characters in the novel and their own lives.

Section Elements

In addition to Pre- and Post-Reading sections, the guide is made up of five core components that support the reading of specific chapters. These components include:

- **Introduction**

  - » *Essential Questions*: the important themes that will be emphasized in both the novel and the materials included in the section.

  - » *Rationale*: the thematic focus of the section and how it connects to both important literary elements in the novel and the historical context.

  - » *Plot Summary*

  - » *ELA Skills Focus*

  - » *Academic Vocabulary List*

- **Exploring the Text**, containing resources to guide students' close examination of the novel and reflection on its themes.

  - » *Before Reading*: brief activities and journal prompts to initiate student thinking about important themes to follow.

» *Using Connection Questions*: primarily text-based questions designed to deepen students' understanding of the novel and to prompt reflection on its themes. Questions are provided for each chapter, as well as a culminating set to help students think about the section as a whole.

» *Activities for Deeper Understanding*: suggestions for writing, reflection, and close reading activities that engage students in deep consideration of important Facing History themes and literary elements in the novel.

- A **Building Historical Context** segment, featuring activities that use primary and secondary source documents, films, images, and other resources to help students understand the historical context that influences the world of Maycomb, Alabama, which is not made explicit in the novel.

Introducing the Central Question

As you and your students progress through your study of *To Kill a Mockingbird*, we recommend that you use the central question to connect classroom discussion and activities back to the larger themes of the novel.

What factors influence our moral growth? What kinds of experiences help us learn how to judge right from wrong?

When we discuss *moral growth* in this guide, we are referring to the development of each individual's ability to judge right from wrong. This process comprises one of the core themes of *To Kill a Mockingbird*. As the story unfolds through the eyes of Scout, the readers watch her and her brother, Jem, come of age in a society whose mores are at odds in crucial ways with the conscience of their father, Atticus. All three Finches—Scout, Jem, and Atticus—are confronted with their community's beliefs about race, class, and gender, and they must figure out how to be both individuals and members of their society. As students explore the ways in which the characters negotiate these tensions, they will have the opportunity to reflect deeply on how all of us grow and mature as moral people.

We recommend that you introduce this question before beginning your unit of study on *To Kill a Mockingbird* and revisit it in your class reflections and discussions throughout the unit. The Post-Reading section includes an assignment in which students analyze the moral growth of one of the characters from the novel. That activity concludes with an opportunity for broader reflection on this central question. You might choose to make the question the basis for a final assessment or writing assignment.

Alignment with the Common Core State Standards

This resource is grounded in the three instructional shifts required by the Common Core State Standards for English Language Arts:

1. *Building knowledge through content-rich nonfiction*

   This resource combines a deep exploration of *To Kill a Mockingbird* with a variety of primary and secondary sources, memoir, and other informational texts that can help enrich students' understanding of the novel's themes. Students build knowledge through their deep investigation of text and content through discussion, writing, and individual and group activities.

2. *Reading, writing, and speaking grounded in evidence from text, both literary and informational*

   Many of the Connection Questions, journal prompts, and other activities throughout this resource require that students explain and defend their responses and analysis using evidence from one or more texts, including both the novel and related informational texts. (One example of this is the culminating writing assignment based on the central question, mentioned above.) In addition, the resource provides a wide variety of opportunities for different forms of writing and discussion.

3. *Regular practice with complex text and academic language*

   Many of the texts included in this resource are indeed complex and highly sophisticated. In order to support students' engagement with these texts, each section highlights key academic vocabulary that students should understand. Each section also includes specific close reading activities, both for passages from the novel and to compare passages from the novel with related nonfiction.

   The close reading activities were created by Dr. David Pook, chair of the history department at the Derryfield School and an educational consultant. Pook was a contributing writer for the Common Core State Standards for English Language Arts, and he consults with several organizations, districts, and schools on work aligned with those standards. For a detailed analysis of how this resource meets specific Common Core State Standards for English Language Arts, see facinghistory.org/mockingbird.

Professional Development, Coaching, and Other Support

Facing History supports all of its core resources with ongoing professional development opportunities, both online and face-to-face. Visit facinghistory.org to find out about upcoming events supporting your teaching of *To Kill a Mockingbird*, including after-school workshops, in-depth seminars, online courses, hour-long webinars, and community events.

After participating in professional development, educators are paired with a Facing History program associate, who can help you apply your professional development experience to develop course syllabi and lesson plans, conduct coaching and follow-up support, and more. To find out more about Facing History's support model and other educator benefits, visit facinghistory.org.

Teaching Mockingbird Online

Facing History and Ourselves has created a complementary online resource for this guide. The website hosts online videos referenced throughout this guide as well as additional multimedia and opportunities for professional development to support teaching *To Kill a Mockingbird*. It will be helpful to check back frequently, as the site will grow to include additional resources, teaching activities, and suggestions for using the resources with parents and the community.

The Missing Ingredient

This curriculum is missing a crucial ingredient of any Facing History and Ourselves resource: the unique voices of your students and you, the teacher. No two Facing History courses are exactly alike, and that is how it should be. Indeed, we have learned that over time, educators' experience guiding students on a Facing History journey—enhanced by their creative energy—helps them use our materials to craft their own unique voice. We continue to learn from the wisdom of the teachers in our network. Thus, we encourage you to share your ideas, lesson plans, student reactions, and questions with us so that we can all benefit from being part of a learning community that shares a commitment to students' intellectual, moral, and social development.

Discussing Sensitive Topics in the Classroom

To Kill a Mockingbird, like many literary works, includes both language and topics that require careful consideration from teachers and students. We believe the best way to prepare to encounter these topics is to create a class contract outlining guidelines for a respectful, reflective classroom discussion. Review "Fostering a Reflective Classroom" on page 221 for suggestions for creating classroom contracts.

Dehumanizing Language

Harper Lee includes the word "nigger" deliberately to illustrate the society she writes about. Therefore, when quoting the text of *To Kill a Mockingbird* and in the historical documents included in this guide, we have chosen to let the word remain as it originally appeared, without any substitution. The dehumanizing power of this term and the ease with which some Americans have used it to describe their fellow human beings is central to understanding the themes of identity and human behavior at the heart of the book.

It is very difficult to use and discuss the term "nigger" in the classroom, but its presence in the novel makes it necessary to acknowledge it and set guidelines for students about whether or not to pronounce it when reading aloud or quoting from the text. Otherwise, this word's presence might distract students from an open discussion about characters and themes. We recommend the following articles to help you determine how to approach the term in your classroom:

- "Exploring the Controversy: The 'N' Word" from *"Huck Finn" in Context: A Teaching Guide* (PBS)

- "Straight Talk about the N-Word" from *Teaching Tolerance* (Southern Poverty Law Center)

- "In Defense of a Loaded Word" by Ta-Nehisi Coates (*New York Times*)

You may also wish to point out the use of the word "negro" in the novel. In earlier times, this was an acceptable term for referring to African Americans. While not offensive in the past, today the term "negro" is outdated and inappropriate unless one is reading aloud directly from a historical document or work of literature.

Accusations of Rape

Accusations of rape play a central role in both the story of *To Kill a Mockingbird* and the history of the Scottsboro Boys, which is included in this guide. While explicit depictions of rape do not appear, the accusations in these stories may simultaneously be difficult to understand for some students and all too real for others.

Discussions of rape are complicated in relation to *To Kill a Mockingbird* and the Scottsboro Boys because both of these stories involve false accusations that play into racial fear and hatred. *Experts tell us that most accusations of rape are not false.* There is material provided later in this guide to help explore the beliefs and stereotypes that led to the false accusations students will learn about.

It is possible that some students will have additional questions or comments on the topic of rape outside of the context of the book. It is important to preview how you might respond to such questions and comments in case they arise. If they do, make sure to return to the class contract you have established with students to guide any discussion that follows. You might also consider alerting your building administrator to the fact that the topic of rape—critical in the analysis of the novel— might be brought up in your class in case any concerns about the discussion arise in the broader school community.

SECTION 1

Pre-Reading: The Individual in Society

Introduction

Essential Questions

- What is identity? To what extent do we determine our own identities? What influence does society have?

- What are stereotypes, and how do they affect how we see ourselves and how others see us?

- How does our need to belong influence our identity? How does it lead to the formation of "in" groups and "out" groups in our society?

Rationale

In this section, students will prepare to read *To Kill a Mockingbird* by first reflecting on the relationship between the individual and society and how that relationship influences one's identity. This reflection will prepare students both for a deep literary analysis of character and setting during their study of the novel and for thoughtful exploration of the novel's themes about caring, growth, justice, and democracy.

The plot of *To Kill a Mockingbird* is driven forward by the conflict that the main characters experience as their beliefs about justice and morality come into conflict with the mores of the society they inhabit. The novel interweaves two primary plots: Atticus Finch's effort to follow his conscience and break the unwritten rules of the Jim Crow criminal justice system, and the socialization of Atticus's children—Scout and Jem—as they negotiate the spoken and unspoken rules of their community. Throughout the novel we observe these three individuals seeking to define their identities both within and in opposition to their society's moral universe.

Therefore, it makes sense that before students begin to read *To Kill a Mockingbird*, they take some time to examine their own experience of the relationship between the individual and society. By starting here, students will be prepared to analyze more deeply the way this tension plays out in the world of Maycomb, Alabama, during the Great Depression. As a result, they will reach a deeper understanding of the characters and setting, as well as how conflicts between the two drive the plot forward. Examining the complexity of their own identities also enables students to make personal connections with the story, deepening their engagement with the text.

Another crucial opportunity for reflection lies within an examination of the individual and society. If, as philosopher George Santayana has written, art provides us an imaginative rehearsal for life,[1] then we might ask as we read *To Kill a Mockingbird* what facets of our own lives this novel can help us reflect on and rehearse. What can we learn about our own lives and our own moral universe from the experiences of Scout, Jem, Atticus, and the other inhabitants of Maycomb, Alabama? It is not so much that we are looking for specific lessons or morals planted in the text by Harper Lee for us to uncover. Rather, we look to the novel to provide us opportunities for reflection on the dilemmas and choices we face in our own lives. For instance:

- How can the characters' responses to the dilemmas they face in a society characterized by sharp divisions around race, class, age, and gender help us think about our choices in the face of similar dilemmas in our own lives?

- What models of moral and ethical behavior do the characters offer to us that we might adopt, modify, or reject in our own lives?

These are questions that students and teachers will explore throughout this guide as they read the novel. But for these questions to have sufficient resonance, it is useful to first engage in an exploration of our own identities and the challenges we face when our own choices and desires come into conflict with the rules and expectations of our society.

This section provides a variety of resources to help students reflect on the interplay between the individual and society. Several readings explore the complexity of identity and will help students consider how each of the following factors influences who we are:

- Individual choices and passions

- Legacies of values, or mores, inherited from community, family, and other important individuals in our lives

- Labels our society uses to organize and categorize its members

---

1   George Santayana, "Justification of Art," in *The Essential Santayana*, ed. Martin A. Coleman (Bloomingdale: Indiana University Press, 2009), 312, excerpt from *Reason in Art* (1905), accessed June 3, 2014, http://books.google.com/books?id=kt59aieu6hkC.

Other resources and activities suggested here will help students think about identity as dynamic, prompting them to reflect on the pivotal moments and turning points from their own stories that influenced who they are today. Finally, this section asks students to consider the impact of our need to belong on how we define ourselves and how that need results in "in" groups and "out" groups in our society. After exploring the resources in this section, students will be better prepared both to analyze the fictional world of Maycomb, Alabama, and to engage in crucial reflection on the roles of compassion, empathy, conscience, and justice in their lives and our society.

Activities for Deeper Understanding

Introduce Identity

Once students begin to read *To Kill a Mockingbird*, they will engage in deep analysis of the characters as well as the factors that influence who the characters are and the choices they make. In a sense, they will be analyzing the characters' identities. Therefore, to prepare students, it is helpful to start by asking them to reflect on their own identities as well as the very concept itself.

One's identity is a combination of many things. It includes the labels others place on us, as well as ideas we have about who we want to be. Gender, ethnicity, religion, occupation, and physical characteristics all contribute to one's identity. So do ties to a particular neighborhood, school, community, or nation. Our values and beliefs are also a part of who we are as individuals, as are the experiences that have shaped our lives.

This section provides resources that will help students explore the variety of factors that influence both our identities and those of the characters in *To Kill a Mockingbird*:

- In **Handout 1.3**, student Jonathan Rodríguez explains that while his name reflects "two worlds" that have influenced who he is, it also fails to capture the full complexity of his identity. As students will discover in *To Kill a Mockingbird*, names can sometimes influence the assumptions people make about an individual's identity and character, but those assumptions are often false.

- In **Handout 1.4**, Lori Duron, author of the book *Raising My Rainbow*, describes how her son C.J.'s identity defies the expectations others have of him because of his gender. Similar questions about what it means to be a boy, a girl, a gentleman, and a lady arise in the novel.

- In **Handout 1.5**, author Julius Lester explains how he discovered his passion for haiku, an interest that many would have not expected an African American boy in the 1950s to have. Lester's story will help students preview the challenges experienced by several characters in *To Kill a Mockingbird* to find their own voices despite others' beliefs about their identities.

- In **Handout 1.6**, sociologist Dalton Conley explains how the categories of race and class that our society uses to "organize our reality" impact our identities. Conley's story can help students begin to think about categories that are also used in the novel by the residents of Maycomb to organize their beliefs about the world.

Each reading is followed by Connection Questions to guide student reflection and class discussion.

Introduce Identity Charts

As students read **Handouts 1.1** through **1.6**, ask them to use evidence from the texts to create identity charts for Jonathan Rodríguez, C.J. Duron, Julius Lester, and Dalton Conley. The diagram in **Handout 1.1** is an example of an identity chart. It includes phrases that individuals use to define themselves, as well as words that others use to define them. Students can include their own analysis as well as direct quotations from the reading on the diagram.

After students complete identity charts for Rodríguez, Duron, Lester, and Conley, they should create one for themselves. **Handout 1.1** provides a series of prompts that can help students complete their personal identity charts.

Explore Identity through Contrasts

Describing his experience growing up as a white person in a majority black and Hispanic neighborhood, Dalton Conley suggests in **Handout 1.6** that one could "define whiteness by putting a light-skinned kid in the midst of a community of color." His statement is reminiscent of Zora Neale Hurston's statement in a 1928 essay: "I feel most colored when I am thrown against a sharp white background."[2] Artist Glenn Ligon has used Hurston's statement as the basis for the untitled etching in **Handout 1.7**.

Consider showing Ligon's etching to students. You might ask them to interpret the work using the Analyzing Visual Images teaching strategy (see facinghistory.org/

---

2   Zora Neale Hurston, "How It Feels to Be Colored Me," 1928, in *I Love Myself When I Am Laughing . . . and Then Again When I Am Looking Mean and Impressive: A Zora Neale Hurston Reader*, ed. Alice Walker (New York: Feminist Press at CUNY, 1979), 154, accessed June 3, 2014, http://books.google.com/books?id=SNfoStBUQ4IC.

mockingbird/strategies). After students develop their own interpretations of the image, ask them to consider the following questions:

- How does the way that we blend in or stand out among those around us change how we define ourselves? How does it change how others define us?

- How does it feel to be the "different" one and how does it influence the choices we make?

- Is our identity influenced more greatly by our similarities to other people or by our differences?

Introduce Moral Growth and Memory Maps

As students read *To Kill a Mockingbird*, this guide will invite them into a deep examination of human behavior. In particular, students will be asked to reflect on the moral growth of the main characters as their senses of right and wrong are challenged by their society's written and unwritten rules about race, class, and gender. After reading the novel, students will be asked to choose a main character and analyze how he or she has changed over the course of the novel. Their task will be to focus especially on the character's moral development.

In order to prepare for this examination of human behavior and moral growth, students should begin by reflecting on some of the pivotal moments in their lives that have contributed to who they are today. In other words, if the identity charts students have created for themselves represent their identities today, what are the most important events in their lives that shaped those identities? Students should choose two to three pivotal moments from their pasts and use them to create a memory map. Use the following steps to help students complete their memory maps:

Step 1: Preparation and brainstorming:

Ask students to write a journal entry describing the important moments and decisions in their lives. In their writing, they should consider factors both within their control (e.g., selection of friends, interests, likes, and dislikes) and outside of their control (e.g., moving, birth of a sibling, breaking a bone).

Step 2: Identifying pivotal moments:

After students have brainstormed a variety of moments, ask them to identify two to three that they think have been *most pivotal* in determining who they are today. Spend a few minutes discussing the word *pivotal* and defining what might qualify a moment as such. You might also use the term *turning point* to describe pivotal moments. As students identify two to three pivotal moments, encourage them to include at least one moment that was within their control and one moment that was beyond their control.

You might show the short, 7-minute video "Custom and Conscience: Margot Stern Strom Reflects on Growing Up in the South" to help students better understand what might make a moment in their lives pivotal. In the video, Strom, co-founder of Facing History and Ourselves, explains how she was impacted by growing up in the South in the 1950s by describing three experiences she had as a child in Memphis, Tennessee. You might ask students to identify those three experiences and look for evidence in Strom's comments for reasons why those experiences stand out to her over others. The video can be streamed from facinghistory.org/mockingbird/videos.

Step 3: Representing pivotal moments:

Either in their journals or on a separate piece of paper (perhaps a piece of chart paper for display purposes), have students draw a picture to represent each of the pivotal moments they have identified. The pictures can be realistic or symbolic. You might also choose to bring in newspapers, magazines, or other art supplies for students to use in constructing images.

Step 4: Analyzing pivotal moments:

Now that students have represented some pivotal moments and choices that have shaped their identities, ask them to think about the factors that may have influenced those moments. For each of the images that students created, they can add details to represent factors that may have influenced their decisions, such as historical events, important relationships, goals, beliefs, and aspects of human behavior (e.g., fear, conformity, prejudice).

Step 5: Sharing and discussing:

Students can share their work through a formal presentation to the class, a small group, or a gallery walk (see facinghistory.org/mockingbird/strategies). As students review the work of their classmates, ask them to pay attention to similarities and differences among moments they selected. Prompts you might use to guide students' reflections and a follow-up discussion include:

>> What factors influence the choices people make?

>> What factors help people move forward and make progress?

>> What factors set people back?

As a final exercise, you can ask students to write a journal entry explaining what they have learned from this activity. In particular, students can reflect on what is unique about one person's life and what seems universal.

After reading *To Kill a Mockingbird*, students will use this same process to create a memory map for a character in the novel as part of their analysis of that character's growth and development.

Define Stereotype

If common categories such as race and class are, as Dalton Conley says, "stories we tell ourselves to get through the world, to organize our reality," we might ask students to consider the consequences of these stories. We can begin by reflecting on the human behavior of categorizing and organizing the world and trying to articulate when that behavior is useful and when it is harmful.

You might begin this discussion with the class by sharing the following quotation by psychologist Deborah Tannen:

> We all know we are unique individuals, but we tend to see others as representatives of groups. It's a natural tendency, since we must see the world in patterns in order to make sense of it; we wouldn't be able to deal with the daily onslaught of people and objects if we couldn't predict a lot about them and feel that we know who or what they are.[3]

Ask students to respond to Tannen in their journals. Do they agree? What is the benefit of seeing the world in patterns and viewing others as representatives of groups? What gets lost when we categorize our experiences in this way? What kinds of stories do we attach to the groups we use to categorize other people? When is it offensive or harmful to see others as representatives of groups?

Finally, ask students to write a working definition for the word *stereotype*. In their definitions, they might reflect on the word's connotation. Is it positive or negative? Does the connotation of the word imply that stereotypes are useful or harmful? When does a judgment about an individual based on the characteristics of a group become offensive? Give students the opportunity to share and refine their definitions with one or more classmates.

---

3   Deborah Tannen, *You Just Don't Understand* (New York: Morrow, 1990), 16.

Explore the Consequences of Stereotypes

The concept of *stereotype threat* explains one significant way that stereotypes can affect one's identity, choices, and behavior. The 8-minute video "How Stereotypes Affect Us and What We Can Do" introduces students to this concept through the accounts of individuals who have experienced it and the research of social psychologist Claude Steele (watch the video at facinghistory.org/mockingbird/videos).

In short, the concept of stereotype threat holds that when we are in a situation in which we believe we might be judged or treated differently because of a negative stereotype about a facet of our identity, we may feel threatened and distracted. This distraction impacts our performance on particular tasks, our enjoyment of various activities, and our choices in specific circumstances. In the video, Steele concludes from his research that stereotypes constitute one way that history impacts our daily lives. This is because the stereotypes that persist from the past affect how we function in the world around us today.

Handout 1.2 provides a series of questions to guide students' note-taking as they view the video. This viewing guide can also serve as a springboard into a deeper discussion about the impact of stereotypes on our identities and the choices we make in our lives.

Explore the Relationship between Identity and the Need to Belong

The essay "The Walking Boy" by Alan Jacobs (**Handout 1.8**), author and Baylor University humanities professor, provides students an opportunity to explore the relationship between our need to belong and our identity. Jacobs tells a story about growing up in segregated Birmingham, Alabama, in the 1960s. The location of one African American boy's home required him to walk through Jacobs's white neighborhood in order to get to school and to see friends in the black section of town. Jacobs describes how his friends harassed the boy and threw rocks at him as he passed by. Jacobs participated, or at least pretended to participate, even though he knew it was wrong.

Examining the moral dilemma Alan Jacobs experienced, and analyzing the ways in which he resolved that dilemma, can provide students the opportunity to think about the following questions:

- How might our need to belong affect our identities?

- How might our need to belong affect how we treat those who do not belong to the "in" group?

- How might our lack of knowledge and familiarity with other individuals or groups enable negative stereotypes to take root? How might it lead us to treat others unfairly?

- How might peer pressure impact our ability and willingness to follow our consciences?

Because these questions will resonate with the moral dilemmas students encounter while reading *To Kill a Mockingbird*, it is worth providing students time to think deeply about them before beginning the novel. Consider using these questions as the basis of a reflection and discussion activity such as the Learn to Listen/ Listen to Learn activity (for more information, see facinghistory.org/mockingbird/ strategies). After reading "The Walking Boy," divide students into small groups and ask them to reflect in their journals on one or more of the above questions. Then provide a short period of time for students to share with their groups part or all of their journal responses. After each group member has shared, provide additional time for open discussion of the question within each group. Finally, ask each group to summarize their discussion for the rest of the class. Repeat this process for one or more of the other questions above.

Finally, you might ask students to respond in their journals to the following statement by a Facing History student named Eve Shalen: "Often being accepted by others is more satisfying than being accepted by oneself, even though the satisfaction does not last." What do you think she means? How does her statement apply to "The Walking Boy"? How does it apply to your own experiences?

This quotation is from Shalen's account of a time when she joined with a group of classmates in the eighth grade to exclude and mock another student. You can learn more about Eve Shalen and her story at Facing History's website, facinghistory.org.

Handout 1.1 Creating an Identity Chart

Use the following steps to create an identity chart for yourself:

1. Draw a circle in the middle of a blank piece of paper or page in your journal.

2. Begin with the words or phrases that describe the way you see yourself. Add those words and phrases to your chart.

3. Most people define themselves by using categories important to their culture. They include not only gender, age, and physical characteristics but also ties to a particular religion, class, neighborhood, school, and nation. Consider if any of these characteristics belong on your chart.

4. You may wish to add new categories to your identity chart. How much of your identity do you create and how much of it is determined by things beyond your control? What other factors influence your identity? What can you add that does not fall into any of the categories listed above?

5. How does the way that other people think about you impact your identity? Consider multiple perspectives. Think about these questions as you think about what else to add to your chart:

   • What labels would others attach to you?

   • Do they see you as a leader or a follower? A conformist or a rebel?

   • Are you a peacemaker, a bully, or a bystander?

   • How do society's labels influence the way you see yourself? The kinds of choices you and others make each day? For example, if a person is known as a bully, how likely is he or she to live up to that label?

Handout 1.2 "How Stereotypes Affect Us and What We Can Do"

Use the following questions to guide your note-taking as you view the video:

1. How does Claude Steele define stereotype threat? What does he say is the threat that stereotypes pose, and how does that threat affect the way people function?

2. Whom does he say stereotype threat affects?

3. Summarize the ways in which Jonathan Lykes says stereotypes have affected him.

4. Why does Sonya Sohn say she lost a lot of confidence when she was the only black girl in a class of white students? What role did stereotypes play?

5. Summarize the experiment Steele describes. What stereotype about women was at the heart of his experiment? What effect did the stereotype have? How was he able to eliminate the effects of stereotype threat in this situation?

6. According to Steele, how does stereotype threat help explain the impact of history on the present?

7. Based on what you have learned from this video, explain in your own words how stereotypes may impact how one thinks about his or her own identity.

Handout 1.3 Two Names, Two Worlds

In the poem below, student Jonathan Rodríguez reflects on how his name represents his identity:

Hi I'm Jon............No—Jonathan

Wait—Jonathan Rodríguez

Hold on—Jonathan *Rodríguez*

My Name, Two names, two worlds

The duality of my identity like two sides of the same coin

With two worlds, there should be plenty of room

But where do I fit?

Where can I sit?

Is this seat taken? Or is that seat taken?

There never is quite enough room is there?

Two names, Two worlds

Where do I come from?

Born in the Washington heights of New York City

But raised in good ol' Connecticut

The smell of freshly mowed grass, autumn leaves

Sancocho, Rice and Beans

The sound from Billy Joel's Piano Keys

And the rhythm from *Juan Luis Guerra*

I'm from the struggle for broken dreams

Of false promises

Of houses with white picket fences

And 2.5 kids

The mountains and *campos de la Republica Dominicana*

And the mango trees

I'm not the typical kid from suburbia

Nor am I a smooth Latin cat

My head's in the clouds, my nose in a comic book

I get lost in the stories and art

I'm kinda awkward—so talkin' to the ladies is hard

I listen to *Fernando Villalona* and *Aventura* every chance I get,

But don't make me dance *Merengue, Bachata*

Or *Salsa*—I don't know the steps

I've learned throughout these past years

A race that is black, white and Taino

I am a mix of cultures, a mix of races

"Una Raza encendida,

Negra, Blanca y Taina"

A song

You can find me in the parts of a song, *en una cancion*

Percussion instrument used in merengue; percussion instrument used in the Dominican Republic

You can feel my African Roots *en la Tambora*

My *Taino* screams *en la guira*

And the melodies of the lyrics are a reminder of my beautiful Spanish heritage

I am African, Taino and Spanish

A Fanboy, an athlete, a nerd, a student, an introvert

I am Dominican

I'm proud to say: *Yo soy Dominicano*

I'm proud to say, I am me

I am beginning to appreciate that I am

A beautiful blend

Una bella mezcla

I am beginning to see that this world is also a beautiful mix

Of people, ideas and stories.

Is this seat taken?

Or is that seat taken?

Join me and take a seat,

Here we'll write our own stories[1]

Connection Questions

1. What does Rodríguez mean when he uses the phrase "two names, two worlds"? What two worlds does his name represent?

2. What assumptions does Rodríguez think others might make about his identity because of his name? Which of those assumptions are true? Which are false?

3. What does your name suggest about your identity? To what extent does it influence how others think about you? How does it affect how you think about yourself?

---

1   Jonathan Rodríguez, untitled poem.

Handout 1.4 A Rainbow Creation

Author Lori Duron and her husband, Matt, have two children, both boys. Duron writes about the reaction of her young son, C.J., the first time he saw a Barbie doll:

For days after C.J. discovered her, Barbie never left his side. When I'd do a final bed check at night before I retired for the evening to watch reality television and sneak chocolate when no one was looking, I'd see his full head of auburn hair sticking out above his covers. Next to him there would be a tiny tuft of blonde hair sticking out as well.

The next time we were at Target near the toy aisle—which I've always tried to pass at warp speed so the kids don't notice and beg me to buy them something—C.J. wanted to see "Barbie stuff." I led him to the appropriate aisle and he stood there transfixed, not touching a thing, just taking it all in. He was so overwhelmed that he didn't ask to buy a single thing. He finally walked away from the aisle speechless, as if he had just seen something so magical and majestic that he needed time to process it.

He had, that day, discovered the pink aisles of the toy department. We had never been down those aisles; we had only frequented the blue aisles, when we ventured down the toy aisles at all. As far as C.J. was concerned, I had been hiding half the world from him.

I felt bad about that, like I had deprived him because of my assumptions and expectations that he was a boy and boys liked boy things. Matt and I noticed that C.J. didn't really like any of the toys we provided for him, which were all handed down from his brother. We noticed that C.J. didn't go through the normal boy toy addictions that Chase [C.J.'s older brother] had gone through: he couldn't care less about balls, cars, dinosaurs, superheroes, The Wiggles, Bob the Builder, or Thomas the Tank Engine. What did he like to play with? We didn't worry ourselves much about finding the answer (a case of the second-born child not getting fussed over quite like the first-born); we trusted that in time something would draw him in. Which it did. It just wasn't at all what we were expecting.

At about the eighteen- to twenty-four-month mark of a child's life, the gender-neutral toys disappear and toys that are marketed specifically to boys or to girls take over. We didn't realize it until later, but that divide in the toy world and our house being filled with only boy toys left C.J. a little lost at playtime. We and the rest of society had been pushing masculine stuff on him and enforcing traditional gender norms, when all he wanted was to brush long blonde hair and dress, undress, and re-dress Barbie . . . .[1]

Reflecting on C.J.'s identity, Duron concludes:

. . . On the gender-variation spectrum of super-macho-masculine on the left all the way to super-girly-feminine on the right, C.J. slides fluidly in the middle; he's neither all pink nor all blue. He's a muddled mess or a rainbow creation, depending on how you look at it. Matt and I have decided to see the rainbow, not the muddle. But we didn't always see it that way.

Initially, the sight of our son playing with girl toys or wearing girl clothes made our chests tighten, forged a lump in our throats, and, at times, made us want to hide him. There was anger, anxiety, and fear. We've evolved as parents as our younger son has evolved into a fascinating, vibrant person who is creative with gender. Sometimes, when I think of how we behaved as parents . . . I'm ashamed and embarrassed.[2]

Connection Questions

1. What is the difference between the toys in the "pink aisle" and those in the "blue aisle"? What assumptions do the toys in those aisles reflect about gender?

2. How do you explain the anxiety, anger, and fear Duron describes feeling when C.J. started playing with "girl toys"?

3. How do you respond to the assumptions people make about your gender? To what extent do you embrace and reflect them? To what extent do you reject them?

1   Lori Duron, *Raising My Rainbow: Adventures in Raising a Fabulous, Gender Creative Son* (New York: Broadway Books, 2013), 9–10.
2   Ibid., 4.

Handout 1.5 Finding One's Voice

Julius Lester, a noted author, describes how discovering an ancient form of poetry helped him find his voice and define his own identity:

I grew up in the forties and fifties in Kansas City, Kansas, and Nashville, Tennessee, with summers spent in Arkansas. The forties and fifties were not pleasant times for blacks and I am offended by white people who get nostalgic for the fifties. I have no nostalgia for segregation, for the "No Colored Allowed" signs covering the landscape like litter on the smooth, green grass of a park, I have no nostalgia for a time when I endangered my life if, while downtown shopping with my parents, I raised my eyes and accidentally met the eyes of a white woman. Black men and boys were lynched for this during my childhood and adolescence . . .

I grew up in a violent world. Segregation was a deathly spiritual violence, not only in its many restrictions on where we could live, eat, go to school, and go after dark. There was also the constant threat of physical death if you looked at a white man in what he considered the wrong way or if he didn't like your attitude. There was also the physical violence of my community. . . .

One of the pivotal experiences of my life came when I was eighteen. I wandered into a bookstore in downtown Nashville one frosted, gray day in late autumn aware that I was looking for something: I was looking for myself, and I generally find myself while wandering through a bookstore, looking at books until I find the one that is calling me. On this particular day I wandered for quite a while until I picked up a paperback with the word *Haiku* on the cover. What is that? I wondered. I opened the book and read,

> On a withered branch
> a crow has settled—
> autumn nightfall.

I trembled and turned the pages hastily until my eyes stopped on these words:

> A giant firefly;
> that way, this way, that way, this—
> and it passes by.

I read more of the brief poems, these voices from seventeenth-century Japan, and I knew: This is my voice. This simplicity, this directness, this way of using words to direct the soul to silence and beyond. This is my voice! I exulted inside. Then I stopped. How could I, a little colored kid from Nashville, Tennessee—and that is all I knew myself to be in those days like perpetual death knells—how could I be feeling that something written in seventeenth-century Japan could be my voice?

I almost put the book back, but that inner prompting which had led me to it would not allow such an act of self-betrayal. I bought the book and began writing haiku, and the study of haiku led to the study of Zen Buddhism, which led to the study of flower arranging, and I suspect I am still following the path that opened to me on that day when I was eighteen, though I no longer write haiku.

I eventually understood that it made perfect sense for a little colored kid from Nashville, Tennessee, to recognize his voice in seventeenth-century Japanese poetry. Who we are by the sociological and political definitions of society has little to do with who we are.[1]

Connection Questions

1. Why does Julius almost put the book of haiku back on the shelf? What factors lead to his momentary doubt that haiku is for him?

2. What does it mean to "find yourself"? Where does Julius Lester say he finds himself? Where do you go to find yourself?

3. What are you passionate about? How do the things you are passionate about help shape who you are?

1   Julius Lester, *Falling Pieces of the Broken Sky* (New York: Little Brown, 1990), 71–73.

Handout 1.6 Stories We Tell Ourselves

Sociologist Dalton Conley reflects on how the ways in which society teaches us to "organize our reality" can affect our identities:

I am not your typical middle-class white male. I am middle class, despite the fact that my parents had no money; I am white, but I grew up in an inner-city housing project where most everyone was black or Hispanic. I enjoyed a range of privileges that were denied my neighbors but that most Americans take for granted. In fact, my childhood was like a social science experiment: Find out what being middle class really means by raising a kid from a so-called good family in a so-called bad neighborhood. Define whiteness by putting a light-skinned kid in the midst of a community of color. If the exception proves the rule, I'm that exception.

Ask any African American to list the adjectives that describe them and they will likely put black or African American at the top of the list. Ask someone of European descent the same question and white will be far down the list, if it's there at all. Not so for me. I've studied whiteness the way I would a foreign language. I know its grammar, its parts of speech; I know the subtleties of its idioms, its vernacular words and phrases to which the native speaker has never given a second thought. There's an old saying that you never really know your own language until you study another. It's the same with race and class.

In fact, race and class are nothing more than a set of stories we tell ourselves to get through the world, to organize our reality . . . . One of [my mother's favorite stories] was how I had wanted a baby sister so badly that I kidnapped a black child in the playground of the housing complex. She told this story each time my real sister, Alexandra, and I were standing, arms crossed, facing away from each other after some squabble or fistfight. The moral of the story for my mother was that I should love my sister, since I had wanted to have her so desperately. The message I took away, however, was one of race. I was fascinated that I could have been oblivious to something that years later feels so natural, so innate as race does.[1]

---

1   Dalton Conley, *Honky* (Berkeley: University of California Press, 2000), xi–xii.

Connection Questions

1. What does Conley say about the difference between how black and white people describe themselves? Why do you think he believes that?

2. Do you agree?

3. Make a list of the adjectives that describe you. Which did you think of first? Which took longer to think of? Why were you were able to think of some adjectives more easily than others?

4. What does Conley mean when he says that "race and class are nothing more than a set of stories we tell ourselves to get through the world"? Do you agree? Write working definitions for the words *race* and *class* in your journal. You can revise or expand your definitions as you read and analyze the novel.

Handout 1.7 "I Feel Most Colored When . . ."

Artist Glenn Ligon created Untitled: Four Etchings [B] *using a quotation from writer Zora Neale Hurston's essay, "How It Feels to Be Colored Me."*

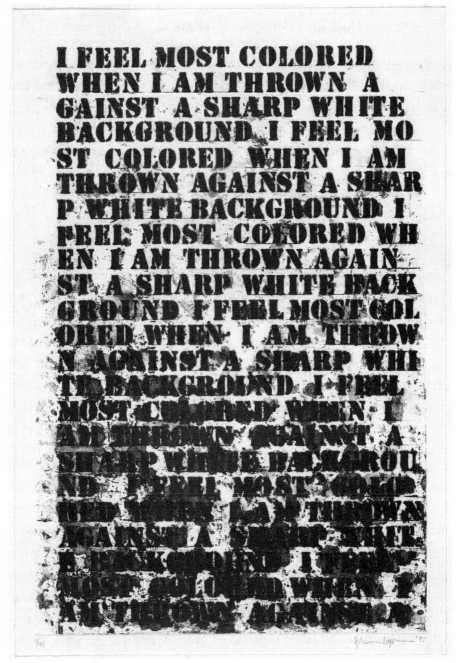

Reproduced with permission from Thomas Dane Gallery

Handout 1.8 "The Walking Boy"

> *Note: We have chosen to include certain racial epithets in this reading in order to honestly communicate the bigoted language of the time. We recommend that teachers review the section "Discussing Sensitive Topics in the Classroom" before using this document.*

The following is excerpted from an essay published on The American Conservative *website by writer and humanities professor Alan Jacobs:*

All I can say in my defense is that I never hurled a stone at him, or shouted abuse. But I stood by, many a time, as others did those things, and I neither walked away nor averted my eyes . . . . I watched it all, gripping a rock in my hand as though I were preparing to use it—so that no one would turn on me with anger or contempt—and I always stood a little behind them so they couldn't see that I wasn't throwing anything. I was smaller and younger than the rest of them, and they were smaller and younger than him. In my memory he seems almost a full-grown man; I suppose he was eleven or twelve.

We called him Nigger Jeff. I have never doubted that Jeff was indeed his name, though as I write this account I find myself asking, for the first time, how we could have known: I never heard any of the boys speak to him except in cries of hatred, and I never knew anyone else who knew him. It occurs to me now that, if his name was Jeff, there had to have been at least a brief moment of human contact and exchange—perhaps not even involving Jeff, perhaps one of the boys' mothers talked to Jeff's mother. But we grasp what's available for support or stability. It's bad to call a boy Nigger Jeff, but worse still to call him just Nigger. A name counts for something.

Arkadelphia Road is a major artery on the west side of Birmingham, Alabama, becoming Highway 78 for a while before 78 veers off to the northwest and heads for Memphis, but for me it was simply a liminal space, a mighty boundary. My house on 11th Court West sat three blocks off Arkadelphia, and when I visited Snappy's Service Station at the corner to buy soft drinks and candy, I could gaze across the four lanes of charging traffic into another world, a world inhabited solely by black people. Often I passed in an automobile through that world, but my feet had never touched its ground, and I knew no one who lived there . . . . [T]hose dark strangers could sometimes be seen hanging clothes on the clotheslines of our neighborhood, or taking the clothes in to iron them

. . . . But really, neither side passed to the other: when they came to labor for us they always left something essential behind; maybe everything essential. I stood sometimes on the hot pavement of the gas station, straddling my bike, and while I drank my coke I would look across the blaring four-lane gulf. Then I would drain the bottle and ride back towards home.

Just past my house, the pavement ended, and a red dirt path, big enough for a single car, extended into fields of high grass that, when my father was a boy, were cotton fields. When I was very young a tiny cinder-block shack a quarter-mile down the path housed a radio station; I remember looking through my bedroom window as the tall antenna was pulled down, frightening the few cows in the field. Soon the cows were gone too, and the grasses grew higher. A hundred yards farther along stood the remains of an old greenhouse, with broken glass and a scattering of plastic pots. And a little further down still, on the other side of the path, stood a ramshackle old house. Jeff and his family lived there. There were no other houses, no other people.

But Jeff's house I never cared to pass, or even to approach. I don't know whether he lived with both parents or one, though I seem to remember references to his mother, who probably worked in some white lady's home. If he had any siblings I never saw them. All I knew was that sometimes, especially in the hot summer days, he would set off along the red dirt path, in his old dungarees and his bare feet, towards our neighborhood.

As I continue to recall these events, I am more and more troubled by my ignorance. Did Jeff go to school? If so, it would have had to be at the all-black school—on the other side of Arkadelphia, of course, up the hill towards Center Street. . . . But I never saw Jeff walking to school. Did his family have a car? I never saw one, and I feel sure that I would have noticed if they had had such transportation. . . .

But that's just one question among many. If they didn't have a car, when and where and how did they get their groceries? Where did his mother, or his mother and father, work, and how did they get there? Did they receive mail? Perhaps they always headed in the other direction, west towards Bush Boulevard: a longer walk, but less likely to find conflict or even attention. I have no idea how these people lived, how they sustained themselves. I must have missed a great deal; there must have been many events to which I was oblivious, as children of course can be—and yet my obliviousness bothers me, because there are some things I remember so well. . . .

Especially I remember Jeff moving at his habitual level pace towards our world, a small world so comfortable to us but surely like some wall of flame to him. Of course we knew where he was going: not to us but through us, through our neighborhood to the one on the other side of Arkadelphia, where there must have been friends glad to see him and houses where he was welcome. But first there were the three blocks of our territory. And when we saw him coming we picked up our rocks.

When he caught sight of us, Jeff would stoop and collect a handful of good throwing-size stones for his own use. In another part of Birmingham, at this very time, Martin Luther King's followers were practicing nonviolent resistance to the water cannons and police dogs of Bull Connor, but Jeff was no pacifist. Yet he never initiated conflict: he had somewhere to get to, and all he wanted was the quickest and most uneventful passage possible. If we threw our rocks he returned fire, and since he was bigger and stronger than any of us, that was something to be reckoned with. So often my friends inadvertently and unwittingly imitated me by simply holding their missiles in their hands; they contented themselves with curses and mockery. And Jeff, then, would simply walk on down the middle of the otherwise quiet little street, slowly and steadily. He never ran, and would only vary his even pace when he had to stop to launch a rock or two—though sometimes he had to walk backwards for a while to be sure we didn't start pelting him when his head was turned.

We could have surrounded him, of course, but we were too cowardly for that. We were pretty sure that, as long as we huddled in a small group, he wouldn't attack; but if we separated he might go for one of us. So we gathered like a Greek chorus to curse, and Jeff kept walking. Eventually his solitary figure grew smaller, and our throats grew tired of launching insults. We dropped our rocks and returned to our children's games.

Sometimes I would be playing alone in my yard, and would look up to see Jeff walking by. My heart would then buck in my chest, but he never turned his head to acknowledge my presence. At the time I wondered if he knew that I never threw rocks at him, that I didn't curse him—for, if my memory is not appeasing my conscience, I avoided that crime as well. But now I realize that he neither knew nor cared about the individual members of our cruel impromptu assembly: with rocks in our hands we were just mobile, noisy impediments to his enjoyment of some of the blessings of life—friendship, comfort, safety—but when unarmed and solitary we posed no threat and therefore, for Jeff, lacked significant substance. He kept his eyes on that day's small but valued prize, and kept on walking.

Why didn't I throw rocks at him? Why didn't I curse him? Well, obviously, because I felt sorry for him. But not sorry enough to walk away, or to turn my back on the scene; and not nearly sorry enough to stay a friend's hand or demand his silence. I was young, and small, and timid. I saw one valid option: to stand as a member of the chorus, grasping the rock that was the badge of our common identity. There's no point now in trying to distinguish myself from the others. But I can't help it.[1]

1   Alan Jacobs, "The Walking Boy," *Alan Jacobs* (blog), July 16, 2013, accessed May 29, 2014, http://www. theamericanconservative.com/jacobs/the-walking-boy/.

SECTION 2

Maycomb's Ways

This section covers Chapters 1 to 7 of the novel.

Introduction

Essential Questions

- How does our identity influence the choices we make? How does analyzing *character* help us understand the choices characters in literature make?

- How does the "moral universe" in which we live affect the choices we make? How does analyzing *setting* help us understand the choices characters in literature make?

Rationale

In the first section of this guide, students prepared to read *To Kill a Mockingbird* by reflecting on the tension between the individual and society in which our identities are formed. In this section, as students read Chapters 1 through 7, they will connect their examination of the individual and society to the characters and setting of the novel.

Literary critic Wayne C. Booth writes that the plots of great stories "are built out of the characters' efforts to face moral choices. In tracing those efforts, we readers stretch our own capacities for thinking about how life should be lived."[1] In order to understand the moral choices depicted in *To Kill a Mockingbird*, we must first look

---

1   Wayne C. Booth, *The Company We Keep: An Ethics of Fiction* (Berkeley: University of California Press, 1988), 187.

at both the identities of those making moral choices and the context in which they are made. In other words, we must start by examining *character* and *setting*.

When Atticus, in Chapter 3, famously advises Scout that "you never really understand a person until you consider things from his point of view," he might as well be offering us advice on understanding character in a work of fiction. As Michael W. Smith and Jeffrey D. Wilhelm assert, "The unique power of literature allows us to pay respectful attention to people and perspectives that are different from us in time, place, and experience."[2] In Chapters 1 through 7 of *To Kill a Mockingbird*, readers will meet and establish first impressions of most of the important characters in the novel, including Scout, Jem, Atticus, Calpurnia, Dill, and Boo Radley. To pay "respectful attention" to these characters—both in the questions and activities of Section 1 and throughout the rest of this guide—is to go beyond their surface traits and to seek to understand as best we can how each thinks about the world around them. By doing so, we can better understand the choices they make in the book and more deeply reflect on ourselves as moral actors in our own world.

But character is not sufficient for fully understanding the choices made by Scout, Jem, Atticus, and the other residents of Maycomb. We must also put those choices into context by examining the circumstances in which they are made. When we examine these circumstances, we are examining setting.

Just as character includes more than surface traits, setting goes well beyond simply establishing the time and place of the novel. To meaningfully understand the setting of *To Kill a Mockingbird* requires understanding the moral universe in which the story takes place. In other words, it requires having a sense of the "rules, constraints, possibilities, potential conflicts and possible consequences"[3] that affect the choices the characters make. Without this knowledge, we cannot adequately analyze, understand, or learn from the behavior of the characters. For instance, to understand the respect Atticus shows for the Cunninghams and the disdain he exhibits for the Ewells, the reader needs to know not only the perspectives and experiences that the character of Atticus represents but also something about what he calls "Maycomb's ways," the effects of the Great Depression, and more. As Smith and Wilhelm write, "Settings don't come from a vacuum . . . . They grow and evolve from the compost of all that we know from the world, from history, from our own experience and that of humanity, and from our experience with other books and movies from the genre we are reading."[4] The better we understand this

---

2   Michael W. Smith and Jeffrey D. Wilhelm, *Fresh Takes on Teaching Literary Elements* (New York: Scholastic, 2010), 25.
3   Ibid., 71.
4   Ibid., 72.

web of factors that makes up setting, the better equipped we are to understand the possibilities, constraints, and rules—both explicit and implicit—that influence the choices that characters make.

In this section, students will begin to understand the moral universe of Maycomb, Alabama, both through analyzing the text itself and through investigating some of the historical context into which Harper Lee has placed her characters. By looking closely at what the characters say and do, as well as how they act toward each other, students will begin in this section to establish an understanding of Maycomb's ways. Sometimes the clues students need to build this understanding are stated explicitly in the text, and other times they are implied in the characters' words and actions. In Section 2, students will use this evidence to piece together the effects of class on the social hierarchy of the town based on the way the characters they meet interact with one another (race and gender will be examined in later sections). They will also consider the way that Scout's first-person narration both enriches our experience of the story and imposes limits on our ability to truly know some of the other characters and events she reports. Finally, through a series of activities using primary source documents and other historical resources, students will learn in this section about the Great Depression and its devastating effects on American society, especially in the rural and small-town South. By examining photographs and hearing firsthand accounts, students will confront the shame, humiliation, and vulnerability experienced by many Americans in the 1930s and consider how these factors help them better understand both the characters in the novel and the moral universe they inhabit.

Plot Summary

Jean Louise "Scout" Finch opens by introducing the setting of Maycomb, Alabama, and some main characters: Jem, Atticus, Calpurnia, and Dill Harris. Jem and Scout tell Dill the story of Boo Radley, and the trio spends the summer playing and daring one another to get closer to the Radley house.

When the summer ends, Scout starts school, and her first day turns out to be a disaster when she is punished by her teacher for knowing how to read. The teacher, who is new to Maycomb, has trouble understanding the dynamics of the different students in the classroom—namely, the difference between two impoverished families: the Cunninghams, who don't like to take things they cannot repay, and the Ewells, who have never done an honest day's work.

At the end of the school year, Dill returns to Maycomb, and he, Jem, and Scout resume their attempts to make Boo Radley come out of his house. They find a series of small trinkets in the knot-hole of a tree at the edge of the Radleys' property. When the three friends make a last attempt to see Boo, Jem loses his pants in the Radleys' yard, only to find them repaired and waiting for him later that night. After Scout and Jem leave a note thanking the person who is leaving them presents in the tree, Mr. Nathan Radley fills the knot-hole with cement.

Skills Focus

- Understanding the Setting as a "Moral Universe"

- Getting to Know the Characters

  » Main characters: Scout, Jem, Atticus

  » Secondary characters: Dill, Calpurnia, Miss Maudie, Miss Caroline, Boo Radley, Walter Cunningham, Burris Ewell

- Investigating the Author's Craft: Descriptive Language

- Deepening Understanding of the Novel through Analysis of Historical Context from Informational Texts

Academic Vocabulary

CHAPTER 1 *dictum, eccentric, quaint, malevolent, morbid, predilection;*
CHAPTER 2 *indigenous, illicit, sentimentality, entailment;* CHAPTER 3 *monosyllabic, misdemeanor, capital felony;* CHAPTER 4 *auspicious;* CHAPTER 5 *benevolence, edification*

Exploring the Text

Before Reading

Before they begin reading Chapters 1 to 7, consider having students reflect in their journals on the following questions:

1. *Think about a community in which you are a member—for instance, your school, religious community, family, or group of friends. What are some of the most important rules in that community? Are these rules written down? What are the most important unwritten rules, those not written down but which everyone knows about?*

2. *Write about a pivotal choice you have made in your life or an experience you have had that was influenced by the setting. What other options might have been available to you if you lived in a different place and time? What circumstances would have influenced you to make a different decision?*

When discussing these questions, explain that understanding the setting of a novel is more than simply knowing the time and place in which the plot takes place. The setting helps us understand the choices the characters make because it helps shape the possibilities and options available. Later in the book, the characters that students meet in this first section will make important and pivotal choices. As they read these opening chapters, the students' primary task is to try to understand the world these characters live in and the rules, both written and unwritten, that will guide their behavior.

Using Connection Questions

Connection Questions, organized by chapter, are provided below to help guide your class's analysis of the text. A similar set of "After Reading Section 2: Connection Questions" is also provided below to help students synthesize their understanding of Chapters 1 through 7 as a whole.

While these questions are mostly text-based, they are designed to probe important themes in the novel. As you assign chapters for students to read, you might designate all or some of these questions for students to respond to in their journals. These questions can also provide the basis for a class discussion of the text. See facinghistory.org/mockingbird/strategies for suggestions about how to structure effective classroom discussions.

Close Reading

An additional set of text-dependent questions is provided in the Appendix to help facilitate the close reading of a passage from Chapter 3 of the novel. This close reading activity is specifically written to align with the Common Core State Standards for English Language Arts. In this passage, Atticus offers his famous advice to Scout about seeing things from others' perspectives. If you choose to implement this close reading activity, we recommend you do so before engaging the class in other activities related to Chapter 3. See "Close Reading for Deep Comprehension" in the Appendix for a suggested procedure for implementing this close reading activity.

Activities for Deeper Understanding

In addition to the Connection Questions, the following activities can help students reach a deeper understanding of Chapters 1 through 7 of *To Kill a Mockingbird* and their essential themes.

Write and Reflect in Journals

Any of the Connection Questions in this section might be used as a prompt for journal writing. Also, consider the following questions for a brief reflective writing assignment before, during, or after reading Chapters 1 to 7:

1. Choose a character that stands out to you—a character you most relate to or a character you are curious about. Write a paragraph describing your first impression of this character. Who is the character? What are the character's circumstances?

2. Who is "the other"? Who are "the others" in Maycomb? Who are "the others" in a community you belong to? What can we do to understand people who are different from us?

3. How does knowing more about the period in history in which a novel is set help you understand the characters and the choices they make?

Create Identity Charts

Identity charts are a graphic tool that helps students consider the many factors that shape the identities of individuals and communities. As part of their examination of identity in the Pre-Reading section of this guide, students created identity charts for themselves. Identity charts can also help students gather and analyze information about the identities of literary characters in order to help them better understand the dilemmas and choices they face throughout the story.

Creating and modifying identity charts for central characters in *To Kill a Mockingbird* will also help prepare students for a culminating activity, suggested in the Post-Reading section of this guide, that asks students to analyze the moral and ethical growth of a character from the novel. Keeping detailed identity charts while reading the novel will give students a head start in this task after completing their reading.

We recommend having students start identity charts for the three main characters of *To Kill a Mockingbird*—Scout, Jem, and Atticus—after reading the first chapter. First, ask students to write the name of the character in the center of a piece of paper or on a blank page in their journals. Then students can look through the text for evidence that helps them answer the question, "Who is this person?" Encourage students to include quotations from the text on their identity charts, as well as their own interpretations of the character or figure based on their reading. Students can complete identity charts individually or in small groups. Alternatively, students could contribute ideas to a class version of an identity chart that you keep on the classroom wall. Students will return to these identity charts throughout the novel to expand and revise them as their understanding of each character deepens.

Use Storyboards to Improve Comprehension

Teachers sometimes notice that the first several chapters of *To Kill a Mockingbird* are challenging for their students. This is likely because these chapters introduce a wide variety of characters by providing a large quantity of background information with references to history and literature to which students may not have been exposed. At the same time, students must adjust to seeing the world through the eyes of six-year-old Scout, who is describing the unwritten rules of Maycomb, rules that she herself does not fully comprehend. Much is left for the reader to infer, and as a result students sometimes struggle to pick up the thread of the narrative as it emerges.

The Storyboard teaching strategy has been valuable for some teachers and students by helping them keep track of the important events and characters early in the novel and creating a resource the class can refer to as the plot and pacing of the novel build momentum later in the book (for more information on this strategy, see facinghistory.org/mockingbird/strategies). Students can work either independently or in small groups to illustrate an important scene from each of the first several chapters. Each image should be accompanied by a caption describing the scene. By sharing and discussing the images they have created, students will be required to verbalize and thus further synthesize their understanding of the narrative.

CHAPTER 1: Connection Questions

1. In the second paragraph of the novel, Scout says that the events leading up to Jem's broken arm started with the Ewells (another family in Maycomb), but Jem "said it started long before that." How does Jem's comment relate to the family history Scout provides over the next couple of pages? What is Harper Lee suggesting about the influence of the past on the events that take place in the novel?

2. Read aloud Scout's description of Maycomb in the first chapter, beginning with "Maycomb was an old town, but it was a tired old town when I first knew it." What words does Harper Lee, with Scout as the narrator, use to paint a picture of Maycomb? If Maycomb were a person, how would you describe its personality?

3. What kind of figurative language does Harper Lee use in the following description?

   > Ladies bathed before noon, after their three-o'clock naps, and by nightfall were like soft teacakes with frostings of sweat and sweet talcum.

   What does this description suggest about the role of women in Maycomb?

4. Harper Lee does not directly tell the reader what years the novel takes place during. What are some clues that she provides to help the reader determine the time period?

5. What facts are revealed about the history of the Radleys in this chapter? What gossip and legend about the Radleys is revealed? How do you know the difference between the facts and the gossip?

CHAPTER 2: Connection Questions

1. Scout tells us the following about her teacher on the first day of school:

   > Miss Caroline was no more than twenty-one. She had bright auburn hair, pink cheeks, and wore crimson fingernail polish. She also wore high-heeled pumps and a red-and-white-striped dress. She looked and smelled like a peppermint drop.

   Analyze the descriptive language Lee uses to describe Miss Caroline. What words or phrases help you visualize her? What figurative language does the author use?

How does the author use the description of Miss Caroline to suggest something about her personality and style as a teacher? How does the description accentuate the personality clash between Scout and her teacher?

2. Scout reflects: "Until I feared I would lose it, I never loved to read. One does not love breathing."

   What comparison is Lee suggesting in these two sentences? What does it suggest about how Scout thinks about reading?

3. When Scout introduces Walter to her teacher by saying, "Miss Caroline, he's a Cunningham," what does Scout assume that Miss Caroline will automatically understand about him? What characteristics do the residents of Maycomb automatically associate with "the Cunningham tribe"?

4. How does our membership in various groups—families, schools, neighborhoods, nations—affect how others think about us? How does it affect how we think about ourselves? Are those impressions ever accurate?

5. How are readers and Miss Caroline similar in their understanding of Maycomb society at this point in the novel? How does Harper Lee use the character of Miss Caroline to introduce readers to what everyone else in Maycomb already "knows"?

6. What words and phrases do Scout and Atticus use to describe the Cunninghams in this chapter? How are the Cunninghams different from the Finches? How are they similar?

CHAPTER 3: Connection Questions

1. What does Scout mean when she says, "By the time we reached our front steps Walter had forgotten he was a Cunningham"?

2. According to Atticus, who are the "common folk" in Maycomb? What characteristics does he say, or imply, are shared by the "common folk"? Who does Atticus say are not included in the "common folk"? Why are they excluded?

3. What do we mean when we talk about someone's social or economic class? What is it supposed to tell you about someone?

4. How does Atticus distinguish between the Cunninghams and the Ewells? Is either family part of the "common folk" of Maycomb? How do the two families differ in class and status from each other and from the Finches? What specific evidence from the text helps explain why his opinion of the two families differs?

5. Compare and contrast the descriptions Scout provides of Burris Ewell and Little Chuck Little. How do the similarities and differences between these two classmates support Atticus's opinion about the Ewell family?

6. In this chapter we learn about more about the Finches, the Cunninghams, and the Ewells. Which of the characters in this chapter have the most power and the highest status in Maycomb? Which have the least power and status? What accounts for those differences?

7. How does Calpurnia fit into the social hierarchy in this chapter? Which characters have more power than she does? Who has less?

8. How do race, class, and gender affect one's position in Maycomb society? How might Atticus use race, class, and gender to describe the "common folk"? What role do they play in determining one's position in your society today?

9. How do particular situations and circumstances affect how our identity is perceived? How might Calpurnia's identity be different in the Finch home from her identity in her own home?

10. Atticus tells Scout, "If you can learn a simple trick, Scout, you'll get along a lot better with all kinds of folks. You never really understand a person until you consider things from his point of view . . . until you climb into his skin and walk around in it."

    Can you ever fully understand another person's point of view? What is the value in trying? How does Atticus's advice relate to empathy? Take a moment to write a working definition for *empathy* in your journal.

CHAPTER 4: Connection Questions

1. Jem and Dill continue to swap gossip, superstition, and exaggeration in this chapter. What are some examples of superstitions that they discuss? What effect do they have on Scout?

2. What do Jem and Scout agree to do with the items they find in the tree on the edge of the Radleys' yard? What conclusions about these items does Jem seem to be making without sharing with Scout? Scout says, "Before Jem went to his room, he looked for a long time at the Radley place. He seemed to be thinking again." What do you think Jem was thinking about?

3. How does the fact that Scout is the narrator affect the reader's ability to understand Jem's point of view?

4. Despite Jem's disagreement, Scout says she thinks that Boo Radley is in the Radley home and watching the kids play. Why does Scout feel so certain? When does Scout share her evidence with the reader? How does Lee foreshadow that revelation?

5. According to Scout, Calpurnia called the Hot Steam superstition that Jem and Dill describe "nigger-talk."* What does Calpurnia mean?

6. How can words divide people? Why do some words create more powerful divisions than others?

7. How does Jem use stereotypes about gender to influence Scout? How does Scout feel about her gender? How do you know?

8. How can stereotypes, especially about race, gender, and class, affect our behavior, even when we are trying to disprove them?

CHAPTER 5: Connection Questions

1. What does Miss Maudie mean when she says that Jem "gets more like Jack Finch every day"? What details in the story she tells about her relationship with Jack help explain why Maudie thinks that Jem and Jack are similar?

2. What does Maudie's comparison between Jem and Jack reveal to us about what Jem might really be thinking about Boo and the items left in the tree?

3. What is the difference between the letter of the law and the spirit of the law? How does Maudie and Scout's discussion about different kinds of Baptists explore that difference? How does the conflict between Jem

---

* We have chosen to include this word in order to honestly communicate the harshness of the bigoted language. We recommend that teachers review "Discussing Sensitive Topics in the Classroom" on page xv before using these questions in class.

and Atticus over playing the Boo Radley game explore that difference? Who in this chapter follows the letter of the law? Who follows the spirit of the law? What is the difference? What are the consequences of each approach for the characters in this chapter?

4. Why does Jem declare at the end of the chapter, "I thought I wanted to be a lawyer but I ain't so sure now"?

CHAPTER 6: Connection Questions

1. Why is it so important to Jem to risk his safety to retrieve his pants from the Radleys' fence in the middle of the night?

2. Scout states in this chapter, "It was then, I suppose, that Jem and I first began to part company." What prompts her to draw this conclusion? What does she mean? As you continue to read the novel, look for evidence that Scout and Jem are growing apart.

CHAPTER 7: Connection Questions

1. Why is Jem moody at the beginning of Chapter 7? Is Scout able to understand by "climbing into Jem's skin"? What does the rest of the chapter reveal about the source of Jem's moodiness?

2. Jem tells Scout that when he retrieved his pants from the Radleys', "they were folded across the fence like they were expectin' me." Of what type of figurative language is this an example? How does this language contribute to the sense of mystery around the Radley house? Does Jem know how his pants ended up that way?

3. What evidence does Chapter 7 provide to help the reader understand how Scout and Jem were "parting company"? What was Jem beginning to understand (about Boo Radley) that Scout could not yet see? Why does Jem keep his feelings secret from Atticus and Scout?

4. How do Jem's responses to the objects left in the tree change in this chapter? What does this suggest about how he feels about the items and the person leaving them?

5. Why does Jem cry at the end of Chapter 7? What does Jem understand about Boo and Mr. Radley that he did not understand before? Find evidence in the text to support your answer.

AFTER READING SECTION 2: Connection Questions

1. What do Scout, Jem, and Dill know about Boo Radley? What parts of their understanding of Boo are based on facts and reliable information? What parts are based on gossip and legend? How can the reader tell the difference between the facts about the Radley family and the legends?

2. How does the relationship between Scout and Jem change over the first seven chapters? How does Scout understand the changes Jem undergoes?

3. In Chapter 3, Atticus and Scout talk about "Maycomb's ways." What stands out to you most about the customs, traditions, and unwritten rules of Maycomb's society?

4. What is "the other"? Who are "the others" in Maycomb? What roles do race, class, and gender play in establishing who is the other? What role does gossip and superstition play? What about stereotypes? What about fear?

5. What events and experiences begin to change Jem's feelings about Boo Radley in these chapters? What does this suggest about how we can better understand people different from us?

6. How does race complicate the circumstances of the characters we have met so far? What role does Calpurnia play in the Finch family? What authority does she have in the Finch household that she might not have elsewhere in Maycomb?

Building Historical Context

To Kill a Mockingbird takes place in Alabama during the Great Depression. Learning historical context about the economic collapse of the 1930s and about some of the effects of the Depression on life in the South can help students better understand the economic circumstances and social tensions woven into the novel. The resources and activities below focus specifically on life in the South. They have been chosen to help students understand the class differences that play out in the first seven chapters of the novel. Historical context about the laws and attitudes about race and gender will be explored in later sections of this guide.

As you explore these resources with the class, remind students that your goal is to reach a deeper understanding of the characters and setting of the novel. After analyzing each resource, revisit the following questions:

- How did this resource deepen your understanding of the characters and setting of *To Kill a Mockingbird*?

- How did this resource help you understand factors that might influence the worldviews and choices of individuals who live in the world of Maycomb, Alabama, during the Great Depression?

The following resources and activities can help you introduce the Great Depression and its effects on life in the South to your students:

Begin a K-W-L Chart to Activate Prior Knowledge

After reading Chapter 1, you might ask students to begin a K-W-L chart for the Great Depression in their journals. They create three columns on a page (or use three separate pages). In the first column they will answer the question: What do you **K**now about the Great Depression? In the second, they will answer the question: What do you **W**ant to know about this era? Students can complete these first two columns before you proceed with any additional activities for building historical context. As students learn more about the Great Depression, provide them with opportunities to stop and add to the third column of their charts, in which they will answer the question: What did you **L**earn about the Great Depression? You can find more details about K-W-L charts at facinghistory.org/mockingbird/strategies.

Read a Historical Overview of the Great Depression

Handout 2.1 provides a brief overview (from the American Experience website for the film *Surviving the Dust Bowl*) of the Great Depression and how it affected

Americans from all walks of life. You might use the information to create a brief lecture or simply ask students to read it, using it to add information to their K-W-L charts.

Read an Excerpt of Franklin D. Roosevelt's 1933 Inaugural Address

In Chapter 1, Scout alludes to the circumstances of the Great Depression and the 1933 inaugural speech by President Franklin D. Roosevelt:

> There was no hurry, for there was nowhere to go, nothing to buy and no money to buy it with, nothing to see outside the boundaries of Maycomb County. But it was a time of vague optimism for some of the people: Maycomb County had recently been told that it had nothing to fear but fear itself.

You might share the excerpt of Roosevelt's speech included in **Handout 2.2** as a way both to illustrate the allusion explicitly and to read the description of the effects of the Depression included in the speech.

Analyze Photographs of the Great Depression in the South

Photographs provide another entry point for students to learn about the Great Depression and its effects. **Handout 2.3** provides several photos taken by Walker Evans for the Farm Security Administration (FSA) in the 1930s. Consider sharing these photographs with students as you read Chapters 2 and 3, when the Cunninghams and Ewells are introduced.

The FSA, a bureau in the federal government, charged Walker Evans with the task of documenting the effects of the Great Depression on film. He took hundreds of photographs across the country. Many of them are available on the website for the Library of Congress (see loc.gov). Several photos that Evans took during this time period became part of his famous collaboration with the writer James Agee, the book *Let Us Now Praise Famous Men*.

We recommend you invite students to look carefully at each image, perhaps using the Analyzing Visual Images teaching strategy (see facinghistory.org/mockingbird/strategies). Remind students that photographs reflect the choices and objectives of the photographer. Ask students to consider not only what they see but also what they think Walker Evans wanted them to see when they look at each image.

You might extend this activity by asking students to search the Library of Congress's online archives at loc.gov for photos during the Depression taken at locations in the North. What similarities and differences do they notice in the conditions in each region during the Depression?

Analyze Firsthand Accounts of the Depression

Writer Studs Terkel published *Hard Times*, an oral history of the Great Depression, in 1970. The firsthand accounts of life in the United States during the Depression were collected from interviews Terkel conducted several decades later. The accounts included here from Virginia Durr, Eileen Barth, and Emma Tiller explore the shame and humiliation experienced by many Americans who found themselves dependent on others, or on government relief programs, for survival. These three accounts can help deepen students' understanding of the Cunningham and Ewell families in *To Kill a Mockingbird*; each family deals with poverty and dependence on others in a different way. Students may also connect the experience of Emma Tiller, an African American sharecropper, to the character Tom Robinson, who will be introduced in the second section of the book.

Excerpts from the transcripts of Terkel's interviews with these three women are included as **Handout 2.4**. However, we recommend that you listen to the interviews online at facinghistory.org/mockingbird. Hearing the actual voices of the women provides students with a richer, more engaging experience. Note that Terkel's transcripts appear to have been lightly edited for clarity, and they do not match the audio transcripts word for word.

Like the Library of Congress's online photo archive, Terkel's collection of oral histories includes accounts from residents of both the South and the North. You might extend this activity by asking students to explore the interviews available at studsterkel.org or in his book *Hard Times* to compare and contrast experiences of Southerners and Northerners.

Handout 2.1 The Great Depression

The following historical overview of the Great Depression was created for the American Experience website for the film Surviving the Dust Bowl:

During the economic boom of the Roaring Twenties the traditional values of rural America were challenged by the Jazz Age, symbolized by women smoking, drinking, and wearing short skirts. The average American was busy buying automobiles and household appliances, and speculating in the stock market, where big money could be made. Those appliances were bought on credit, however. Although businesses had made huge gains—65 percent—from the mechanization of manufacturing, the average worker's wages had only increased 8 percent.

The imbalance between the rich and the poor, with 0.1 percent of society earning the same total income as 42 percent, combined with production of more and more goods and rising personal debt, could not be sustained. On Black Tuesday, October 29, 1929, the stock market crashed, triggering the Great Depression, the worst economic collapse in the history of the modern industrial world. It spread from the United States to the rest of the world, lasting from the end of 1929 until the early 1940s. With banks failing and businesses closing, more than 15 million Americans (one-quarter of the workforce) became unemployed.

President Herbert Hoover, underestimating the seriousness of the crisis, called it "a passing incident in our national lives," and assured Americans that it would be over in 60 days. A strong believer in rugged individualism, Hoover did not think the federal government should offer relief to the poverty-stricken population. Focusing on a trickle-down economic program to help finance businesses and banks, Hoover met with resistance from business executives who preferred to lay off workers. Blamed by many for the Great Depression, Hoover was widely ridiculed: an empty pocket turned inside out was called a "Hoover flag"; the decrepit shantytowns springing up around the country were called "Hoovervilles." Franklin Delano Roosevelt offered Americans a New Deal, and was elected in a landslide victory in 1932. He took quick action to attack the Depression, declaring a four-day bank holiday, during which Congress passed the Emergency Banking Relief Act to stabilize the banking system. During the first 100 days of his administration, Roosevelt laid the groundwork for his New Deal remedies that would rescue the country from the depths of despair.

The New Deal programs created a liberal political alliance of labor unions, blacks and other minorities, some farmers and others receiving government relief, and intellectuals. The hardship brought on by the Depression affected Americans deeply. Since the prevailing attitude of the 1920s was that success was earned, it followed that failure was deserved. The unemployment brought on by the Depression caused self-blame and self-doubt. Men were harder hit psychologically than women were. Since men were expected to provide for their families, it was humiliating to have to ask for assistance. Although some argued that women should not be given jobs when many men were unemployed, the percentage of women working increased slightly during the Depression. Traditionally female fields of teaching and social services grew under New Deal programs. Children took on more responsibilities, sometimes finding work when their parents could not. As a result of living through the Depression, some people developed habits of careful saving and frugality, others determined to create a comfortable life for themselves.

African Americans suffered more than whites, since their jobs were often taken away from them and given to whites. In 1930, 50 percent of blacks were unemployed. However, Eleanor Roosevelt championed black rights, and New Deal programs prohibited discrimination. Discrimination continued in the South, however, [and] as a result a large number of black voters switched from the Republican to the Democrat party during the Depression.

The Great Depression and the New Deal changed forever the relationship between Americans and their government. Government involvement and responsibility in caring for the needy and regulating the economy came to be expected. [1]

---

1   Reproduced from the American Experience website for the film *Surviving the Dust Bowl,* accessed April 17, 2014, http:// www.pbs.org/wgbh/americanexperience/features/general-article/dustbowl-great-depression/.

Handout 2.2 President Franklin D. Roosevelt's First Inaugural Speech

This excerpt is from the beginning of Roosevelt's address, delivered on March 4, 1933:

This is a day of national consecration. And I am certain that on this day my fellow Americans expect that on my induction into the Presidency, I will address them with a candor and a decision which the present situation of our people impels. This is preeminently the time to speak the truth, the whole truth, frankly and boldly. Nor need we shrink from honestly facing conditions in our country today. This great Nation will endure, as it has endured, will revive and will prosper. So, first of all, let me assert my firm belief that the only thing we have to fear is fear itself—nameless, unreasoning, unjustified terror which paralyzes needed efforts to convert retreat into advance. In every dark hour of our national life, a leadership of frankness and of vigor has met with that understanding and support of the people themselves which is essential to victory. And I am convinced that you will again give that support to leadership in these critical days.

In such a spirit on my part and on yours we face our common difficulties. They concern, thank God, only material things. Values have shrunk to fantastic levels; taxes have risen; our ability to pay has fallen; government of all kinds is faced by serious curtailment of income; the means of exchange are frozen in the currents of trade; the withered leaves of industrial enterprise lie on every side; farmers find no markets for their produce; and the savings of many years in thousands of families are gone. More important, a host of unemployed citizens face the grim problem of existence, and an equally great number toil with little return. Only a foolish optimist can deny the dark realities of the moment.

And yet our distress comes from no failure of substance. We are stricken by no plague of locusts. Compared with the perils which our forefathers conquered, because they believed and were not afraid, we have still much to be thankful for. Nature still offers her bounty and human efforts have multiplied it. Plenty is at our doorstep, but a generous use of it languishes in the very sight of the supply. . . .[1]

---

1   Franklin D. Roosevelt, first inaugural address, March 4, 1933, retrieved April 22, 2014, from http://www.americanrhetoric. com/speeches/fdrfirstinaugural.html.

Handout 2.3 Photographs of the South During the Depression

Walker Evans is one of the most famous photographers to document the effects of the Great Depression in the United States. He took the following photos in the South while working for a branch of the federal government called the Farm Security Administration in the 1930s.

Bud Fields and His Family: Alabama Sharecroppers

Library of Congress

Floyd Burroughs and Tengle Children, Hale County, Alabama

General Store in Moundville, Alabama

Negro Cabin in Hale County, Alabama

Library of Congress

Negro Farming Near Tupelo, Mississippi

Library of Congress

Negroes Wait in Line for Food at Camp for Flood Refugees in Alabama

Street in Marion, Alabama

Children Receive Food in Alabama Camp for Flood Refugees

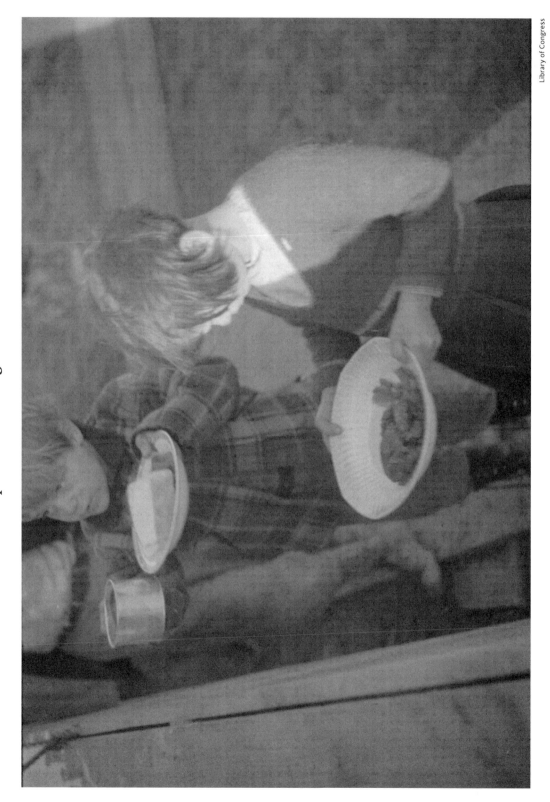

Handout 2.4 Firsthand Accounts of the Great Depression

Virginia Durr, who later became a civil rights activist, describes the shame and humiliation people experienced:

It was a time of terrible suffering. The contradictions were so obvious that it didn't take a very bright person to realize something was terribly wrong.

Have you ever seen a child with rickets? Shaking as with palsy. No proteins, no milk. And the companies pouring milk into gutters. People with nothing to wear, and they were plowing up cotton. People with nothing to eat, and they killed the pigs. If that wasn't the craziest system in the world, could you imagine anything more idiotic? This was just insane.

And people blamed themselves, not the system. They felt they had been at fault: . . . "if we hadn't bought that old radio" . . . "if we hadn't bought that old secondhand car." Among the things that horrified me were the preachers— the fundamentalists. They would tell the people they suffered because of their sins. And the people believed it. God was punishing them. Their children were starving because of their sins.

People who were independent, who thought they were masters and mistresses of their lives, were all of a sudden dependent on others. Relatives or relief. People of pride went into shock and sanitoriums. My mother was one.

Up to this time, I had been a conformist, a Southern snob. I actually thought the only people who amounted to anything were the very small group which I belonged to. The fact that my family wasn't as well off as those of the girls I went with—I was vice president of the Junior League—made me value even more the idea of being well-born . . . .

What I learned during the Depression changed all that. I saw a blinding light like Saul on the road to Damascus. (Laughs.) It was the first time I had seen the other side of the tracks. The rickets, the pellagra—it shook me up. I saw the world as it really was . . . .

The Depression affected people in two different ways. The great majority reacted by thinking money is the most important thing in the world. Get yours. And get it for your children. Nothing else matters. Not having that stark terror come at you again . . . .

And then there was a small number of people who felt the whole system was lousy. You have to change it. The kids come along and they want to change it, too. But they don't seem to know what to put in its place. I'm not so sure I know, either. I do think it has to be responsive to people's needs. And it has to be done by democratic means, if possible.[1]

Eileen Barth worked as a case worker in Chicago. Her job was to work with those who needed government assistance during the Great Depression. In one case, a family asked for government assistance in getting clothing, and Barth was instructed by her supervisor to look in their closets to determine how badly they needed the clothing they asked for. She describes what happened:

I'll never forget one of the first families I visited. The father was a railroad man who had lost his job. I was told by my supervisor that I really had to *see* the poverty. If a family needed clothing, I was to investigate how much clothing they had at hand. So I looked into this man's closet—[pauses, it becomes difficult]—he was a tall, gray-haired man, though not terribly old. He let me look in his closet—he was so insulted. [She weeps angrily.] He said, "Why are you doing this?" I remember his feeling of humiliation . . . the terrible humiliation. [She can't continue. After a pause, she resumes.] He said, "I really haven't anything to hide, but if you really must look into it. . . ." I could see he was very proud. He was so deeply humiliated. And I was, too. . . ."[2]

Emma Tiller describes sharecropping during the Depression:

In 1929, me and my husband were sharecroppers. We made a crop that year, the owners takin' all of the crop.

This horrible way of liven' with almost nothin' lasted up until Roosevelt. There was another strangest thing. I didn't suffer for food through the Thirties, because there was plenty of people that really suffered much worse. When you go through a lot, you in better condition to survive through all these kinds of things.

I picked cotton. We weren't getting but thirty-five cents a hundred, but I was able to make it. 'Cause I also worked peoples homes, where they give you old clothes and shoes.

At this time, I worked in private homes a lot and when the white people kill hogs, they always get the Negroes to help. The cleanin' of the insides and the

1   Studs Terkel, *Hard Times: An Oral History of the Great Depression* (New York: The New Press, 2005), 461–462.
2   Ibid., 420.

clean up the mess afterwards. And then they would give you a lot of scraps. A pretty adequate amount of meat for the whole family. The majority of the Negroes on the farm were in the same shape we were in. The crops were eaten by these worms. And they had no other jobs except farming.

In 1934, in this Texas town, the farmers was all out of food. The government gave us a slip, where you could pick up food. For a week, they had people who would come and stand in line, and they couldn't get waited on. This was a small town, mostly white. Only five of us in that line were Negroes, the rest was white. We would stand all day and wait and wait and wait. And get nothin' or if you did, it was spoiled meat. . . .

The Government sent two men out there to find out why the trouble. They found out his man and a couple others had rented a huge warehouse and was stackin' that food and sellin' it. The food that was supposed to be issued to these people. These three men was sent to the pen.[3]

3 Ibid., 232–233.

Connecting to the Central Question

Before beginning Section 3, consider taking time to ask students to review the central question introduced at the beginning of this guide:

What factors influence our moral growth? What kinds of experiences help us learn how to judge right from wrong?

Give students some time to reflect on what they have learned in the first seven chapters of *To Kill a Mockingbird*. You might give them an opportunity to review their notes and reflections in response to the activities and questions in this section as a way to help them brainstorm factors that might influence the main characters' moral growth. They should record references to events from the novel and historical documents that they think can help them answer the question. Then ask students to write a preliminary response to the central question, based on both the novel and the historical context they have explored so far. Make sure to remind them that they will have several opportunities to revise their thinking as they continue to read the novel.

Their preliminary response and their notes will help prepare students for a culminating activity, suggested in the Post-Reading section of this guide, that asks them to analyze the moral growth of a character from the novel.

SECTION 3

It's a Sin to Kill a Mockingbird

This section covers Chapters 8 to 11 of the novel.

Introduction

Essential Questions

- How does a community determine who belongs and who does not? How does a society determine its "universe of obligation"?

- What are the consequences for those who choose to challenge a community's rules—written and unwritten—about who belongs?

- What dilemmas do individuals confront when their consciences conflict with the rules and expectations of their communities? What conflicts arise in literature out of the tension between characters and their setting?

Rationale

In the previous section, students explored the first seven chapters of *To Kill a Mockingbird*, established first impressions of the novel's central characters, and used both textual analysis and historical context to begin to understand the "moral universe" of the fictional Maycomb, Alabama, during the Great Depression. In this section, students will continue to explore the characters and setting of the novel. They will also begin to explore more deeply the novel's themes by engaging in some of the ongoing, unresolved cultural conversations at the core of *To Kill a Mockingbird*.

Few novels, much less one as culturally and historically rich as *To Kill a Mockingbird*, can be reduced to a single theme. Likewise, no single theme in a novel can be expressed elegantly in a single phrase or sentence. According to Michael W. Smith and Jeffrey D. Wilhelm, a theme is not a category or an idea but a conversation, and it is a conversation that cannot be easily or quickly resolved. They write:

> Stating the theme isn't the end of conversation—it's the start of one. . . . If the conversation is ongoing, then no one can be silenced, no one perspective holds the trump card or the answer. Exploring theme opens up discussion instead of closing it down. Even a compelling argument is taken as categorically tentative: Is this always true? Or is it true only under certain conditions? Responding to those questions makes a theme more than an aphorism or a bumper sticker.[1]

In this way, themes are generative—like essential questions—and they explore issues that resonate with readers even before they pick up the novel, and their resonance persists long after reading is complete.

In Chapters 8 through 11, readers continue to learn about "Maycomb's ways" as well as the people who live within its moral universe. The plot begins to gain momentum as it is revealed that Atticus has taken on a difficult and unpopular case in defending a black man, Tom Robinson. Although we do not yet learn about the details of the charges he must defend Robinson against, a variety of themes begin to emerge from the growing tension between the characters and their setting. The ongoing conversations that emerge in this section are perhaps best expressed in the form of questions:

- How do communities determine who belongs and who doesn't belong?

- How do society's rules—written and unwritten—differ depending on your family, race, gender, or class?

- How do those rules become accepted by many people as normal?

- What are the consequences of challenging the rules that determine who belongs and who does not?

By observing the choices characters make and the consequences that result, and by bringing their own prior knowledge and experiences to bear, students can begin to formulate answers to the questions above. As they continue to read the novel, they will test those ideas.

---

1   Michael W. Smith and Jeffrey D. Wilhelm, *Fresh Takes on Teaching Literary Elements* (New York: Scholastic, 2010), 156–157.

At the same time, Section 3 provides historical context that will help deepen students' exploration of the themes at play as well as their understanding of some of the important actions, events, and dialogue in Chapters 8 through 11. This section includes informational texts and primary documents that will help students continue to explore the explicit and implicit rules of Depression-era Southern society around the characteristics of race, gender, and class. In particular, students will learn about the following topics:

- The legal and social structure of Jim Crow segregation

- The social ideals embodied by the proper *Southern lady* and *Southern gentleman* social types

- The roles and status of black women in Depression-era Southern society

This historical context will help students understand the complexity of the rules and expectations of Maycomb society, a complexity that is not explained explicitly in the novel. In Maycomb, these rules are understood, so there is little reason for Scout or any other character to discuss them explicitly. The rules differ not only depending on whether one is white or black, but also whether one is rich or poor and whether one is a man or a woman. Note that the role and status of black men will be explored deeply in subsequent sections of this guide as the Tom Robinson trial becomes a primary focus of the plot.

Plot Summary

The night after the first snow in Maycomb since 1885, Miss Maudie's house is destroyed by a fire. While Scout and Jem are outside watching the attempts to contain the fire, Boo Radley puts a blanket on Scout's shoulders, but neither Jem nor Scout realizes he has done so.

Scout gets in fights with peers who call Atticus a "nigger-lover"—including one with her cousin Francis on Christmas while she, Atticus, Jem, and her Uncle Jack are visiting Aunt Alexandra and Uncle Jimmy—because he intends to defend a black man in court. A few weeks later, Jem and Scout are surprised by Atticus's skill when he shoots a mad dog on their street.

When Mrs. Dubose insults Jem and Scout because Atticus is defending Tom Robinson, Jem ruins all her flower bushes, and as punishment, he reads to her every afternoon for a month. Atticus explains that Jem reading to Mrs. Dubose served as a distraction as she slowly weaned herself off of the morphine to which she was addicted. Atticus points to her as an example of courage for the way she overcame her addiction.

Skills Focus

- Identifying and Analyzing Theme

- Getting to Know the Characters

  » Newly introduced characters: Mrs. Dubose, Uncle Jack, Aunt Alexandra, Francis, Heck Tate, Link Deas

- Understanding Setting as a Moral Universe

- Investigating the Author's Craft: Symbolism

- Deepening Understanding of the Novel through Analysis of Historical Context from Informational Texts

Academic Vocabulary

CHAPTER 8 *aberration, libel, morphodite;* CHAPTER 9 *lineaments, analogous, relativity, provocation, guileless, obstreperous, invective;* CHAPTER 10 *feeble, alist;* CHAPTER 11 *passé, wrathful, ruthless, melancholy, apoplectic, degeneration, umbrage, rectitude, disposition, interdict, palliation, propensity, contrary, escapade, beholden, cantankerous*

Exploring the Text

Before Reading

Before they begin reading Chapters 8 to 11, consider having students reflect in their journals on the following questions:

1. *What is courage? Write about a person or group from your own personal experience, the news, or history who behaved courageously. What made his or her actions courageous?*

2. *How do you define conscience? Write about a time when you or someone you know chose to act according to conscience. What were the circumstances of the choice? What were the consequences?*

Using Connection Questions

Connection Questions, organized by chapter, are provided below to help guide your class's analysis of the text. A similar set of "After Reading Section 3: Connection Questions" is also provided below to help students synthesize their understanding of Chapters 8 through 11 as a whole.

While these questions are mostly text-based, they are designed to probe important themes in the novel. As you assign chapters for students to read, you might designate all or some of these questions for students to respond to in their journals. These questions can also provide the basis for a class discussion of the text. See facinghistory.org/mockingbird/strategies for suggestions about how to structure effective classroom discussions.

Close Reading

An additional set of text-dependent questions is provided in the Appendix to help facilitate the close reading of a passage from Chapter 9 of the novel. This close reading activity is specifically written to align with the Common Core State Standards for English Language Arts. In this passage, Atticus explains to Scout why he must take seriously the task of defending Tom Robinson. If you choose to implement this close reading activity, we recommend you do so before engaging the class in other activities related to Chapter 9. See "Close Reading for Deep Comprehension" in the Appendix for a suggested procedure for implementing this close reading activity.

Activities for Deeper Understanding

In addition to the Connection Questions, the following activities can help students reach a deeper understanding of Chapters 8 to 11 of *To Kill a Mockingbird* and its essential themes.

Introduce "Universe of Obligation"

One way to help students understand the moral universe of a community such as Maycomb in *To Kill a Mockingbird* is by introducing the concept of "universe of obligation," a term coined by scholar Helen Fein. Consider using the following procedure to introduce this concept:

1. Share the following definition with students:

    Universe of obligation: The circle of individuals and groups toward whom obligations are owed, to whom rules apply, and whose injuries call for amends. In other words, those that a society believes have rights that are worthy of respect and protection.

    Ask students to record the definition in their journals and then discuss its meaning with a classmate. They might also discuss briefly who they think is included in Maycomb's universe of obligation and who they think is excluded.

2. Pass out **Handout 3.1**: "'Universe of Obligation': Maycomb, Alabama, in the 1930s." This handout provides a graphic organizer of concentric circles that can help students map Maycomb's universe of obligation in more detail. Prompt them to start inside the center circle (Circle #1) and describe there the residents of Maycomb who receive the most respect and protection from the community's spoken and unspoken rules. They can add descriptions of those who receive different levels of respect and protection to each of the next three levels in the diagram. If there are any residents of Maycomb who they believe don't receive any respect or protection, students can write them outside of the outermost circle.

3. After they complete their diagrams, have students share their thinking with one or more classmates. What similarities and differences do they notice in the ways that they mapped Maycomb's universe of obligation? What differences account for the positions of different groups of residents in Maycomb's universe of obligation? What characteristics seem to define one's place?

4. Consider following up this activity by asking students to reflect in their journals about what they learned about the ways in which communities confer more rights and privileges on some members than on others. You might also ask them to choose a community to which they belong—a school, neighborhood, nation, or a different group—and reflect on its universe of obligation.

Write and Reflect in Journals

Any of the Connection Questions in this section might be used as a prompt for journal writing. Also, consider the following questions for a brief reflective writing assignment before, during, or after reading Chapters 8 through 11:

1. Everything we know about the events in *To Kill a Mockingbird* is filtered through Scout's perspective. Take a moment to imagine what some of the other characters might think about the events you have read about. Write a diary entry about the mad dog incident from either Jem's or Atticus's point of view. How do you think their perspective would be different from Scout's?

2. When Atticus shoots the mad dog, Scout and Jem see their father in a new way. Write about an experience that changed your impression of someone. What did you think about the person before the experience? What happened to change that impression?

3. Miss Maudie describes Atticus as "civilized in his heart." What does she mean? Do you know anyone who, like Atticus, is "civilized in his or her heart"? Describe him or her.

4. When Scout tells Atticus he must be wrong to defend Tom Robinson because everyone in the town seems to think they are right, Atticus replies, "The one thing that doesn't abide by majority rule is a person's conscience." What does Atticus mean? What does it mean to be a person of conscience? What are the consequences? Describe someone from your world who "marches to his/her own drummer" even if it goes against what everyone else thinks, says, and does.

Explore Levels of Questions and Theme

One way to engage students in determining the themes, or generative universal conversations, at the heart of *To Kill a Mockingbird* is to explicitly teach them about the levels of questions they encounter in this guide. Students have been responding to three types of questions: factual, inferential, and universal. If they understand the difference between these three types of questions, they can then make the connection between the particular details of the novel and universal themes. They can also engage in the more difficult task of determining important themes by writing their own questions. Consider the following suggestions for engaging students in this process:

- Before students respond to the Connection Questions provided here for each chapter, you might first ask them to label each question as *factual*, *inferential*, or *universal*. You can also help students understand that their answers to the factual questions typically provide evidence that they can use to form their answers for the higher-level questions. The process of answering the universal questions forces them to move beyond the particular details of the story and engage with a theme of the novel.

- As students become more comfortable with the three levels of questions, you might ask them to generate their own chapter-based questions before exploring the questions provided in this guide. Require students to attempt to generate at least a few questions for each level. By creating universal questions based on a chapter or a group of chapters, students will be wrestling with theme.

More suggestions are available in the description of the levels of questions at facinghistory.org/mockingbird/strategies.

Revisit Identity Charts

In Section 1, students began identity charts for Scout, Jem, and Atticus (see facinghistory.org/mockingbird/strategies for more information about identity charts). Throughout Chapters 8 to 11, new details are revealed about all three characters. Give students the opportunity to revisit the identity charts. What information might they add? What information might they change or revise?

Encourage students to include quotations from the text on their identity charts, as well as their own interpretations of the character or figure based on their reading.

Keep in mind that creating and revising identity charts for the central characters in *To Kill a Mockingbird* will help prepare students for a culminating activity, suggested in the Post-Reading section of this guide, that asks students to analyze the moral and ethical growth of a character from the novel.

CHAPTER 8: Connection Questions

1. How does Jem respond to Atticus's compliment about the snowman? What does this suggest about their relationship?

2. What does the town's response to the fire at Miss Maudie's house reveal about Maycomb's universe of obligation in this chapter? A community's universe of obligation includes the circle of individuals and groups toward whom obligations are owed, to whom rules apply, and whose injuries call for amends. In other words, a community's universe of obligation consists of those its members believe are worthy of respect and protection.

3. Based on what you know so far, who do you think is included in Maycomb's universe of obligation? Who do you think is excluded? Look for evidence in the text to support your answers.

4. Individuals can also have a universe of obligation (or circle of responsibility), consisting of the people for whose safety and well-being they feel responsible. What do we learn about Boo Radley's universe of obligation in this chapter? Do his actions in this chapter reveal him to be similar to or different from the person Scout and Jem think he is? How does this refute the gossip and legend about the Radleys that the children spread?

5. Is it easy or difficult for Jem and Scout to change their apparent misconceptions about Boo? Find evidence in the chapter to support your answer for each character.

CHAPTER 9: Connection Questions

1. What is Aunt Alexandra's vision for what is "lady-like"? How does Scout respond to that vision? What does Atticus think about Scout's conformity to gender roles?

2. What metaphor does Alexandra use to describe the role that Scout should play in her father's life because she is a girl? How does her repetition of the metaphor help establish her tone and indicate her feelings about Alexandra's attempt to influence her?

3. Telling her side of the fight with Francis to Uncle Jack, Scout says, "A nigger-lover.* I ain't very sure what it means, but the way Francis said

---

* We have chosen to include this word in order to honestly communicate the harshness of the bigoted language. We recommend that teachers review "Discussing Sensitive Topics in the Classroom" on page xv before using these questions in class.

it—tell you one thing right now, Uncle Jack, I'll be—I swear before God if I'll sit there and let him say something about Atticus." What does it say about the power of the "N" word that Scout is moved to anger by the insult, even though she does not know what it means?

4. What does "nigger-lover"* mean to the residents of Maycomb? Why is it such a powerful insult?

5. Discussing the Tom Robinson case with Uncle Jack, Atticus refers to "Maycomb's usual disease." What does he mean? Why doesn't he suffer from it?

6. What does it mean to be a "Finch"? What does it mean to Aunt Alexandra? What does it mean to Atticus?

7. How would you describe the relationship between Atticus and Aunt Alexandra? How does Scout make sense of the differences between Atticus and Alexandra?

8. How does Atticus explain his reasons for defending Tom Robinson? What factors influenced his choice to take the case seriously? How does he expect the case will turn out?

9. Atticus explains to Scout: "This time we aren't fighting the Yankees, we're fighting our friends. But remember this, no matter how bitter things get, they're still our friends and this is still our home."

Are there some fights you can have with friends that make it impossible to remain friends? What types of fights are those? What does it say about Atticus that he doesn't view the insults he receives for defending Tom Robinson as reason enough to end any friendships? How can you respond when friends or family members express views that you find abhorrent?

CHAPTER 10: Connection Questions

1. What do we learn at the beginning of Chapter 10 about the way that Scout and Jem feel about Atticus? How does Atticus's defense of Tom Robinson reinforce those feelings?

2. Atticus instructs Scout and Jem that "it's a sin to kill a mockingbird." What does this advice mean? Look for evidence in the text to help you explain

---

* We have chosen to include this word in order to honestly communicate the harshness of the bigoted language. We recommend that teachers review "Discussing Sensitive Topics in the Classroom" on page xv before using these questions in class.

it. How does this advice help explain why Scout and Jem did not know that their father was "the deadest shot in Maycomb County"? How does Miss Maudie explain Atticus's feelings about his sharpshooting skills?

3. Both the mockingbird and the mad dog are symbols. Based on what you have read so far, what or who in this story might the mockingbird symbolize? What or who might the mad dog symbolize? Look for evidence to support or refute your hypothesis as you read the rest of the novel.

4. How does Harper Lee describe Atticus's movement after he takes the rifle from Heck Tate? How does she use simile and personification to describe how Scout perceives the passage of time? What does this indicate about the importance of the events that follow?

5. What does it mean to be a "man"? Based on your reading of this chapter, how might Scout answer this question? How might Atticus? Do you think Jem agrees more with Scout or with Atticus?

6. How do Scout and Jem continue to "part ways" in this chapter? How do they interpret the revelation of Atticus's sharpshooting skills differently?

7. Describe the pacing of this chapter. What does the pacing suggest about how Harper Lee views the importance of the events in this chapter?

CHAPTER 11: Connection Questions

1. What does Mrs. Dubose mean when she says, "What's this world coming to when a Finch goes against his raising?" In what ways does Atticus go against his raising? When is "going against your raising" a good thing? When is it bad?

2. After Jem vandalizes Mrs. Dubose's flower bed, he and Scout wait in their living room for Atticus to come home. Scout narrates:

   > Two geological ages later, we heard the soles of Atticus's shoes scrape the front steps. The screen door slammed, there was a pause—Atticus was at the hat rack in the hall—and we heard him call "Jem!" His voice was like the winter wind.
   >
   > Atticus switched on the ceiling light in the livingroom and found us there, frozen still.

What literary devices does Harper Lee use to communicate how Scout and Jem feel upon Atticus's arrival?

3. Why does Atticus think Mrs. Dubose is a "great lady"? Do you agree with him?

4. Jem responds to Atticus's praise of Mrs. Dubose by saying: "A lady? After all those things she said about you, a lady?" Why does he question whether or not Atticus should refer to her as a "lady"? How does Maycomb society define a proper lady? Does Atticus agree? Do you agree?

5. What lesson do you think Atticus wants Jem to learn by having him read to Mrs. Dubose?

6. How did you define *courage* at the beginning of this section? How does Atticus define "real courage"? What metaphor does he use to describe what he believes is the wrong idea about courage? Which characters in the novel so far display courage?

7. Scout tells Atticus that he must be wrong to represent Tom Robinson because most people in Maycomb think it is wrong. How does Atticus respond?

8. How did you define *conscience* at the beginning of this section? How would you refine your definition based on what you have read in this chapter? What does it mean to be able to live with one's self?

9. How does Atticus explain the insult "nigger-lover"* to Scout? How does he answer the accusation?

10. Atticus advises Scout: "It's never an insult to be called what somebody thinks is a bad name. It just shows you how poor that person is, it doesn't hurt you." Do you agree? Are insults harmless? When might they cause real damage?

AFTER READING SECTION 3: Connection Questions

1. How would you describe Atticus's universe of obligation? How can he respect both his racist neighbors, such as Mrs. Dubose, and the black man he will defend in court, Tom Robinson?

* We have chosen to include this word in order to honestly communicate the harshness of the bigoted language. We recommend that teachers review "Discussing Sensitive Topics in the Classroom" on page xv before using these questions in class.

2. Discussing the Tom Robinson case with Scout, Atticus says: "When you and Jem are grown, maybe you'll look back on this with some compassion and some feeling that I didn't let you down." Scout, as the narrator, *is* older as she tells us the story. Look for evidence in the text that suggests how the adult Jean Louise views these events.

3. What is courage? Compare Atticus's decision to represent Tom Robinson with Mrs. Dubose's decision to kick her morphine habit before her death. In what ways are their convictions similar? In what ways are they different? Are they both courageous?

4. What messages does Scout receive about the proper behavior of a young Southern girl? How does she respond to these messages? What do Scout's responses tell you about her character?

5. How are the ways people view gender roles in Maycomb different from the way we view gender roles today? How are they similar?

6. How does race complicate the circumstances of the characters we have met so far? What role does Calpurnia play in the Finch family? What authority does she have in the Finch household that she might not have elsewhere in Maycomb?

7. Give an example from this section of the novel of obstacles that prevent people in Maycomb from understanding and getting to know people who are different from them.

8. The novel is divided into two distinct parts. Now that you have finished Part 1, what title would you give it? Explain why your title is compelling. How does it connect to one of the major themes of *To Kill a Mockingbird*?

Building Historical Context

The historical context of the small-town and rural South in the 1930s continues to serve as an essential backdrop to the events that take place in Chapters 8 through 11. Many of the choices, conversations, and events that occur in Chapters 8 through 11 reflect characters' preoccupation with status in Maycomb society. In particular, the moral universe of the small-town and rural South that continues to come into focus in this section includes rules—written and unwritten—about family, gender, age, class, and race. Throughout the novel, the characters concern themselves with the following questions:

- What does it mean to be part of a particular family? What are the consequences of "going against your raising"?

- What does it mean to be a lady? What does it mean to be a gentleman?

- How do society's rules differ depending on whether you are black or white? How are they the same?

The resources and activities below will help you explore with your students some of the historical context from which the answers to these questions emerge.

As you explore the resources below with the class, remind students that your goal is to reach a deeper understanding of the characters, setting, plot, and themes of the novel. After analyzing each resource, revisit the following questions:

- How did this resource deepen your understanding of the characters and setting of *To Kill a Mockingbird*?

- How did this resource help you understand factors that might influence the choices made by an individual who lives in the world of Maycomb, Alabama, in the 1930s?

Explore the Importance of Family Heritage in the Age of Eugenics

What does it mean to be a "Finch," a "Ewell," or a "Cunningham"? Several times in the first 11 chapters of the novel, characters imply that the simple fact of one's family affiliation accounts for an unchangeable part of one's identity and character. Part of this belief reflects an emphasis in some parts of American history and culture on social status tied to family lineage. However, these statements may also reflect a different understanding of heritage that was prevalent in both the United States and Europe in the first half of the twentieth century and has since been discredited. As part of the eugenics movement, many scientists advanced the now-disproved idea that not only disease and disability but also intelligence and morality are biologically determined from generation to generation. According to this misunderstanding of biology, intelligence and moral judgment are part of our genetic inheritance, and thus a "feebleminded" parent (a label some scientists used to describe one unable to make intelligent and moral choices in his or her life) could pass on a similar propensity to his or her child, regardless of upbringing or other social forces. Such reasoning buttressed the beliefs of some that their families were superior, not only socially or economically but also biologically, to other families. For more on the eugenics movement, see the Eugenics, Race and Membership Resource Collection at facinghistory.org.

After reading and discussing Chapter 3, you might share **Handout 3.3**, "Being Well Born," with the class. This document is an excerpt from a high-school textbook titled *New Civic Biology*, in use from 1915 until the 1930s, that explains to students the supposedly scientific basis for these beliefs. You might ask students to discuss what the author of this textbook hopes to convince the readers about their responsibilities. Students can also highlight words and phrases in this document that the author uses to try to convince them of the importance of those responsibilities. Ask students to consider whether or not the author of this textbook would believe that a member of an impoverished family such as the Cunninghams or Ewells could rise above his or her circumstances. Finally, explain to students that, while scientists eventually discredited the ideas in this textbook, many people at the time were suspicious of the conclusions of the eugenics movement. Ask them which characters in *To Kill a Mockingbird* might be suspicious of these ideas.

Watch and Discuss "Setting the Setting of To Kill a Mockingbird"

This 7-minute video provides an overview of Jim Crow segregation in the small-town and rural South. By exploring the history presented here, students can understand more deeply the consequences of Atticus's representation of Tom Robinson and the reaction of the townspeople. Consider showing the video as the class discusses Chapters 9, 10, or 11. As students watch the video, have them take notes on the viewing guide included below (**Handout 3.2**). After they complete the viewing guide, lead a discussion connecting the information from the video back to the characters and setting of the novel. See facinghistory.org/mockingbird/videos to watch the video.

Analyze Firsthand Accounts of Growing Up in a Segregated Society

The novel provides a fictional account of what it was like to grow up in a segregated society. Firsthand accounts, from both sides of the color line, are readily available from a variety of resources and on the Internet. Two additional accounts are included in this section, both reflections by women (one white and one black) who used the options available to them, however limited, to resist the rules of segregation as soon as they became apparent to them.

After reading Chapters 9, 10, or 11, have students read **Handout 3.4** and **Handout 3.5**. This short, 7-minute video "Custom and Conscience: Margot Stern Strom Reflects on Growing Up in the South" also provides a valuable account of growing up in a segregated society. This video was previously suggested as part of the "Introduce Moral Growth and Memory Maps" activity in Section 1; you might review the movie with students now, or show it in its entirety if you did not show it during the previous activity. The video, which can be streamed from facinghistory.org/mockingbird/videos, begins with an excerpt from Lillian Smith's book *Killers of the Dream*, yet another powerful account of the effects of segregation.

After reading these documents, you might lead a class discussion focusing on the following questions:

- How does each author learn about her *place* in segregated society? What does each think about her place?

- Once they become aware of the limitations that segregation places on them, what options are available to each of the authors? What choices do they make in response?

- What else is surprising, interesting, or troubling to you about these accounts? Which characters in *To Kill a Mockingbird* do these accounts help you better understand? How?

Acknowledge the Variety of Jim Crow Experiences

It is important to help students realize that not all individuals who lived in Jim Crow society had the same experiences. This is especially important to note when discussing the experiences of African Americans. The stories told in both the novel and the historical documents we have provided to help students better understand the novel reflect some common experiences of black Americans in the South in the 1930s, but there are other experiences that students should know about. Not all black Southerners worked in agriculture as sharecroppers or in white households as maids. In fact, many found a measure of success through education and professional careers. Some blacks made reasonable livings as teachers and professors, doctors, lawyers, and business owners. In addition, between 1915 and 1970, millions of black Southerners responded to discrimination and segregation by moving to the

North as part of the Great Migration. Therefore, while it is not fully reflected in the story of *To Kill a Mockingbird*, it is essential to at least acknowledge with students the variety of the experiences of black Southerners during this time period.

Isabel Wilkerson's chronicle of the Great Migration, *The Warmth of Other Suns*, provides an in-depth look at the experiences of three black Americans in the Jim Crow era. **Handout 3.6**, "Proving Oneself," provides an excerpt from this book in which Wilkerson describes the childhood of Pershing Foster. Foster grew up in Monroe, Louisiana, the child of two respected educators in the community. He married the daughter of the president of a prominent black university and earned his medical degree at an all-black medical school before migrating to Los Angeles. You might share this excerpt with students and compare and contrast it with the experiences of Calpurnia, Tom Robinson, and other black Southerners they learn about through the historical context provided in this guide.

Make Connections through Close Reading

The Appendix includes a set of text-dependent questions, entitled "Close Reading Pairing: Virginia Durr and Scout," that you can use to guide student analysis of both Virginia Durr's and Scout's experiences as children awakening to the racial divisions in their societies. By engaging in the process of close reading to make connections between the informational text by Durr (**Handout 3.4**, "The Birthday Party") and the fictional conversation between Scout and Atticus in Chapter 9 of the novel, students can reach a deeper understanding of both texts. This close reading activity is specifically written to align with the Common Core State Standards for English Language Arts. See "Close Reading for Deep Comprehension" in the Appendix for a suggested procedure for implementing this close reading activity.

Explore Social Types and Gender Expectations in the South

Even as Atticus's representation of Tom Robinson exposes Scout and Jem to divisions along the color line in Maycomb, they also continue to encounter beliefs, expectations, and tensions around gender in Chapters 8 through 11. Both characters are learning what it means in their society to be a gentleman and a lady. While Scout resists Aunt Alexandra's demands for her to be more "lady-like" in Chapter 9, Jem embraces Atticus's example of gentlemanly behavior after the mad dog incident in Chapter 10. They are learning about two sets of expectations—the *Southern gentleman* and the *Southern lady*—that have a long history as social types in Southern culture.

Sociologist John Shelton Reed distinguishes between *social types* and pernicious *stereotypes*. A social type is a label we use to identify "certain noticeable clusters of behaviors and attributes within any human population." We attach an ideal to that label, an image of a person that embodies all of the characteristics that define the social type, even though no such pure example may exist in reality. Reed maintains that this process is useful because it can help us describe, organize, and communicate about the social world we observe. However, he also points out a danger: "Sometimes what we have are vicious stereotypes that have long outlived their usefulness (if, indeed, they ever had any), or that are used to justify discrimination and hard-dealing of various sorts."[2] In *To Kill a Mockingbird*, students will encounter examples of both social types and stereotypes, and it is important to help them consider the difference.

Handout 3.7 and **Handout 3.8** provide students with brief descriptions of the Southern gentleman and Southern lady social types. After sharing these descriptions with students, challenge them to think about the extent to which some of the characters in *To Kill a Mockingbird* are consistent with them. For instance, you might discuss the following questions:

- In what ways does Atticus represent the ideal "Southern gentleman"? In what ways does his character differ from that ideal?

- Which character best represents the ideals of the "Southern lady"?

Explore the Roles of Black Women in Southern Society

It is important to note that the ideal images of the Southern gentleman and Southern lady throughout American history have always been images of white people, even though those ideals influenced Americans of all backgrounds. Obviously, the experiences of black Southerners have differed enormously from those of white Southerners. The limited opportunities available to African Americans throughout history have led to different social types, and also to pernicious stereotypes. The following documents in this section can help students better understand the experience of black women working as domestic servants in white households (resources exploring the experience of black men are included in Section 4):

- **Handout 3.5**: "You Worked Long Hours"

- **Handout 3.9**: The Black Nurse in the White Household

When sharing these resources with students, it is crucial to acknowledge the variety of experiences that black women had in the Jim Crow South (as well as the segregated cities of the North during this time period). In other words, it is

---

2   John Shelton Reed, *Southern Folk Plain and Fancy: Native White Social Types* (Athens: University of Georgia Press, 1986), 5–6.

important for students to understand that despite assumptions and stereotypes to the contrary, black women during this time worked not only as maids but also as lawyers, writers, nurses, doctors, and in a variety of other professions. Because the primary black female character in *To Kill a Mockingbird* is Calpurnia, the Finches' maid, we have provided resources in this section to help students gain a deeper understanding of her experience. Her experience, however, does not represent that of all black women who lived in similar places at this time in history.

These resources can be used in a variety of ways to help students better imagine the experience of Calpurnia. They can also help deepen students' understanding of the setting and moral universe of Maycomb. In **Handout 3.5**, an African American woman describes her career as a domestic worker for white families, while in **Handout 3.9**, a white woman describes the role of black nurses in white households. Ask students to compare and contrast the two accounts and consider the following questions:

- To what extent do the two accounts support, or corroborate, each other? On which points do they differ?

- What conclusions might we draw from these two accounts about the experiences of black women who worked as domestic employees in white households?

- What additional questions do you have about the experiences?

Handout 3.1 "Universe of Obligation": Maycomb, Alabama, in the 1930s

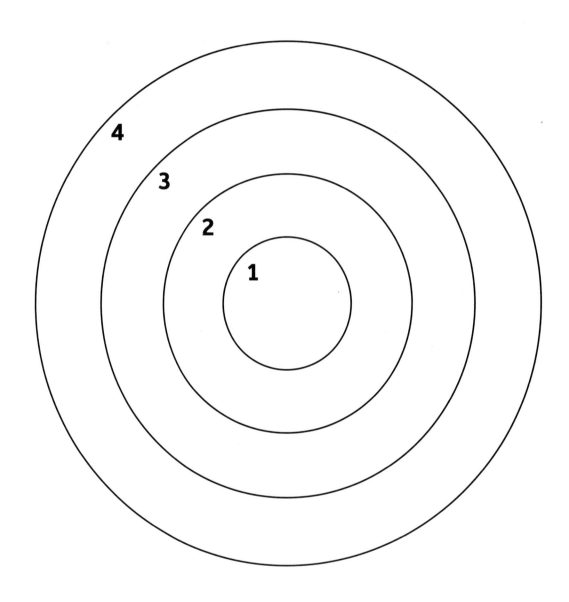

Handout 3.2 "Setting the Setting of *To Kill a Mockingbird*"

Use the following questions to guide your note-taking and reflection on the video "Setting the Setting of To Kill a Mockingbird*":*

1. David Cunningham describes Jim Crow segregation as both a system of laws and a system of customs. What is the difference between laws and customs? Which are more difficult to change?

2. Why did Mississippi and Alabama have fewer formal Jim Crow laws than other states in the South?

3. In what ways did black and white lives overlap in Alabama in the 1930s? In what ways were they completely separated?

4. What was the effect of the Depression on the relationships between whites and blacks in the Jim Crow South? Why?

5. What were some of the unwritten rules of segregation? What were some of the complications around those rules?

6. How were gender roles different between white and black Americans?

7. What were the consequences of questioning Jim Crow? How do you think they were different for blacks and whites?

8. How did this video help shed light on written and unwritten rules of life in Maycomb? What characters, choices, and events in the book so far did this video help you better understand?

Handout 3.3 Being Well Born

What does it mean to be a "Finch," a "Ewell," or a "Cunningham"? Many of the residents of Maycomb express the belief that the family one is born into carries great significance in determining one's character or behavior. This was an especially common belief in the first half of the twentieth century, as many scientists advanced the now-disproved idea that not only disease and disability but also intelligence and morality are biologically inherited from generation to generation.

In New Civic Biology, *a textbook first published in 1914, author George William Hunter alerted young people to the "menace of feeblemindedness" (the inability to make intelligent, moral choices) and the value of "breeding the best with the best" by using the language of science to heighten real fears about the spread of diseases and the threat of possible disabilities.*

Since our knowledge of heredity has been increased, the demand has become more urgent that we do something to prevent the race from handing down diseases and other defects, and that we apply to man some of the methods we employ in breeding plants and animals. This is not a new idea; the Greeks in Sparta had it, Sir Thomas More wrote of it in his *Utopia*, and today it has been brought to us in the science of eugenics. The word comes from the Greek word *eugenes*, which means well born. Eugenics is the science of being well born, or born well, healthy, fit in every way. A tendency to cancer, or tuberculosis, or chorea, or feeblemindedness, is a handicap which it is not merely unfair, but criminal, to hand down to posterity.

Two Notorious Families

Studies have been made on a number of different families in the country, in which mental and moral defects were present in one or both of the parents as far back as was possible to trace the family. The "Jukes" family is a notorious example. "Margaret, the mother of criminals," is the first mother in the family of whom we have record. Up to 1915 there were 2094 members of this family; 1600 were feebleminded or epileptic, 310 were paupers, more than 300 were immoral women, and 140 were criminals. The family has cost the state of New York more than $2,500,000, besides immensely lowering the moral tone of the communities which the family contaminated.

Another careful investigation (up to 1912) concerned the "Kallikak" family. This family was traced to the union of Martin Kallikak, a young solider of the War of the Revolution, with a feebleminded girl. She had a feebleminded son, who had 480 descendants. Of these 33 were sexually immoral, 24 confirmed drunkards, 3 epileptics, and 143 feebleminded. The man who started this terrible line of immorality and feeblemindedness later married a normal Quaker girl. From this couple, a line of 496 descendants was traced, with no cases of feeblemindedness. The evidence and the moral speak for themselves!

Parasitism and Its Cost to Society

Hundreds of bad families such as those described exist today, spreading disease, immorality, and crime to all parts of this country. The cost to society of such families is very severe. Just as certain animals or plants become parasitic on other plants or animals, these families have become parasitic on society. They not only do harm to others by corrupting, by stealing, and by spreading disease, but they are actually protected and cared for by the state out of public money. It is estimated that between 25% and 50% of all prisoners in penal institutions are feebleminded. They take from society, but they give nothing in return. They are true parasites. . . .

Blood Tells

Eugenics shows us, on the other hand, in a study of families in which brilliant men and women are found, that the descendants have received the good inheritance from their ancestors. . . . Although we do not know the precise method of inheritance, we do know that musical and literary ability, calculating ability, remarkable memory, and many other mental and physical characteristics are inheritable and "run in families." The Wedgewood family, from which three generations of Darwins have descended, and the Galton family are examples of scientific inheritance; the Arnolds, Hallams, and Lowells were prominent in literature; the Balfours were political leaders; the Bach and Mendelssohn families were examples showing inheritance of musical genius. A comparison of fathers' and sons' college records at Oxford University shows [that] . . . fathers who did well had sons who did well also. It is said that 26 out of 46 men chosen to the Hall of Fame of New York University had distinguished relatives. Blood does tell!

How to Use Our Knowledge of Heredity

Two applications of this knowledge of heredity stand out for us as high school students. One is in the choice of a mate, the other in the choice of a vocation. As to the first, no better advice can be given than the old adage, "Look before you leap." If this advice were followed, there would be fewer unhappy marriages and divorces. Remember that marriage should mean love, respect, and companionship for life. The heredity of a husband or wife counts for much in making this possible. And, even though you are in high school, it is only fair to yourselves that you should remember the responsibility that marriage brings. You should be parents. Will you choose to have children well born? Or will you send them into the world with an inheritance that will handicap them for life?[1]

1   George William Hunter, *New Civic Biology: Presented in Problems* (New York: American Book Co., 1926).

Handout 3.4 "The Birthday Party"

> *Note: We have chosen to include certain racial epithets in this reading in order to honestly communicate the bigoted language of the time. We recommend that teachers review the page "Discussing Sensitive Topics in the Classroom" before using this document.*

In her autobiography, Outside the Magic Circle, *white Southerner Virginia Foster Durr recalls how the customs of the Jim Crow South affected her seventh birthday party:*

During the summer of Aunt May's visit, she heard the little black children in the backyard calling my sister "Sis." My brother called her Sis, and I called her Sister. Well, Aunt May sent Grandmother's house servant, Easter, out to tell the little black children they couldn't call Josephine Sis. They had to call her Miss Josephine. We were astonished and hurt and didn't know what this was about. Here Sister, who had been playing with the black children all her life, had to be called Miss Josephine all of a sudden. But Sister solved the problem by telling them, "Now, you don't have to call me Miss Josephine; you just call me Miss Sis." So after that all the children, white and black, called her Miss Sis. She solved the problem by not hurting anybody's feelings. She spent her life doing that.

That incident was a warning that our idyllic days were over, but the great trauma of my early life came with my seventh birthday. I had always celebrated my birthday in Union Springs because it was in August. We would have a barbecue in the backyard with the black children. We would dig a pit in the backyard, which was sandy, and place a grill over the hole and build a fire. Then the cook would give us chickens, which we were allowed to baste and turn. Of course, by the time we got through, the chickens were full of sand, but to me this was a great event. Here I was presiding over the chickens! But on my seventh birthday my mother and grandmother and aunts all said I had to have my birthday in the front yard and have just white children. No black children could come to the party. Well, I got very angry about that. Mostly, I wanted the barbecue. I was thinking of food, as usual.

I had been planning the party for months. I'd had typhoid fever and had spent the whole time that I was ill planning my birthday party. I was going to have a pink cake and pink slippers and pink socks and a pink dress and a pink sash and a pink bow in my hair and a pink cake and strawberry ice cream. When August arrived, I had a pink dress, the pink socks, the pink everything, except the strawberries, which weren't available in August, but I was told none of the black children could come to the party. Only white children—perfect strangers they had picked up in Union Springs. So I had a temper fit early that morning and they finally agreed that I could have the barbecue in the morning and the party in the afternoon. The barbecue would be in the backyard with the black children, and the party would be in the front yard with the white children.

Elizabeth, Aunt May's daughter, was there. Aunt May had brought a French maid with her to Union Springs, too, if you can imagine. Aunt May really put on airs. Elizabeth was always dressed up in beautiful dresses with sashes and everything matching and her hair curled. She was a little older than I was, about my sister's age.

We had the birthday barbecue and everything was going fine. One of the little black girls was tearing up the chicken, and she offered a piece to Elizabeth. Elizabeth, who must have felt like an outcast in this group, all of a sudden said, "Don't you give me any chicken out of that black hand of yours. I'm not going to eat any chicken that your black hand has touched, you little nigger." I told Elizabeth to go to hell. I was just furious. You see, the black girl was Nursie's little girl, Sarah. She and I played together all the time. I was raised with her. The grown-ups put me to bed and said *I* was going to hell for being so bad.

When the afternoon came, I went to the birthday party with all these strange white children. I had another temper fit and screamed and yelled. I bashed the cake in and was put to bed again. By that time, the seventh birthday was pretty well shot, cake and all. That night at the supper table, my aunt said I was the worst child she had ever known. She told my mother, "I really think you have got to do something about her because she's so high-tempered, such a bad child." I was sitting right there listening to her, so I took a knife and threw it at her. Well, I was really a disgrace then, so they sent me away from the table. I went out to the back porch and sat in Nursie's lap. We could hear Aunt May through the window saying, "Annie, the trouble with Virginia is that nurse. She spoils her to death. And besides, I think it's terrible that you let her sit in her lap and sleep with her and kiss her and hug her. You know all those black women are diseased."[1]

1 Hollinger F. Barnard, ed., *Outside the Magic Circle: The Autobiography of Virginia Foster Durr* (Tuscaloosa: University of Alabama Press, 1985), 16–17.

Handout 3.5 "You Worked Long Hours"

Born in 1910, Essie Favrot worked for several decades for Southern white families as a domestic worker. In an interview, she described some of the situations in which she worked:

I finished out the eighth grade in the country. But by then my very oldest sister had come to stay with my aunt, and she decided it was time I came, too.

The onliest thing then was for a black girl to do was to get domestic work. So, I worked. First it was just about a two-hour job per day, five days a week for this lady that just had come up to me and asked me to work. I'd go down there to her house, clean up the house, do a little washing, and that was it. Fifty cent a day was what I made. They were poor people. They were probably just about as poor as I was, but the lady worked for a department store!

Then, I think, my brother's mother-in-law told me that this lady needed somebody to keep her kids. So I went there and worked. I was living on the place, and that's when I met my husband. This was in '39, and I remember the salary had gone up to a dollar a day. I was making seven dollars [a week] because I was living on the place. And I worked every day from seven to seven. You worked long hours, but you were making a dollar a day.

I slept up in the bedroom with the little boy. There was a servant house in the backyard, but it was occupied by the cook, which was a male. It was considered his house, but I used the bathroom there.

They were rich people. I guess they owned stock. And when my mother-in-law decided to sell half her land, I don't know why but it came for me to borrow the money. My husband had been working for his people much longer than I had. Anyway I asked them for fifty dollars to pay for the property, and they readily gave it to me. But they said they wouldn't help me to build a house. They had got stung with another maid borrowing from them. We paid the money back right quick, and they were surprised.

After that, I worked thirteen years for the Elliots. Now they weren't rich people. They both worked, and they had six children. I took over the running of the house. I did everything for them—the groceries, the cleaning up, the kids. I did all for the kids—took them to the park, to school, bought their clothes, saw that they wore the right clothes to parties, all that. My neighbors used to laugh because those Elliots were such poor people. Everyone knew they were. I mean not poor white trash—no. Just working people like myself. I was fond of those kids. I still am. I worked for them until my son was born. We still keep in touch. One of the girls just died. She had cancer; that was very sad. And their mother, I worry about her. She's had a hard time. Working for them—since they had all those kids, it was more like family for me there. I feel still sort of protective and maternal towards them. Not like I do my own family, no, but like I would any children I'd cared for that much, watched grow up. I'd help them still anyway I could. I would . . . not go back to work, but I'd help them any other way I could.

After that, I worked days till my son got old enough to go to school. Then I worked for the Helms. I worked there for a while. And they had four kids. Two were up in age, school-age children. And they had two little kids. And I just figured, since I was taking care of her kids and cooking for them, I'd have supper done when they got there and the kids fed and clean. They both worked. And they were so congenial at first. So, when my son started school not far from where they lived, I figured they wouldn't mind him coming down there after school and then going home with me.

But the first day after I did it, Mr. Helms say, "What happened, Essie? Did your son miss his bus?" I say, "No, he didn't miss his bus. It's nobody at home in the evening, so I just took your two children, and when we were on our way back from the park, we picked him up."

"I don't think it's going to be such a good idea, him coming down here. That lady next door . . . . Mind you now, it's not us," he said. "But that lady next door don't want him playing down here."

So his wife she thought she could come home early so I could go home early, too. And the next evening she said, "I think I might enjoy coming on home, getting here early." I didn't say a word, because I knew I wasn't going to work for nobody who had two that were not toilet trained and I had to clean both of them up and I had to cook dinner for the whole family and clean the apartment and wash their clothes. I felt if I was doing all of that for her children and her, and mine couldn't come there in the evening, that they could have their job. After she paid me, I said, "Now you be sure and get you somebody." I was headed to my car when I said it. And I left there and never went back. . . .[1]

---

1   Susan Tucker, *Telling Memories Among Southern Women* (Baton Rouge: Louisiana State University Press, 1988), 118–119.

Handout 3.6 Proving Oneself

In her book The Warmth of Other Suns, *author Isabel Wilkerson describes the Monroe, Louisiana, childhood of Pershing Foster, an African American man who later migrated to Los Angeles and became a successful physician:*

The only way that someone as proud and particular as Pershing could survive in the time and place he was in was to put his mind somewhere else. He grew up watching his parents exercise exquisite control over the few things they were permitted to preside over in life. Their domain was the Monroe Colored High School, where Madison [his father] was principal and Ottie [his mother] taught seventh grade. It was a small brick building with 1,139 pupils and a teacher for each grade, from kindergarten to eleventh, and run with the precision of a military institution.

. . . Monroe was a quietly hierarchal town with its two castes remaining in their places and separated by two sets of railroad tracks. The town had been founded by French traders in the nineteenth century and became a mill town serving the nearby cotton plantations and lumber concerns by the time the Fosters got there . . .

. . . It was in Monroe that Madison and Ottie Foster spent their honeymoon hoping to prosper despite the limits of their era, a time when Jim Crow was closing in on them and mutating all over the South. Madison took a position as principal and she as a teacher of the colored children who spilled out of the shotgun houses on the colored side of the Kansas City Southern and Union Pacific railroad tracks. They eventually bought a white frame bungalow on Louise Anne Avenue surrounded by icemen, barbers, sawmill workers, and domestics. The colored people took to calling the husband "Professor Foster" out of an overinflated respect for his bachelor's degree and the position he held over them. It came out "'Fessor Foster," though, by the time people got through saying it.

He cut a tight-buttoned bearing in his Kuppenheimer suits and Arrow shirts with detachable white collars and cuff links, always gold cuff links. By the late twenties, he was in a position of some prestige among colored people in town, the president of the Louisiana Colored Teachers Association, and was regularly mentioned in the Louisiana News section of the Chicago *Defender* [newspaper] for attending or speaking at some important colored meeting or convention.

He rose early to open his school and greeted the people on their porches as he passed. He had authority of some sort over practically every child in New Town. Some Sundays, he preached at Zion Traveler Baptist Church. It was a world unto itself. The striving colored people in town, stooped and trodden the rest of the week, invested their very beings into the church and quarreled over how things should be run and who should be in charge of the one thing they had total control over . . .

On school mornings, he stood at the front steps of the school with a pocket watch in one hand and a paddle in the other. Sometimes the students came running across the school yard late and out of breath.

"The trains cut us off, 'Fessor Foster," the children would tell him.

"I'm gon' cut you off," he'd say, raising his paddle. "Get up early. Get up early."

. . . His wife, Ottie Alberta Wright Foster, was a prim and ambitious woman, who made the society pages of the colored papers as president of the Golden Seal Embroidery Club and for hosting such things as a wedding breakfast for a bridal party in what the *Defender* called a "lovely home . . . prettily decorated for the occasion." Ottie was raised in New Orleans, a magic circus of a place compared to Monroe, braided with openly mixed-race Creole people and their patois and jambalaya . . . . She was a small woman with skin the color of chestnuts and wavy black hair. It was said she would have been considered quite a beauty if it weren't for the tight bun she wore low on her head with the severe center part at her forehead and the fact that she seemed rarely to smile at anyone other than her children.

All of the children were bright. But in the family hierarchy, there was not much Pershing could do to distinguish himself with one big brother off in medical school and another a star athlete. He played softball with the neighborhood kids, where they used broomsticks for bats and made their own rules because nobody had seen an official baseball game. But he wasn't especially good at it.

Pershing looked for a way to prove himself. There were three fig trees in their yard, and he picked the figs and sold them to the neighbors, thirty-five cents for a gallon bucket. He gave them a broad smile and charmed them into believing they needed the figs for breakfast or for preserves or to can for the coming winter.

He practiced smiling in the mirror and writing with his left hand even though he didn't need to. He lived for the pat on the head from his father but especially his mother for washing out the washtub or any little thing that he did. He took to cleaning the house to make them happy and to keep the compliments coming, but it only felt good as long as he did it before they could ask.

He was crushed whenever he fell short. His parents punished him by making him go to the back steps and sit there. He sat hugging his dog and cried. Sometimes his mother got tired of him sitting on the steps and called him in. Otherwise, he couldn't leave until his father said so.

"Alright," Professor Foster would say. "Come back in."

It was true he couldn't milk a cow, but he didn't mind churning. He churned the milk as it soured and clabbered. Ottie skimmed the butter off, and he proceeded to go door to door, selling the butter and the buttermilk in a lard bucket with a cultivated earnestness and the crisp airs he was beginning to master.

Mrs. Poe, don't you wanna buy some milk from me? Can I start bringing you milk on Thursdays?

He found that he could get people to like him and that if people liked him he could get what he wanted.[1]

1   Isabel Wilkerson, *The Warmth of Other Suns: The Epic Story of America's Great Migration* (New York: Knopf Doubleday Publishing Group, 2010), 77–82.

Handout 3.7 The Southern Gentleman

In their book The Companion to Southern Literature, *Joseph Flora and Lucinda MacKethan describe the characteristics of the Southern gentleman, a social type that first emerged in the earliest days of European settlement in Virginia and was viewed as an ideal against which generations of Southern men would measure themselves.*

The first commandment of the code of the gentleman . . . dictated a recognition of the inherent inequality of man and the acceptance of the idea that certain men were born to lead and that others, the great majority, were born to follow and serve. Assured of his own superiority, a gentleman was expected at all times to be graceful and dignified in his deportment, as well as courteous and thoughtful toward all men, regardless of their social status. In designing a moral code to complement their dignified bearing, Virginia gentlemen, like their English counterparts, sought to attain qualities of fortitude, temperance, prudence, justice, liberality, and courtesy . . .

Observers of manner and conduct agreed that learning was an essential quality for a gentleman . . . . Learning was an adornment, worn lightly and gracefully, which—along with dancing, fencing, hunting, riding, and occasionally the playing of a musical instrument—combined to produce a complete and smoothly functioning social creature . . . .

There was a widespread agreement that the gentleman's primary purpose in following his code was to possess and maintain a personal honor that commanded the respect of all his peers as well as of all those of lower social order. . . .

The gentlemanly code expressed an ideal of character, an ideal roughly translated from the English rural gentry to southern planters who presided over moderate-to-large landholdings cultivated by slave labor. . . . As the institution of slavery came to be viewed by northerners with increasing moral opprobrium in the decades preceding the Civil War, it became more essential for southern planters to view themselves as refined individuals practicing a humane and noble code of conduct. Slavery could thus be justified as a paternalistic system that produced twin social paragons—the patriarchal planter aristocrat and his consort, the exquisitely pure and submissive southern lady.[1]

---

1   Joseph M. Flora and Lucinda H. MacKethan, eds., *The Companion to Southern Literature: Themes, Genres, Places, People, Movements, and Motifs* (Baton Rouge: Lousiana State University Press, 2002), 292–293.

Handout 3.8 The Southern Lady and Belle

In their book The Companion to Southern Literature, *Joseph Flora and Lucinda MacKethan describe the Southern lady and the younger Southern belle, social types that exuded the traditional characteristics to which many white Southerners expected girls to aspire for much of the twentieth century.*

Ideally a patrician, privileged white woman, she served her husband, bending to him in all matters; she was maternal, bearing children regularly and caring for them lovingly; she possessed great skill in the domestic sphere, running kitchen and nursery, overseeing the household in all areas, dispensing medicine, always hospitable. Most important, perhaps, she was the moral center of the household, pious, self-effacing, and kind. An expert with the needle, she could also play a musical instrument and sing melodies for the family. She was essential to the patriarchy, assuring well-brought-up children, a well-run home, and complete comfort for her husband. . . .[1]

Following the Civil War, [the] vision of a plantation South took on mythic proportions as southerners grew defensive and nostalgic about the Old South. In particular, the southern woman of the Old South was presented, through the image of the southern lady, as the ideal of nineteenth-century womanhood.

. . . A marble figure on a pedestal, she was static. A more appealing character, in this idealized vision of the South, was the southern belle, the younger, unmarried, and hence incomplete version of the southern lady . . . .

If trained right, the belle had, by her early teen years, already acquired most of the makings of the southern lady: she was beautiful or potentially beautiful, graceful, charming, virtuous, loyal to family, submissive to father, in need of men's protection, yet resourceful and brave when unusual circumstances called on her to be. But even in her late teens, she might not yet have perfected self-sacrifice and calm self-possession. These characteristics would come, or must come, once she married—and marrying was supposed to be her goal in life.[2]

---

1   Joseph M. Flora and Lucinda H. MacKethan, eds., *The Companion to Southern Literature: Themes, Genres, Places, People, Movements, and Motifs* (Baton Rouge: Lousiana State University Press, 2002), 413.

2   Ibid., 95.

Handout 3.9 The Black Nurse in the White Household

In her memoir about growing up in the segregated South, Killers of the Dream, *Lillian Smith describes the place that black nurses occupied in white households like hers:*

It was customary in the South, if a family possessed a moderate income, to have a colored nurse for the children. Sometimes such a one came with the first child and lived in the family until the last one was grown. Her role in the family was involved and of tangled contradictions. She always knew her "place," but neither she nor her employers could have defined it. She was given a limited authority, but it was elastic enough to stretch into dictatorship over not only children but the white mother and sometimes even the male head of the family. They leaned on her strength because they had so little of their own or because she had so much, and once leaning they could not free themselves from subjection. Many an old nurse, knowing all there was to know of her white folks, familiar with every bone of every skeleton in their closets, gradually became so dominating that her employers actually feared her power. Yet she was a necessary part of these big sprawling households; her knowledge, alone, of how to grow children was too precious a thing to throw away lightly, and her value extended far beyond child rearing. She nursed old and young when they were sick, counseled them when they were unhappy . . . and following her precepts we prospered as did her own children. Sometimes Mr. White Man himself did not deem it beneath him to call on her for help. "Mammy, come in here and talk to Miss Sarah [his wife]. Talk sense to her, Mammy," and he'd leave for the cotton gin downtown or the sawmill, hoping to God that Mammy could straighten Sarah out. And usually she did, and Sarah would be as meek and gentle as a wife should be when her husband returned that evening . . .

. . . These intimacies fill our memories and do strange things now to our segregated grown-up lives.[1]

---

1   Lillian Smith, *Killers of the Dream* (New York: Norton, 1994), 128–130.

Connecting to the Central Question

Before beginning Section 4, consider pausing to ask students to review the central question introduced at the beginning of this guide:

What factors influence our moral growth? What kinds of experiences help us learn how to judge right from wrong?

Give students the opportunity to review the preliminary response to this question that they recorded after completing Section 2 of this guide. What evidence have they found in this section that confirms their previous response? What evidence have they found that might prompt them to revise their thinking?

Ask students to take a few minutes to reflect on whether or not their thinking has changed, revise their preliminary responses, and record new evidence from Section 3 that can help them answer the question.

Remind students that they will have several opportunities to revise their thinking as they continue to read the novel. Their revised responses and notes will help prepare students for a culminating activity, suggested in the Post-Reading section of this guide, that asks them to analyze the moral growth of a character from the novel.

Do You Really Think So?

This section covers Chapters 12 to 15 of the novel.

Introduction

Essential Questions

- How does bias limit our understanding of the world? What kind of experiences can widen our perspective?

- What are the consequences for individuals and groups who are considered outside of a community's "universe of obligation"?

Rationale

In the previous section, students continued to learn about the characters of *To Kill a Mockingbird* as well as the "moral universe" of Maycomb. They also began to consider the novel's central themes—the essential cultural conversations embedded in the narrative. In this section, students will continue to explore the characters, setting, and themes. They will also look more closely at *point of view* and its impact on both the reader's experience of the book and, more broadly, our beliefs and the choices we make in our own lives.

The events related in Chapters 12 through 15 continue to open Scout's and Jem's eyes to written and unwritten rules about family, gender, class, and race in ever more dramatic and surprising ways. As Scout and Jem confront the issues of difference and belonging embedded in their community—beginning with their trip to Calpurnia's church, continuing through Aunt Alexandra's residency in the Finch household, and culminating in the confrontation with a lynch mob at the jailhouse—Harper Lee's choice to tell the story through the eyes of Scout becomes more crucial. Scout's wide-eyed naïveté heightens the impact of both the social expectations she resists and the injustices she sees unfold. Indeed, one of the primary narrative arcs of the novel is Scout's "coming of age" through these experiences. At the same time, Scout's lack of life experience and knowledge about the world she inhabits leaves readers with gaps to fill in their own understanding of several important events and characters in the book. In this section, students will explore the limits of Scout's point of view by considering the following questions:

- To what extent does Scout understand the events and people she describes for readers?

- How does her lack of understanding affect the extent to which readers need to look for information outside of her narrative to understand the people and events in the novel?

By answering these questions, students are beginning to assess Scout's reliability as a narrator.

Assessing Scout's reliability is essential for two reasons. First, it prompts us to look both within the novel and to other sources to seek a deeper understanding of the characters and events in the moral universe of Maycomb. As Michael W. Smith and Jeffrey D. Wilhelm point out, "We . . . need to think about what didn't or couldn't get told from [the narrator's] point of view. If something could have been told but wasn't, we realize that it's our job as readers to try to find out."[1] While we occasionally hear the reflective voice of a much older Jean Louise, the key events of this novel are seen through the eyes of Scout in her childhood. Therefore, many of the Connection Questions in this section prompt students to use the evidence Harper Lee provides within the novel to put together a fuller picture of the story than Scout herself understands. Additionally, the historical resources in this section were chosen to help students learn more about experiences, customs, and beliefs that influence the events in these chapters but go unexplained in Scout's narration. These include the experiences of a black man like Tom Robinson in the Jim Crow South, the stereotypes and myths about black men that were widely shared in the first half of the twentieth century, and the practice of lynching that those myths and stereotypes were used to justify. After synthesizing all of this information from both the novel and historical texts, students will be able to understand the dramatic irony* created by Scout's limited understanding in key moments of the story. They

---

1   Michael W. Smith and Jeffrey D. Wilhelm, *Fresh Takes on Teaching Literary Elements* (New York: Scholastic, 2010), 119.

* *Dramatic irony* occurs when the reader possesses greater knowledge or understanding of the story than the characters do.

will also be able to reach a deeper appreciation of the themes of caring, growth, justice, and democracy at the heart of *To Kill a Mockingbird*.

The second reason why Scout's reliability as the narrator is important to understand is because of what it shows about both the value and limitations of attempting to "walk in someone else's skin." As students simultaneously grapple with Scout's limited perspective and observe it slowly expand as the story unfolds, they might reflect on the ways in which their own perspectives are limited, as are everyone's. As the questions in this section will prompt them to do, students can reflect on how we might expand our perspectives, consider new points of view, and learn about people who are different from us. Finally, we might also ask to what extent it is truly possible to "walk in someone else's skin," and what the value is in trying. By wrestling with these questions, students can begin to strengthen their understanding and practice of empathy.

Plot Summary

After Jem turns 12, he begins to act differently and spend less time with Scout. One Sunday, Calpurnia brings Jem and Scout to church with her, and the children learn more about Cal's "double life" during the excursion. Aunt Alexandra comes to stay with the Finches for a while and brings a philosophy for raising children that contrasts with Atticus's, frustrating Scout. As the Tom Robinson trial approaches, Scout and Jem are confused by the way their peers and other townsfolk criticize Atticus. The children grow more curious about the case and the charge of rape against Tom Robinson.

One night, Atticus leaves the house with little explanation, so Jem, Scout, and Dill sneak out to find Atticus sitting outside of the jail. They watch as a crowd arrives and demands that Atticus give them Tom Robinson. Unaware of the danger the men pose, Scout runs to Atticus, surprising everyone. While Atticus is trying to convince the children to leave, Scout recognizes Mr. Cunningham, and she tries to talk to him. After a little while, her reaction seems to break the tension, and the whole crowd leaves before violence erupts. After realizing that Mr. Underwood, who lives next to the jail, is keeping an eye on the situation with his shotgun, Atticus walks home with Jem, Scout, and Dill.

Skills Focus

- Understanding Point of View

- Getting to Know the Characters

  » Newly introduced characters: Reverend Sykes, Mr. Underwood

- Understanding Setting as a Moral Universe

- Deepening Understanding of the Novel through Analysis of Historical Context from Informational Texts

Academic Vocabulary

CHAPTER 12 *alien, ecclesiastical, denunciation, austere, heady;* CHAPTER 13 *tactful, incestuous, myopic;* CHAPTER 14 *carnal, consent, antagonize, infallible, fortitude;* CHAPTER 15 *defendant, begrudge, venue, discreet, uncouth, impassive*

Exploring the Text

Before Reading

Before they begin reading Chapters 12 to 15, consider having students reflect in their journals on the following questions:

1. *Describe a significant event in your life (such as a conflict or transition) that you understand better now than you did when it happened. Why was the event significant? What is the difference between how you understood it then and how you do now? How do you account for the change?*

2. *Have you ever been a part of a group that treated someone disrespectfully or unfairly? Why do you think the group behaved the way it did? What role did emotion play? What role did reason play? How did you respond?*

Using Connection Questions

Connection Questions, organized by chapter, are provided below to help guide your class's analysis of the text. A similar set of "After Reading Section 4: Connection Questions" is also provided below to help students synthesize their understanding of Chapters 12 through 15 as a whole.

While these questions are mostly text-based, they are designed to probe important themes in the novel. As you assign chapters for students to read, you might designate all or some of these questions for students to respond to in their journals. These questions can also provide the basis for a class discussion of the text. See facinghistory.org/mockingbird/strategies for suggestions about how to structure effective classroom discussions.

Close Reading

Additional sets of text-dependent questions are provided in the Appendix to help facilitate the close reading of two passages from the novel, one from Chapter 12 and one from Chapter 15. These close reading activities are specifically written to align with the Common Core State Standards for English Language Arts. The Chapter 12 passage describes Scout's realization that Calpurnia lives a "secret double life." The Chapter 15 passage describes the confrontation with the mob at the jailhouse on the night before the trial. If you choose to facilitate these close reading activities, we recommend that you do so before engaging the class in other activities related to their respective chapters. See "Close Reading for Deep Comprehension" in the Appendix of this guide for a suggested procedure for implementing these close reading activities.

Activities for Deeper Understanding

In addition to the Connection Questions, the following activities can help students reach a deeper understanding of Chapters 12 through 15 of *To Kill a Mockingbird* and its essential themes.

Introduce the Concept of Code-Switching

When Scout and Jem accompany Calpurnia to church, one part of the experience that especially surprises them is the discovery that the language, vocabulary, and tone Calpurnia uses to speak to other African Americans are different from what she uses when she speaks to white people. This phenomenon is called *code-switching*, and everyone does it in their lives. It is worth exploring this concept with students and asking them to think about when, how, and why they use code-switching.

Handout 4.1, "How Code-Switching Explains the World," can provide students with a clear and concise explanation of the phenomenon. You might also watch with students some of the videos on National Public Radio's *Code-Switch* blog that illustrate the practice (see facinghistory.org/mockingbird/links for more information). Then ask students to reflect on the following prompt in their journals:

- How do you use code-switching? Describe an example of how your language is different when you address different people or groups of people. Why does your language change? Are you conscious or unconscious of the change?

In **Handout 4.1**, journalist Gene Demby concludes, "When you're attuned to the phenomenon of code-switching, you start to see it everywhere, and you begin to see the way race, ethnicity, and culture plays out all over the place."[2] You might ask students to look for other, perhaps more subtle, examples of code-switching in *To Kill a Mockingbird*. What do these examples tell us about the divisions in Maycomb bound by race, gender, class, and even age?

Explore Different Perspectives on Maycomb

Students can deepen their understanding of how the story of *To Kill a Mockingbird* is constructed through Scout's point of view by pausing to consider the perspectives of other characters. Everything we know about the setting of Maycomb, Alabama, is filtered through Scout's perspective. Ask students to imagine how other characters in the book might describe Maycomb differently than Scout. Students can then

---

2 Gene Demby, "How Code-Switching Explains the World," *Code Switch: Frontiers of Race, Culture, and Ethnicity*, last modified April 8, 2013, accessed June 4, 2014, http://www.npr.org/blogs/codeswitch/2013/04/08/176064688/how-code-switching-explains-the-world.

choose a character and create an identity chart, not for that character but for Maycomb from that character's point of view. Students can then share their identity charts with classmates who worked with different characters to explore the identity of Maycomb from a variety of perspectives. You might follow up with a brief class discussion that focuses on the following questions:

- Which characters have a perspective on Maycomb similar to Scout's? Which characters' perspectives are different from Scout's? What evidence do we have to support our answers?

- Which version of Maycomb is the "real" Maycomb? How do we know?

Rewrite the Scene at the Jailhouse

Another way to help students understand Scout's limitations as the narrator is to ask them to consider how a different character might have described the jailhouse scene. Ask them to rewrite the scene from the perspective of another character who was there: Tom Robinson, Walter Cunningham, Atticus, or Jem. Note that writing from the perspective of Tom Robinson, in particular, gives students the challenge of synthesizing what they have learned both from the novel and from the historical context resources included with this section.

Regardless of the character that students choose or are assigned, they should include responses to the following questions in their work:

- How does the character understand what the men intend to do when they arrive at the courthouse?

- How does the character feel when Scout runs to Atticus? How does he respond?

- How would the character explain why the men decided to leave? To whom does the character give credit for convincing them to back down?

Write and Reflect in Journals

Any of the Connection Questions in this section might be used as a prompt for journal writing. Also, consider the following questions for a brief reflective writing assignment before, during, or after reading Chapters 12 through 15:

- To what extent do you think that people can really understand the perspective of someone whose life experiences differ from theirs? What has taken place in the first 15 chapters of the book that makes you optimistic about the possibility that one can truly understand those who are different? What has made you question that possibility?

- In Chapters 12 through 15, it becomes clear to Scout that many people, from Aunt Alexandra to the group of men led by Mr. Cunningham, think Atticus is wrong to defend Tom Robinson. Write about a time that you witnessed someone disagree or argue with an adult that you trust, such as a parent, teacher, older sibling, or friend. What did they disagree over? Who do you think was right? Did the disagreement change how you thought about the adult? If so, how? If not, why not? What did it feel like to see someone you trust challenged?

- In Chapter 12, Scout and Jem begin to think differently about Calpurnia and her life after they attend church with her. Write about a time that you learned something new about a close friend or family member that changed how you thought about him or her. How did you find out about this new information? How did you respond? How did it change your relationship with that person?

Revisit Identity Charts

In Section 1, students began identity charts for Scout, Jem, and Atticus (see facinghistory.org/mockingbird/strategies for more information about this teaching strategy). Throughout Chapters 12 to 15, new details are revealed about all three characters. Give students the opportunity to revisit the identity charts. What information might they add? What information might they change or revise?

Encourage students to include quotations from the text on their identity charts, as well as their own interpretations of the character or figure based on their reading.

You might also choose to have students begin new identity charts for some of the characters they learn more about in this section. In particular, they now have a significant amount of detail from which to create identity charts for Calpurnia, Aunt Alexandra, and Tom Robinson.

Keep in mind that creating and revising identity charts for the central characters in *To Kill a Mockingbird* will help prepare students for a culminating activity, suggested in the Post-Reading section of this guide, that asks students to analyze the moral and ethical growth of a character from the novel.

CHAPTER 12: Connection Questions

1. Scout notices that Jem, who has turned 12 at the beginning of Chapter 12, has changed. Describe how Jem is different. How has the relationship between the siblings changed?

2. Calpurnia changes the way she addresses Jem at the beginning of Chapter 12. What does she call him now? Why?

3. Scout tells us that when Calpurnia stays overnight at the Finches', she sleeps on a cot in the kitchen. Why do you think Harper Lee chose to include this detail in this chapter? What is she trying to show us about the Finches and the rules of Maycomb society?

4. What are the differences between the white church that Scout and Jem usually attend and the black church where Calpurnia takes them?

5. What do Scout and Jem notice about the way that Calpurnia talks when she is among other African Americans at church? How does Calpurnia explain the difference? Do Scout and Jem approve of the way she talks to other African Americans?

6. How would you describe the First Purchase Church community's universe of obligation? Use specific evidence from the book to support your answer.

7. How does the woman named Lula react when she sees Scout and Jem arrive at the First Purchase Church with Calpurnia? Why do you think she reacts as she does? How do the other congregants of First Purchase react to Scout and Jem's presence?

8. After going to Calpurnia's church, Scout states, "That Calpurnia led a modest double life never dawned on me." In what sense does Calpurnia lead a double life?

9. What does Scout learn when she accompanies Calpurnia to church? Why might this be a pivotal moment for Scout?

10. What is naïveté? How do Jem and Scout show naïveté in their questions and comments at church? How do their questions reflect assumptions that turn out not to be true?

11. What do we learn about Tom Robinson in this chapter? What can the reader piece together about Tom Robinson and his family that Scout does not understand?

12. Why do you think that Harper Lee chose to write a scene in which Scout and Jem go to church with Calpurnia? How does this scene help us better understand the complexity of the characters? What themes does it prompt us to think more deeply about?

CHAPTER 13: Connection Questions

1. What evidence is there in this chapter that Jem is continuing to try to live up to the idea of being a gentleman? What evidence is there that Scout continues to resist the idea of being a proper lady?

2. Describe Aunt Alexandra. In what ways is she a proper "Southern lady"? Why do you think Atticus asks her to come live with the family? What concerns does Aunt Alexandra have about the way Atticus is raising his children?

3. Early in the chapter, Scout recognizes that she asked Alexandra a question that is not tactful. What is tact? What other evidence can you find in this chapter that Scout is learning to be more tactful?

4. Scout tells us that, according to Aunt Alexandra, "Everybody in Maycomb, it seemed, had a Streak: a Drinking Streak, a Gambling Streak, a Mean Streak, a Funny Streak." What is a "streak"? How does she account for these "streaks"? What does this reveal about her assumptions about human behavior? How is Alexandra's theory about "streaks" different from Scout's theory that "Fine folks were ones who did the best they could with the sense they had"?

5. Do you think these "streaks" are a form of stereotyping? Why or why not? How might believing in "streaks" affect the relationships between townspeople?

6. Scout tells us, "Aunt Alexandra fitted into the world of Maycomb like a hand into a glove, but never into the world of Jem and me." Based on what you have learned so far, how is the world of Scout and Jem different from the "world of Maycomb"? What factors make these worlds different?

7. How does Atticus feel when he delivers his lecture to Scout and Jem about their family's "gentle breeding"? What does Scout notice that leads her to conclude, "This was not my father"? Point to evidence in the text that signals to you how Atticus feels about what he is saying.

8. Scout, as a narrator looking back many years later, concludes, "I know what he was trying to do, but Atticus was only a man. It takes a woman to do that kind of work." What does she mean? Has Scout, as an adult, accepted the gender roles that Aunt Alexandra tries so hard to teach her? How do you interpret her tone in this statement?

CHAPTER 14: Connection Questions

1. When seeing Scout and Jem in town, a man on the street mumbles, "They c'n go loose and rape* up the countryside for all of 'em who run this county care." What does he mean? Why does this man say such a thing at the sight of Scout and Jem? Who is this man accusing of being rapists?

2. How does Atticus explain rape to Scout? Do you think Scout understands him? Do you think Atticus intends for her to understand it?

3. Why does Atticus reprimand Scout after her disclosure about going with Calpurnia to church? What rule did she break that makes Atticus angry?

4. What does Alexandra mean when she calls Atticus "soft-hearted"? What has he done, in Alexandra's view, that is soft-hearted?

5. What is the difference between the way Atticus defines family and the way Alexandra does? What factors have you learned about so far in your study of *To Kill a Mockingbird* that might help explain each of their perspectives? How does Alexandra's universe of obligation differ from Atticus's?

6. How does Jem show in this chapter that he has become more mature and responsible than his younger sister? In what ways is he still a child? How does Scout prove to herself that they are "still equals"?

7. What does this chapter reveal to us about Scout's point of view? What is she learning about herself, her family, and her community? What is she struggling to understand? What parts of the story might the reader

* We recommend that teachers review "Discussing Sensitive Topics in the Classroom" on page xv before using these questions in class.

understand better than Scout? How does this dramatic irony affect the experience of reading the novel?

CHAPTER 15: Connection Questions

1. Why do Heck Tate, Link Deas, and others come to the Finches' house? What do they discuss with Atticus? What do they hope to avoid?

2. What does Scout mean when she says that "Do you really think so?" is Atticus's "dangerous question"? When does he ask that question in this chapter? How do you imagine his tone of voice sounds when he asks it?

3. When Link questions Atticus's judgment for defending Tom Robinson, Atticus replies: "Link, that boy might go to the chair, but he's not going till the truth's told . . . . And you know what the truth is." What is the truth? How might the reader understand this situation better than Scout?

4. Why do you think Jem comes to the door to tell Atticus the phone is ringing, when he could have answered it himself? Why do the men "jump a little"? Does Jem understand the conversation the men are having? Why is he scared for Atticus?

5. What does Atticus mean when he tells Alexandra that he is "in favor of preserving Southern womanhood as much as anybody, but not for preserving polite fiction at the expense of human life"? What is the polite fiction he refers to, and whose life does it threaten?

6. When a group of men, led by Mr. Cunningham, shows up at the Maycomb jailhouse the night before the Tom Robinson trial, what have they come to do? Why is Atticus there waiting? How do you think the men's ideas about justice differ from Atticus's?

7. When the group of men arrives, Atticus confirms that Tom Robinson is inside the jailhouse sleeping and tells the men not to awaken him. Scout reports: "In obedience to my father, there followed what I later realized was a sickeningly comic aspect of an unfunny situation: the men talked in near-whispers." What is "sickeningly comic" about the situation? Why is it ironic that the men agree to talk in whispers?

8. What is a mob? What is mob mentality? Is the group of men that Atticus confronts at the jailhouse a mob?

9. Why does Jem refuse to leave the jailhouse? How does his defiance of Atticus's order to leave make him similar to Atticus in Scout's estimation?

10. When one of the men tries to grab Jem, Scout kicks him while Atticus tells her, "Don't kick folks." Who do you think had the more appropriate response to the man, Atticus or Scout? If not for Scout's actions, how might Atticus have responded to the man trying to grab Jem?

11. Analyze Scout's attempts to engage Mr. Cunningham in conversation. Why does this exchange convince Mr. Cunningham and the other men to leave?

12. How would you characterize Atticus's actions on the night the men came to the jailhouse? What do his actions tell you about his character? What do you think would have happened if the children hadn't arrived at the jailhouse when they did?

13. Early in the chapter, Atticus describes how Sam Levy made the Ku Klux Klan members so ashamed of themselves that they left him alone. How does Atticus suggest Levy made the Klansmen feel ashamed? How does that story parallel the scene at the jailhouse? What do both of these incidents suggest about mob mentality and how Harper Lee thinks it might be defeated? Compare Harper Lee's perspectives with the insights shared by historian Paula Lee Giddings in the video "The Origins of Lynching Culture." (This video can be streamed from facinghistory.org/mockingbird/videos.)

14. How does Scout's limited understanding of the events in this chapter affect the reader? What parts of the story must the reader piece together on his or her own? What does this process reveal about her reliability as a narrator?

AFTER READING SECTION 4: Connection Questions

1. Does Atticus have a choice about being Tom Robinson's attorney? Does he have a choice about how seriously he takes this role?

2. How do you evaluate the decision Atticus makes in response to the choices available to him in Question 1? Set up two columns in your journal. Label the left column "Risks" and the right column "Benefits." List as many examples of risks and benefits as you can think of, and then use those risks and benefits to help you analyze his choice.

3. Is Atticus living up to his definition of *courage*? Who else behaves courageously in Chapters 12 through 15?

4. How well does Scout, the narrator, understand the story she is telling us? How might the way that she tells the story bias the reader toward or against other characters? How does she limit what we know about the story, the setting, and the other characters? What would you most like to know that Scout hasn't told us?

5. What can we learn about point of view in "real life" by analyzing Scout's limitations as the narrator of *To Kill a Mockingbird*? How can it help us better understand the stories that others tell us? How can acknowledging the perspective of the narrator in a work of fiction help us acknowledge our own limited perspective?

6. Who is Tom Robinson? What do we know about him? What important questions about him has the novel left unanswered? If you lived in Maycomb in the 1930s, how might you find out more about Tom? How would your identity influence your options for finding out more about him? What role would race, gender, age, and class play?

7. In Chapter 15, a group of men from Maycomb sets out to lynch Tom Robinson. Such killings are often referred to as acts of "mob justice." How is "mob justice" different from the type of justice Atticus believes in? What are the risks to society when mob justice overrides legal justice? What other beliefs about justice have you found so far in the novel?

Building Historical Context

In Chapters 12 through 15, the written and unwritten rules about family, gender, and class continue to play a significant role in the choices, conversations, and events that take place. However, as readers learn more in these chapters about Tom Robinson, the charges against him, and the rules governing the color line in Maycomb, providing additional historical context about race and Jim Crow society becomes necessary to help students understand the moral universe reflected in the novel. In this section, students will explore historical resources that deepen their knowledge about the following aspects of Maycomb in the 1930s:

- The range of experiences of African Americans under Jim Crow

- The myths, fears, and stereotypes about black men that were prevalent in white society

- The history and purpose of the practice of lynching

As you explore the resources below with the class, remind students that your goal is to reach a deeper understanding of the characters and setting of the novel. After analyzing each resource, revisit the following questions:

- How did this resource deepen your understanding of the characters and setting of *To Kill a Mockingbird*?

- How did this resource help you understand factors that might influence the choices made by an individual who lives in the world of Maycomb, Alabama, in the 1930s?

Explore Firsthand Accounts to Deepen Our Understanding of Tom Robinson

One of the criticisms that has been leveled against *To Kill a Mockingbird*, even by those who cherish the novel, is that Harper Lee does not give the character of Tom Robinson sufficient depth. Readers are left with little sense of his life and experience, or of the devastating consequences the injustices he suffers must have on his family. Writer James McBride, a great admirer of this novel, says of Harper Lee: "She wrote about what she knew, but that doesn't absolve her of handling the character Tom better."[3] Indeed, perhaps one of the greatest consequences of telling the story of *To Kill a Mockingbird* through the narration of Scout is that readers have little opportunity to see, or even draw inferences about, the experiences of the black residents of Maycomb. The primary exception, of course, is Calpurnia, but

---

3   In Mary McDonagh Murphy, ed., *Scout, Atticus, and Boo: A Celebration of Fifty Years of* To Kill a Mockingbird (New York: Harper, 2010), 133.

even after the scene in church, readers are perhaps left with more questions about her life than answers.

Therefore, it is important to provide students with the opportunity to investigate historical context that helps them ascertain who Tom Robinson, were he a real man who lived in this place and time, might have been. This section provides excerpts from interviews with two African American men who lived in Alabama and Mississippi in the 1930s. The two stories these transcripts tell illustrate what is an essential point to underscore with students: there is not a single, generalized experience shared by all black Americans living in the segregated South during the Great Depression. Rather, there are a variety of unique experiences that have similarities and differences. Analyzing moments from the lives of just the two men included here, however, can help students imagine some of the circumstances of a character such as Tom Robinson. If you would like to add to the source material provided here, hundreds of additional interviews of African Americans who lived through the Jim Crow era are available on Duke University's *Behind the Veil* website. (See facinghistory.org/mockingbird/links for more information.)

Handouts 4.3 to **4.16** include excerpts from longer interviews of two men, who are unrelated despite having the same last name: H. J. Williams, who was born in 1910 and lived mostly in Alabama, and Roosevelt Williams, who was born in 1912 and lived in Mississippi.

Both men were interviewed in the 1990s about their experiences in the segregated South. It is important to note that while both men discuss segregation and lynching in some of these documents, in others they recall other facets of their lives at the time, including school, work, church, entertainment, and political participation.

One way to help students investigate these documents is to set up a gallery walk. (See facinghistory.org/mockingbird/strategies for information on teaching strategies.) Post the documents in a way that allows students to disperse themselves around the room, with multiple students clustering around a particular text. Documents can be hung on walls or placed on tables. The most important factor is that the texts are spread far enough apart to reduce significant crowding. You may find it necessary to group the documents by theme (i.e., education, church, segregation) in order to create a smaller, more manageable number of stations.

Have students walk through the gallery in pairs to read the firsthand accounts and note the similarities and differences between the experiences of H. J. and Roosevelt Williams. You might provide students with a graphic organizer such as a simple

Venn diagram to help them organize their thoughts about what the two men had in common and how their experiences differed.

Follow up the gallery walk by leading a discussion in which you ask students to apply what they have learned about H. J. Williams and Roosevelt Williams to their analysis of Tom Robinson. You might use the following questions to guide the discussion:

- Based on what you have pieced together about Tom so far, do you notice any similarities between his life and the lives of the two men you learned about?

- Using what you have just learned, what can you imagine or infer about Tom's life that the book does not tell us?

As we learn more about Tom Robinson in the coming chapters, have students return to their notes from this activity and reevaluate their thinking.

Explore the History of Lynching

In Chapter 15, Scout and Jem naïvely step between Atticus and a mob that has arrived at the jailhouse to lynch Tom Robinson. Although it is clear that Scout does not understand the situation, her presence and interaction with the leader of the mob convinces the men to leave. Because students learn about this event through the eyes of Scout, they also might not be fully aware of the historical context that makes this one of the most dramatic scenes of the novel.

This section provides two resources to help students better understand the history of lynching as well as the ways that its perpetrators attempted to justify their actions.

- The 10-minute video "The Origins of Lynching Culture" provides an overview of the history of lynching and mob justice in the United States. In the video, scholar Paula Giddings explains how the perpetrators of lynching in the late nineteenth and early twentieth centuries used ideas about Southern womanhood, eugenics, and racial stereotypes to attempt to justify their actions. Visit facinghistory.org/mockingbird/videos to watch the video.

  Note that the video contains some graphic images and descriptions of lynchings and a frank discussion of stereotypes about white women and black men that are important to understanding the history of lynching and the charge at the center of Tom Robinson's trial. Therefore, we recommend that you preview the video before sharing it with your class. After showing the video to the class, you might ask the students to spend a few minutes writing in their journals about how it felt to see the images and learn about this disturbing practice. Students can then select a word or phrase from their journal entry to share with the class as part of a Wraparound activity. (See facinghistory.org/mockingbird/strategies for information on teaching strategies.)

Finally, **Handout 4.2** provides a series of questions to guide students' note-taking as they watch the video. Alternatively, you might use the questions as the basis for a discussion after viewing.

Handout 4.1 How Code-Switching Explains the World

The following is an excerpt explaining the phenomenon of code-switching from the National Public Radio blog Code Switch*:*

> So you're at work one day and you're talking to your colleagues in that professional, polite, kind of buttoned-up voice that people use when they're doing professional work stuff.
>
> Your mom or your friend or your partner calls on the phone and you answer. And without thinking, you start talking to them in an entirely different voice— still distinctly *your voice*, but a certain kind of *your voice* less suited for the office. You drop the g's at the end of your verbs. Your previously undetectable accent—your easy Southern drawl or your sing-songy Caribbean lilt or your Spanish-inflected vowels or your New Yawker—is suddenly turned way, way up. You rush your mom or whomever off the phone in some less formal syntax ("Yo, I'mma holler at you later"), hang up and get back to work.
>
> Then you look up and you see your co-workers looking at you and wondering who the hell you'd morphed into for the last few minutes. That right there? That's what it means to code-switch.
>
> . . . [M]any of us subtly, reflexively change the way we express ourselves all the time. We're hop-scotching between different cultural and linguistic spaces and different parts of our own identities—sometimes within a single interaction.
>
> When you're attuned to the phenomenon of code-switching, you start to see it everywhere, and you begin to see the way race, ethnicity and culture plays out all over the place.[1]

---

1   Gene Demby, "How Code-Switching Explains the World," *Code Switch*, April 8, 2013, http://www.npr.org/blogs/codeswitch/2013/04/08/176064688/how-code-switching-explains-the-world.

Handout 4.2 "The Origins of Lynching Culture"

After viewing the video "The Origins of Lynching Culture," take a few moments to record your thoughts and feelings about what you saw in your journal. Then use the following questions to guide your note-taking and reflection.

1. What is the legal definition of lynching? What constitutes a mob?

2. What action did the NAACP take against lynching in the 1920s?

3. How did the majority of lynching victims before 1890 differ from the majority after that year?

4. What is one of the functions of a racial stereotype, according to Paula Giddings? How do stereotypes relate to "first-class" citizenship?

5. How does Giddings distinguish between rights and privileges? Is "first-class" citizenship a right or a privilege?

6. How did prejudices toward black Americans change in the late nineteenth century? How was science used to justify those prejudices?

7. What myths and fears were used to justify the lynching of black men?

8. What experiences influenced Ida B. Wells to challenge the custom of lynching?

9. What strategy did Wells use to challenge the practice and disprove the myths used to justify it?

10. According to Wells's observations, what were the real reasons that blacks were being lynched? What is the reality that her work uncovered about the relationships that black lynching victims typically had with white women?

11. What does Giddings define as the primary function that lynching played in Jim Crow society?

Handout 4.3 H. J. Williams Recalls Work and School In Yazoo County, Mississippi

H. J. WILLIAMS: In 1933 we were working for fifty cents a day. 1933. That was.

MAUSIKI SCALES (INTERVIEWER): What were you doing?

H. J. WILLIAMS: Chopping cotton. Plowing a mule. And that's what they paid. That was the wages they was paying. Fifty cents a day at that time in the '30s. And up in the '40s, and like I said after President Roosevelt come in power it was a little change made. They were finally moved up to a $1 a day.

MAUSIKI SCALES: Did you go to school while you were growing up on the farm?

H. J. WILLIAMS: Yeah. Yeah. I went to school.

MAUSIKI SCALES: How long was the school session?

H. J. WILLIAMS: I went to school. I went as high as 8th grade. I didn't complete the 8th grade, but I went to 8th grade when I was going to school. That's as high as I went. As I might have said because of my daddy, we were living on the farm then and we had a bad year and my daddy wasn't able to buy me school books and that's when I dropped out of school. Didn't go no further. I went high as 8th grade. That's as far as I could go. When I was in the 8th grade, I was studying in the books with some of the other children at school what was able to have books and that's where I was studying.

MAUSIKI SCALES: Did you go to school nine months out of the year?

H. J. WILLIAMS: Something like that. Yep. Nine months out of a year.

MAUSIKI SCALES: What type of things did you learn in school?

H. J. WILLIAMS: What type did I learn in school? Well, far as jobs and so on like that I didn't learn nothing about jobs or nothing like that at school cause we was on the farm. In other words, they wadn't teaching at that time, they weren't teaching mechanical work, you know, in the public schools. They wadn't teaching that at that time out there. So they'd teach us about agriculture and so on like that, what we was doing, so on and like that. They'd teach us that. So that's as far as we could go at that time what they was teaching. But far as mechanical work and so on like that they wadn't teaching nothing like that at that time.

MAUSIKI SCALES: Were your parents educated people?

H. J. WILLIAMS: Nope. They wadn't. Neither one.

MAUSIKI SCALES: How about your grandparents? Were they?

H. J. WILLIAMS: Well, the grandparents could read and write. That's as far as I know. I can draw on that.

MAUSIKI SCALES: Did they ever talk about their experiences when they were coming along?

H. J. WILLIAMS: Oh yeah. They talked about their experiences because some of the grandparents was under slavery. Yeah. They was under slavery when they was coming along at that time. Some of 'em.[1]

---

1   H. J. Williams, interview by Mausiki S. Scales, August 8, 1995, "H. J. Williams interview," *Behind the Veil*, Duke University Digitial Libraries, accessed May 6, 2014, http://library.duke.edu/digitalcollections/behindtheveil_btvct04042/#info.

Handout 4.4 H. J. Williams Recalls the Depression in Yazoo County, Mississippi

MAUSIKI SCALES (INTERVIEWER): How did your family make it through the depression?

H. J. WILLIAMS: You talking about what now, back in the '30s? '29 and back in there?

MAUSIKI SCALES: Yes sir.

H. J. WILLIAMS: Well, we made it through by the help of God. That's all. That's all that brought us through by the help of God because they wadn't paying nothing for wages, no money. There wadn't no work unless it was farming and after that why as I fore said, Roosevelt took over, taken over. Okay. The white man in the south, we was just talking about that a few minutes ago, he got rid of the labor out there on the farms. You couldn't rent no land from them. They got the white faced cows and fenced off the land out there and put white faced cows in that pasture, you see, and the black people had to move from out there. And when they moved from out there that's what happened. They had to come to the cities or had to come somewhere and there wadn't but few jobs in the city and that's what made it so bad and kept the wages down so low cause there's so many people here. That's what kept it so low. And that man put them white faced cows out there and then the next step after he did that he went in the machinery business and got three or four tractors and hired him three or four tractor drivers and while they were working, when we had the team out there in the field, he was working probably 100 acres of land, he's two or three thousand acres with them three tractor drivers. That's right.

MAUSIKI SCALES: So the tractor replaced blacks.

H. J. WILLIAMS: Yes sir. Yes sir. Replaced the black. The tractors.[1]

---

1   H. J. Williams, interview by Mausiki S. Scales, August 8, 1995, "H. J. Williams interview," *Behind the Veil*, Duke University Digitial Libraries, accessed May 6, 2014, http://library.duke.edu/digitalcollections/behindtheveil_btvct04042/#info.

Handout 4.5 H. J. Williams Recalls Segregation in Business and Transportation in Yazoo County, Mississippi

MAUSIKI SCALES (INTERVIEWER): When you were growing up here did the blacks own their own businesses?

H. J. WILLIAMS: No. No black business when I was growing up here. None whatever. Nothing but white was in business at that time when I was growing up here 85 years ago. Nothing but white business.

MAUSIKI SCALES: Were there places that you couldn't go into because they . . .

H. J. WILLIAMS: Yes sir. Lots of places we couldn't go into and those what we could go into like a cafe or a drug store or something like that the white would be on that side and the black on the other side, the right side. That's the way it was here at that time. Absolutely. And there was some you couldn't go in at all. That's right. And in the bus stations you couldn't drink out of the water fountains what a white man dranked out of. You couldn't go to that fountain and get a drink of water. In other words if you get on the bus to go, I'll say Memphis and Chicago, or any place, okay. You'd go about middle ways of that bus and take your seat. And, traveling on as many white, if whites get on there, okay, you'd have to continue moving back to the back. Moving back, and back, and back until you get to the last seat and have to get behind this if any more whites got on there. That's the way it was then.

MAUSIKI SCALES: They had room behind the last seat?

H. J. WILLIAMS: What? No, just crowd you back up in the back. That's right. Crowd you back up in the back and you'd have to stand up. You didn't have no seat as long as some white got on there that's the way you were. And it was like that I'd say it was in the armed forces in '43, that's when I went to the army and we had trouble right there in Yazoo City concerning us riding the bus. That's right. Concern of that. They put some colored boys off in Jackson, Mississippi. I come here on a furlough and they put some black boys off the bus because they wouldn't get back and they had us pushed in there like cows and they couldn't get back no further and they put 'em off the bus. That's right. That was the way it was. That was in 1943. Sure was.

MAUSIKI SCALES: Blacks own cars here?

H. J. WILLIAMS: At that time? A few. A few. A very few owned cars at that time in the '40s. A few.[1]

1   H. J. Williams, interview by Mausiki S. Scales, August 8, 1995, "H. J. Williams interview," *Behind the Veil*, Duke University Digitial Libraries, accessed May 6, 2014, http://library.duke.edu/digitalcollections/behindtheveil_btvct04042/#info.

Handout 4.6 H. J. Williams Recalls Learning About the Rules of Jim Crow in Yazoo County, Mississippi

MAUSIKI SCALES (INTERVIEWER): When did you first realize that the way blacks and whites were treated was different?

H. J. WILLIAMS: When I first realized that? Well, I been knowing that . . . all my days. I realize that all my days when I was a small boy coming up I'd say around 10 or 12 years, you know, I knowed the difference, you know, in the treatments of human beings. I knowed the treatment at that time, but we wadn't allowed to say anything. That's right. We wadn't allowed to say anything. I remember back there in those days and new to that time if you was driving a horse to a buggy, okay, and white ladies was in a buggy, you couldn't pull around them and go in the front of them. Because my sisters did it and the man's place what we was living on was Tom Preseton and his daughter was coming back from Yazoo City, coming back out in the country where we lived. And my sisters was in a buggy and they pulled around. They went home and told their daddy that the Williams girls pulled by them and dusted them up. And they daddy got on his horse and come over there and told my daddy that Miss Letty and Miss Eva said your girls pulled around them and dusted them up. Don't let that happen no more. That's right. That's just the way it was in those days. Absolutely. That is around about '30, '32, 1932. That's right. So that's the way things was at that time. I realize that, you know, it is nothing but Jim Crow, you know. But years, man, when I was a small boy, but we couldn't say nothing because if you did the first things they'd holler about was a lynching or whipping up a black person. And then just like you see today about the Ku Klux Klan person, it was the same thing at that time. The same identical thing at that time.[1]

---

1   H. J. Williams, interview by Mausiki S. Scales, August 8, 1995, "H. J. Williams interview," *Behind the Veil*, Duke University Digitial Libraries, accessed May 6, 2014, http://library.duke.edu/digitalcollections/behindtheveil_btvct04042/#info.

Handout 4.7 H. J. Williams Recalls Lynching in Yazoo County, Mississippi

MAUSIKI SCALES (INTERVIEWER): Did they have lynchings down here that you recall?

H. J. WILLIAMS: Oh yeah, they had some lynchings. Yeah. Sure. I can take you to a place right on there on Shorty Creek where they lynched a man. That's right. Hung him to a limb. Sure did. Oh yeah. That's right. There was lynching back then in those days.

MAUSIKI SCALES: Why did they hang him?

H. J. WILLIAMS: Huh?

MAUSIKI SCALES: Why did they hang him?

H. J. WILLIAMS: Well, they claim that he was a friend to a white lady. That's what they claim. Now whether it was true or not, I don't know and I haven't heard anybody else say they knowed, but that's what they claimed and they lynched him. That's right. Well, due to the fact as I was coming up, back in those days I remember this . . . .[1]

---

1   H. J. Williams, interview by Mausiki S. Scales, August 8, 1995, "H. J. Williams interview," *Behind the Veil*, Duke University Digitial Libraries, accessed May 6, 2014, http://library.duke.edu/digitalcollections/behindtheveil_btvct04042/#info.

Handout 4.8 H. J. Williams Recalls Church in Yazoo County, Mississippi

MAUSIKI SCALES (INTERVIEWER): When you were growing up, was church mandatory for you? Did you have to go to church?

H. J. WILLIAMS: Oh yeah. Yeah. We had to go to church. When we were kids, we had to go to church cause that daddy of mine he was going to get his book and he's going to say come on, let's go, and we were going to follow behind him. Had to go. That's right. We were raised up in the church. I was raised up in the Baptist church and the Methodist church too.

MAUSIKI SCALES: Okay. And do you remember revivals and thanksgivings?

H. J. WILLIAMS: Yes sir. Sure I remember the revivals. They had revivals every year. They mostly had revival in the fall of the year. Uh huh. Every fall they'd have revival. Of course, now they have, it's anytime. They have it in the spring and then have another one in the fall. They have it all the time now, but we . . . only have revival from church to church due to the fact in the fall.

MAUSIKI SCALES: Did you get baptized?

H. J. WILLIAMS: Yes sir. Yes sir. I was baptized. That's right.

MAUSIKI SCALES: Was it an outside service?

H. J. WILLIAMS: Yeah, I was baptized in a creek. Holy water. That's where they baptized at and then went to the church and was fellowshiped in the temple.

MAUSIKI SCALES: Okay. Did a lot of people come?

H. J. WILLIAMS: Uh huh. Lot of people come to see me get baptized. Sure did.[1]

---

1   H. J. Williams, interview by Mausiki S. Scales, August 8, 1995, "H. J. Williams interview," *Behind the Veil*, Duke University Digitial Libraries, accessed May 6, 2014, http://library.duke.edu/digitalcollections/behindtheveil_btvct04042/#info.

Handout 4.9 H. J. Williams Reflects on Manhood in Yazoo County, Mississippi

MAUSIKI SCALES (INTERVIEWER): In those times what did it mean to be a man, what was manhood?

H. J. WILLIAMS: What did it mean to be a man?

MAUSIKI SCALES: Yes sir.

H. J. WILLIAMS: Well, I tell you brother, it didn't mean too much to the black race because he didn't have no power to express his self and no position. That's right. It didn't mean nothing in a way to be a man. You was just a person had done growed up of age and that was it. Just had growed up of age and that was it. You couldn't express yourself. You couldn't say no more than that man allow you to say. That's the way it was. Absolutely. And I remember back there in those times, when a white boy got 16 years old the boss man would tell the labor or whoever was on that farm or on that place whatever they call him, say now my son is coming 16 years old or my daughter is 16 years old. It's time for y'all to start saying Miss So and So, Mr. So and So. That's what the boss man did say. The white man would tell the black people and they wadn't but 16 years old and you'd have to be saying Miss So and So and Mr. So and So and So.

MAUSIKI SCALES: And you would be a lot older than them?

H. J. WILLIAMS: Yes sir. You would be a grown man 25 or 30 years old or maybe 50 years old, but you had to say it. And what they used to call the black people then was uncle and auntie. That's what they would call the black. Uncle So and So and So and Aunt So and So and So. Uh huh. That's right. In those days. Yeah, I remember that.

MAUSIKI SCALES: How did you feel about having to do that?

H. J. WILLIAMS: You would feel bad, very bad, but it wasn't nothing you could do about it, because if you said anything to them the first thing they were going to do in those days was going to get a mob crowd and come beat that Negro up. That's right. Beat that Negro up or kill him or hang him. He's a smart Negro. That's what they was going to say. Uh huh. Absolutely. Yeah, I remember those days. Sure do.[1]

---

1   H. J. Williams, interview by Mausiki S. Scales, August 8, 1995, "H. J. Williams interview," *Behind the Veil*, Duke University Digitial Libraries, accessed May 6, 2014, http://library.duke.edu/digitalcollections/behindtheveil_btvct04042/#info.

Handout 4.10 Roosevelt Williams Recalls His Youth in Alabama

R. WILLIAMS: I was born in Pickens County, and I lived on a farm. Of course, we did own our own place. It was pretty rough out on the farm, because cotton and stuff, that's the biggest thing we had to depend on as far as a cash crop, and it wasn't no price for nothing. We did very well, I guess, considering. As far as living, we had plenty to eat and everything. It just wasn't all the time what we wanted, but we had plenty because we raised mostly everything. I lived down there and went to school down there and everything.

In 1940, I left there and I went to Meridian, Mississippi, and I worked there about a year. I didn't like it. I was doing sawmill work and everything. I didn't like that. And so then I got a chance to come to Birmingham and I got a job with U.S. Steel. I stayed there until I retired, U.S. Steel, Ensley Works. I did better there. After I got the job, making a little money, I did very well.

But now, this is a real segregated town, Birmingham was. Well, we found it all over that way in Pickens County, as far as that goes. You know, we come up in it, so we got along very well. I didn't never have no trouble, because I always tried to stay within the law and do what I thought was right. So I didn't never have no trouble with nobody, but it was really going on, that segregation. We had to stay what they called then "in our place." But then, of course, I got along very well.[1]

---

1 Roosevelt Williams, interview by Paul Ortiz, June 24, 1993, "Roosevelt Williams interview," *Behind the Veil*, Duke University Digital Collections, accessed May 6, 2014, http://library.duke.edu/digitalcollections/behindtheveil_btvct02027/.

Handout 4.11 Roosevelt Williams Recalls School in Alabama

ORTIZ (INTERVIEWER): What kind of education was available to you?

R. WILLIAMS: Well, it was available, but actually, I didn't go all the way through, because at that time we had to—well, we didn't have but three months' school at that time, and having to carry the farm on and everything, a lot of times I wasn't able to go all of that semester. So I wound up about tenth grade. I didn't quite finish.

ORTIZ: Do you remember the names of your schools?

R. WILLIAMS: Yeah. Pickens County Training School was one I went to. Of course, now, I went to some local school before then, Cumberland Presbyterian Church. I went to that before I went to Pickens County Training School.

ORTIZ: Pickens County Training School was like a high school?

R. WILLIAMS: Yes, it was a high school.

ORTIZ: And the Presbyterian church was kind of like a grade school for black students?

R. WILLIAMS: Yeah, that's right.

ORTIZ: Do you remember anything about the teachers, about the books, where you got the books from?

R. WILLIAMS: Well, I don't know exactly where we got the books from, but at that time, we didn't get the first—the books was different from what the whites got, I know that. I don't remember exactly where they got them or how they got them, but anyway, they were different.

ORTIZ: As students, did you and your friends talk about that during the time?

R. WILLIAMS: Well, we didn't know much better way back there. We just thought that's the way it's supposed to be, as far as we knew then, because we wasn't taught. Until I got a little older, I didn't know anything about it. Back then, especially in grammar school and all, we didn't know any better. We thought that's the way it's supposed to be, as far as we knew.

But anyway, I went to Pickens County Training School. This was about four or five miles, and we had to walk there because there wasn't no bus available for blacks at all then. They'd pass right by you, these other buses with the white, but you couldn't get on, we couldn't get on.

ORTIZ: So you would watch the whites—

R. WILLIAMS: Oh, yeah, the whites would pass by and go on to their buses, take them to school and bringing them back home.

ORTIZ: What did you think about that?

R. WILLIAMS: It was rough. It was rough. Oh, yeah, I knew it wasn't right, but it seemed to be nothing they could do about it then. But they'd pass right by you, but you couldn't get on that bus.

ORTIZ: Did you ever talk with the white kids?

R. WILLIAMS: Well, yeah, sometimes I talked to them, but, well, I guess they felt like that was right, too, for it to be like that, and so I didn't get much sympathy from them.[1]

1   Roosevelt Williams, interview by Paul Ortiz, June 24, 1993, "Roosevelt Williams interview," *Behind the Veil*, Duke University Digital Collections, accessed May 6, 2014, http://library.duke.edu/digitalcollections/behindtheveil_btvct02027/.

Handout 4.12 Roosevelt Williams Recalls Learning About the Rules of Jim Crow in Alabama

ORTIZ (INTERVIEWER): Were there fights?

R. WILLIAMS: Well, we didn't have many fights among the races. We got along pretty good. Once in a while you'd have a fight, but we didn't have lots of fights. I'll tell you, once in a while some of them you grew up with, they don't live far apart, and when you're small, you play together. But now, quick as he gets a little age on him, then he wants you to call him Mister, you know. That was a few fights about that. You've got to call him Mister. That's what he wanted. So we'd have little squabbles about that sometimes. I'm getting of age now. I'm Mr. So-and-so. Sometimes you might be older than him, but he still wanted you to call him Mister.

ORTIZ: The white kid would actually say—

R. WILLIAMS: Yeah, yeah, call him Mister. He didn't care if you were older than he is. But he's just going to call you by your name. In other words, coming up there, you never was, I'd say, considered a man. You was a boy. If you got old, you was uncle or something like that they'd call you, anything but Mister. That's just the way it was.[1]

---

1 Roosevelt Williams, interview by Paul Ortiz, June 24, 1993, "Roosevelt Williams interview," *Behind the Veil*, Duke University Digital Collections, accessed May 6, 2014, http://library.duke.edu/digitalcollections/behindtheveil_btvct02027/.

Handout 4.13 Roosevelt Williams Recalls Community Events in Alabama

ORTIZ (INTERVIEWER): When you were growing up in Pickens County, do you remember any times or events that would bring people together, like any celebrations?

R. WILLIAMS: You mean both races or just—

ORTIZ: Perhaps just black people.

R. WILLIAMS: Oh, yeah, black, they'd often have big meetings and things, or associations, they called them. Days like that, there'd be lots of people gathered on those days, particular days. We'd celebrate like the 4th of July. They had a little sandlot ball teams and everything that would meet. We call ourselves had a good time. We had a lot of gatherings like that, you know.

ORTIZ: Who would organize those?

R. WILLIAMS: Well, they had different ones in the community there would do that, mostly. They'd just get together and just organize a ball team or whatever it is. As far as big turnouts and everything, the leading church folks, the ministers and things, they'd have these association meetings, they called them. All the churches would meet together and have a big time, have a big dinner and all like that, a turnout. Yeah, we had some nice gatherings, had a big time together that way.[1]

---

1 Roosevelt Williams, interview by Paul Ortiz, June 24, 1993, "Roosevelt Williams interview," *Behind the Veil*, Duke University Digital Collections, accessed May 6, 2014, http://library.duke.edu/digitalcollections/behindtheveil_btvct02027/.

Handout 4.14 Roosevelt Williams Recalls Farming During His Youth in Alabama

ORTIZ (INTERVIEWER): What year did you get married?

R. WILLIAMS: I got married in 1931.

ORTIZ: So you had your own land?

R. WILLIAMS: Yeah.

ORTIZ: Did you purchase that?

R. WILLIAMS: I inherited twenty acres from my grandparents and I bought another forty acres myself. That was sixty acres. I had that to farm on, see.

ORTIZ: I've heard that those were very difficult years.

R. WILLIAMS: Oh, it was. They were difficult years. You see, cotton got as low as 5 cents a pound. It'd take lots of work to make a bale of cotton, and so you didn't get nothing much out of it for what you were doing. And you'd have to have money to farm on. By the time you support your farm and everything, when gathering time come, you had to pay it all out, whatever you made, most of it, so you didn't hardly clear no money. Mighty little, if any.

ORTIZ: Who would you sell your crop to?

R. WILLIAMS: Well, they had an open market, you know, in a little old town, like Carrollton and Aliceville. They had regular buyers to buy this cotton. Of course, we had to take it to the gin. You'd take it there and have it ginned, and they'd give you a sample, what they called. When you'd get ready to sell it, you'd take it before this buyer, and he'll examine that cotton, and depend on what length it was and everything, and he'll pay you accordingly, but it wasn't much.

That was about the biggest cash crop you had, because you could raise a lot of other stuff, but you couldn't sell it. You didn't have nobody to buy it. And so cotton, as I said, that was the biggest thing we had to depend on as far as cash. But we'd raise corn and we had grits meal, make our own meal and stuff, as far as that goes, and things like that, and raise our own hogs and kill hogs and have plenty meat and stuff like that.

It's just the way we had to come up. As I said, we'd have plenty of that, whatever it was, but all this other fancy stuff, maybe what we wanted, we wasn't able to buy it. We'd raise cows and things. If you killed a cow, you didn't have no refrigeration, nothing much. You couldn't keep your meat and stuff. Now, that pork, that hog, we would cure that, smoke it, and you could keep that.[1]

1 Roosevelt Williams, interview by Paul Ortiz, June 24, 1993, "Roosevelt Williams interview," *Behind the Veil*, Duke University Digital Collections, accessed May 6, 2014, http://library.duke.edu/digitalcollections/behindtheveil_btvct02027/.

Handout 4.15 Roosevelt Williams Recalls Moving for Work in Alabama and Mississippi

ORTIZ (INTERVIEWER): Was that your first job outside of the house?

R. WILLIAMS: Well, my first regular job. Like I said, during my spare time, when I wasn't farming, I'd get a little job around sawmills and things like that. I had left home one time and went up in Detroit, but at that time, I stayed up about three months during the winter. I tried to get a job, but I wasn't able to get one. That was somewhere along about 1936 or '7. I didn't get no job then. I come back and farmed about two or three years before I left there, you see.

[. . .]

ORTIZ: There must have been a point when you were farming after you married that you felt like things were getting especially hard and it was hard to make a living.

R. WILLIAMS: Oh, yeah, it was. Yeah, it was, that's right.

ORTIZ: How did you come to the decision to go to Meridian [Mississippi]?

R. WILLIAMS: As I said, I had a cousin down there. He was working at—well, he was sort of in charge of the lumber department down there, and so he kept on after me and told me, "Come on down here. We'll give you a job down here, and you can make some money."

Well, I went on down there, but they wasn't paying nothing much, and working from sunup to sundown. I didn't like that. Then I had a guy over here, one of her cousins, he told me—it was TCI at that time, the steel mill, TCI. He said, "They're fixing to hire some people. Why don't you come on over there? You might get a job over there."

And so I did. I left there one weekend, and that Monday morning they were hiring out there. It was sort of hard to get a job then. That was just after the war had broke out—just before the war broke out. So they finally, he hired me. It was lots of people there, but somehow or another, through all that I did get a job there. I stayed there for thirty-five years.[1]

---

1   Roosevelt Williams, interview by Paul Ortiz, June 24, 1993, "Roosevelt Williams interview," *Behind the Veil*, Duke University Digital Collections, accessed May 6, 2014, http://library.duke.edu/digitalcollections/behindtheveil_btvct02027/.

Handout 4.16 Roosevelt Williams Recalls Voting in Alabama

ORTIZ (INTERVIEWER): Were you involved or did you follow the politics of the day—Roosevelt, New Deal? Were you voting at that time?

R. WILLIAMS: I started voting way back. I'll tell you, at that time, you know, they had such strict laws. You had what they called poll tax, and you had to pay poll tax. I even paid poll tax. And you had to pass the board of examiners. They asked you all kind of strict questions and everything. But I was determined to vote, and I kept on until I got to be a voter. As I said, I had to pay poll tax for so many years. Then they cut out the poll tax.

ORTIZ: Did you start trying to vote in Birmingham?

R. WILLIAMS: Yeah, in Birmingham [in the early 1940s] I started. I didn't even make no attempt down in there, because, I don't know, I don't think they had no black voting down in Pickens County [in the 1930s]. That was out of the question.

ORTIZ: Did anybody ever try?

R. WILLIAMS: I don't know. I don't think it was open for black, as far as I know, then. After I come here to Birmingham, it was rough then. They didn't have but just a few black voters here, and as I said, you had a tough time trying to pass the vote or register.

ORTIZ: What kind of experience was that? What did you have to go through?

R. WILLIAMS: Well, see, you'd go before the examiner. They asked you all kind of questions about the Constitution of the United States, things they know you didn't know. They'd ask you all those silly questions, and if you couldn't answer them all, well, you were turned down.

Now, what we did, we had a voting rights school we'd go to, and they would teach us lots of them things that they might would ask, you know. We had it set up at our church. We'd have people coming in there and trying to learn them, train them to answer these questions. So we got quite a few voters qualified through that.[1]

---

1   Roosevelt Williams, interview by Paul Ortiz, June 24, 1993, "Roosevelt Williams interview," *Behind the Veil*, Duke University Digital Collections, accessed May 6, 2014, http://library.duke.edu/digitalcollections/behindtheveil_btvct02027/.

Connecting to the Central Question

Before beginning Section 5, consider pausing to ask students to review the central question introduced at the beginning of this guide:

What factors influence our moral growth? What kinds of experiences help us learn how to judge right from wrong?

Give students the opportunity to review the response to this question that they wrote and revised in previous sections of this guide. What evidence have they found in this section that confirms their previous response? What evidence have they found that might prompt them to revise their thinking?

Ask students to take a few minutes to reflect on whether or not their thinking has changed, revise their preliminary responses, and record new evidence from Section 4 that can help them answer the question.

Remind students that they will have several opportunities to revise their thinking as they continue to read the novel. Their revised responses and notes will help prepare students for a culminating activity, suggested in the Post-Reading section of this guide, that asks them to analyze the moral growth of a character from the novel.

SECTION 5
Stand Up

This section covers Chapters 16 to 21 of the novel.

Introduction

Essential Questions

- What is justice? What roles do laws and individuals play in creating a just society?

- How do encounters with injustice shape our beliefs about justice and morality?

- How does the existence of "in" groups and "out" groups affect the strength of a democracy?

Rationale

In previous sections, students investigated the relationships between the main characters of *To Kill a Mockingbird* and the setting, or "moral universe," they inhabit. In particular, they explored how the tension between the characters and the unwritten rules of their society draws the reader into ongoing cultural conversations, or themes, about identity, belonging, and the consequences of standing apart from the crowd. In this section, students will spiral back to all of these essential elements of the novel as they reach the climax of the story, the trial and conviction of Tom Robinson.

In many respects, *To Kill a Mockingbird* follows a traditional plot structure, with the Tom Robinson trial and verdict serving as the climax. For the main characters—Scout, Jem, and Atticus—the trial serves as a moment of peak dramatic tension and a turning point in the conflicts they face in the story. Atticus stands before his fellow townspeople and breaks Jim Crow's unwritten rules by mounting a vigorous defense of Tom Robinson. Scout and Jem observe the trial from the front row of the "colored balcony" as their developing senses of right and wrong conflict with the attitudes and assumptions of so many of their fellow townspeople.

As students explore Chapters 16 through 21, it is worth reviewing traditional plot elements (exposition, conflict, rising action, climax, falling action, and resolution) so that they can situate this section into the overall structure of the novel. In particular, students should consider the ways in which Harper Lee signals that these chapters constitute the climax of the story. While it is often helpful to have finished the book before determining the climax (and with this book, some might argue that another climax arrives near the end when Boo Radley rescues the children from Bob Ewell's attack), clues abound that the Tom Robinson trial is going to be a crucial event—a turning point and a formative moment in the lives of the protagonists. Students will certainly notice that the thematic and dramatic tension has mounted in the story ever since Atticus was assigned to the Tom Robinson case, making the trial itself an important and highly anticipated event for both the characters and the reader. Students should also notice the change in the pacing of the novel—the events of the trial take place in one day but span six chapters in the book—and recognize that change as a sign that we have reached a climax in the plot.

The questions and activities in this section help students analyze the Tom Robinson trial and the role it plays in the novel. Such moments of tension and conflict in literature pose important questions for the reader to consider. Students might reflect on the formative experiences and turning points in their own lives as they consider the following questions about the trial and verdict:

- What does the trial reveal about the setting, or moral universe, in which the event is taking place?

- What does it reveal about the characters?

- Who and what will change as a result of the trial, and who or what will stay the same? Will the characters grow and mature? Will the community change?

- How does this climax draw us more deeply into the ongoing cultural conversations, the themes, at the heart of this novel?

We will not be able to fully answer some of these questions until we reach the resolution of the plot at the end of the book, but the tension of the trial and the disconnect between the hopes and expectations of the main characters and the reality of Maycomb society is rich terrain to explore. As a result, students will return to and deepen their consideration of themes that emerged throughout the novel about identity, belonging, and following one's conscience. In addition, some new themes about justice, equality, and democracy emerge more strongly in this section:

- What is justice? Do laws or the hearts and minds of individuals play a greater role in creating a just society?

- What is equality? What forms of equality are necessary for a just, democratic society? Are some forms of inequality natural and acceptable?

The historical context provided in this section will deepen students' consideration of these themes and help them understand the Tom Robinson trial not as an aberration but as an example of a common and integral component of Jim Crow justice, the "courtroom lynching." By learning about the infamous trials in the 1930s of the Scottsboro Boys, nine young African American men falsely accused of raping two white women on a train, students will see how the Tom Robinson trial reflects real challenges to justice, equality, and democracy that existed in Jim Crow courtrooms.

Plot Summary

On the day of the trial, Scout, Jem, and Dill go to the courthouse to watch, despite the fact that Atticus told them to stay home. When they arrive, all the seats are full, so they sit in the "colored balcony" with Reverend Sykes. The court hears testimony from Sheriff Tate, Mr. Bob Ewell, and Mayella Ewell, and as Atticus cross-examines each of the witnesses, he attempts to cast doubt on Mayella's version of events. It becomes clear that Atticus is suggesting that Mr. Ewell beat Mayella. When Tom Robinson takes the stand, he denies the charges and explains that he in fact tried to resist Mayella's advances.

In his closing argument, Atticus invokes the Declaration of Independence and urges the jury to find Tom not guilty. The jury deliberates so long that the children fall asleep in the balcony waiting for the verdict. Finally, the jury returns and delivers a guilty verdict. As Atticus leaves the courtroom, all of the people in the "colored balcony" stand as he passes.

Skills Focus

- Deepening Understanding of the Novel through Analysis of Historical Context from Informational Texts

- Investigating the Author's Craft: Plot, Pace, Suspense

- Understanding the Setting as a Moral Universe

- Getting to Know the Characters (continued from previous section)

  » Newly introduced characters: Judge Taylor, Mayella Ewell, Bob Ewell, Dolphus Raymond, Mr. Gilmer

Academic Vocabulary

CHAPTER 16 *profane, subpoena, elucidate, vista, sundry, solicitor, amiable, dispelled, equity, academic, eccentricities, connivance, litigant;* CHAPTER 17 *namesake, congenital, indigenous, glean, quell, dictum, import, defendant, haughty, complacent;* CHAPTER 18 *immaterial, chronic, subsided, grudging, scrutiny;* CHAPTER 20 *corroborative, detachment, cynical;* CHAPTER 21 *acquit, indignant, tacit*

Exploring the Text

Before Reading

Before reading Chapters 16 to 21, ask students to reflect on the following statements, indicate whether or not they agree, and briefly explain their responses:

- Laws play an important role in shaping who I am.

- It is possible to create a fully equal society.

- People, not laws, are most responsible for creating a just society.

- Culture, custom, and tradition are more powerful than laws.

Note that these statements are included on **Handout 5.1** with space for students to indicate and explain their responses.

After students respond to the statements, consider having the class share their thinking with a Four Corners activity. Post signs in the corners of the room reading "Strongly Agree," "Agree," "Disagree," and "Strongly Disagree." As you read each sentence in the Anticipation Guide, students will move to the sign that indicates how they responded to the statement. Select a few students from each corner to explain their responses. Repeat this process for all six statements or for only a couple. More detailed descriptions of both the Anticipation Guide and the Four Corners strategy are available at facinghistory.org/mockingbird/strategies.

Using Connection Questions

Connection Questions, organized by chapter, are provided below to help guide your class's analysis of the text. A similar set of "After Reading Section 5: Connection Questions" is also provided below to help students synthesize their understanding of Chapters 16 through 21 as a whole.

While these questions are mostly text-based, they are designed to probe important themes in the novel. As you assign chapters for students to read, you might designate all or some of these questions for students to respond to in their journals. These questions can also provide the basis for a class discussion of the text. See facinghistory.org/mockingbird/strategies for suggestions about how to structure effective classroom discussions.

Close Reading

An additional set of text-dependent questions is provided in the Appendix to help facilitate the close reading of a passage from Chapter 20 of the novel. This close reading activity is specifically written to align with the Common Core State Standards for English Language Arts. This passage focuses on Atticus's closing argument in the Tom Robinson trial. If you choose to implement this close reading activity, we recommend you do so before engaging the class in other activities related to Chapter 20. See "Close Reading for Deep Comprehension" in the Appendix for a suggested procedure for implementing this close reading activity.

Activities for Deeper Understanding

In addition to the Connection Questions, the following activities can help students reach a deeper understanding of Chapters 12 through 15 of *To Kill a Mockingbird* and its essential themes.

Reflect on the Trial and Process Responses

The resolution to the Tom Robinson trial is one of two moments often cited as the climax of *To Kill a Mockingbird* (in addition to Boo Radley saving Scout and Jem from Mr. Ewell). Students may have an emotional reaction to this moment when the injustice embedded within Maycomb society is laid bare.

Consider reading aloud to the class the passage from Chapter 21 in which the jury delivers the verdict in order to help students understand the dramatic nature of this moment in the story. Start reading with the paragraph that begins "But I must have been reasonably awake . . . " and continue to the end of the chapter.

After reading about the verdict, consider having students do a "quick write" in their journals for a few minutes to capture their thoughts and feelings about the trial and its outcome. Then ask students to select one or more words from their writing that represent how they feel in response to the trial.

One way to have students share their responses is to use the Wraparound teaching strategy. With this strategy, the students form a line or a circle in the classroom and simply say aloud the words and phrases they have chosen from their reflections in succession.

Another option to help students further process and share their responses is to have them work in pairs to model the words that they have chosen from their reflections kinesthetically. This strategy, called Bodysculpting, can provide a powerful way for students to respond nonverbally to the Tom Robinson verdict. We recommend reading the detailed guidelines for both of these strategies at facinghistory.org/mockingbird/strategies.

Analyze the Verdict through the Lens of History and Human Behavior

An iceberg diagram is a graphic organizer that can help students analyze a complex event, such as the verdict in the Tom Robinson trial, and understand both its more obvious causes as well as those that are not immediately apparent. The guilty verdict is the result of choices made by a variety of individuals, influenced by powerful forces embedded in the fabric of Maycomb, the American South, and the United States as a whole in the 1930s. Like Jem, some students may focus on the presentation of facts and arguments in the trial and expect Robinson to be acquitted. It is therefore important to take the time to consider all of the factors that made the guilty verdict not only possible but the most likely outcome given the setting of *To Kill a Mockingbird*.

Handout 5.3 contains a simple diagram of an iceberg, with the tip extending above the water and the much larger base hidden beneath. Students can write the details of the Tom Robinson case in the tip of the iceberg. Questions they should answer include: What happened? What choices were made in this situation? By whom? Who was affected? When did it happen? Where did it happen?

Students can then think about the outcome of the trial and its causes. In doing so, they should consider the following question: What factors influenced the particular choices made by the individuals and groups involved in this event? They can record their answers on the iceberg below the water line. Answers should include historical factors, such as the Great Depression and Jim Crow laws, or aspects of human behavior such as racism and conformity.

For more details about the Iceberg Diagram teaching strategy, see facinghistory.org/mockingbird/strategies.

Respond to Judge Learned Hand's Quotation on the Nature of Liberty

Share the following quotation from a 1944 speech by Judge Learned Hand, a federal judge and one of the most significant American legal thinkers of the twentieth century (also included on **Handout 5.2**):

> I often wonder whether we do not rest our hopes too much upon constitutions, upon laws, and upon courts. These are false hopes; believe me, these are false hopes. Liberty lies in the hearts of men and women; when it dies there, no constitution, no law, no court can save it; no constitution, no law, no court can even do much to help it. While it lies there, it needs no constitution, no law, no court to save it.

Ask students to reflect in their journals on the meaning of Hand's statement. To what extent does the Tom Robinson trial and its verdict illustrate Hand's belief? What do students think is a more powerful force in society: the law or the hearts and mind of citizens? Remind students to cite the text of the novel as well as their own experiences in their responses.

Return to Pre-Reading Anticipation Guide

You might ask students to return to the Anticipation Guide statements (**Handout 5.1**) that they reflected on before reading these chapters. After reading and analyzing Chapters 16 to 21, and learning about the additional historical context included in this section, have any of their opinions changed? If so, how did they change and why?

Write and Reflect in Journals

Any of the Connection Questions in this section might be used as a prompt for journal writing. Also, consider the following questions for a brief reflective writing assignment before, during, or after reading Chapters 16 through 21:

- Whom do you think Harper Lee intended to be the hero of the story? Who is the hero in the story from your point of view? Who or what is the antagonist of the story?

- Scout, Jem, and Dill all respond differently to the trial. When you read the courtroom scene, did you feel more like Scout, Jem, or Dill? Why?

- Atticus appeals to the jury by declaring, "A court is only as sound as its jury, and a jury is only as sound as the men who make it up." Are the men who make up the jury in Tom Robinson's case "sound"? Explain your answer. Imagine that you are writing an appeal of the decision to a higher court. Make an argument that the verdict should be overturned because the jury wasn't "sound."

- How do you think this encounter with injustice affects Jem? Write a summary of the trial from Jem's perspective. What did he learn from watching the witnesses testify? What did he learn about Atticus from watching him mount the defense? What moments stood out to him most strongly? What was he thinking as the verdict was read?

Revisit Identity Charts

In the previous three sections, students began identity charts for Scout, Jem, and Atticus. (See facinghistory.org/mockingbird/strategies for more information about this particular strategy.) Throughout Chapters 16 to 21, new details are revealed about all three characters. Give students the opportunity to revisit the identity charts. What information might they add? What information might they change or revise? Encourage students to include quotations from the text on their identity charts, as well as their own interpretations of the character or figure based on their reading.

You might also choose to have students begin new identity charts for some of the characters they learn more about in this section. In particular, they now have additional detail from which to create identity charts for Bob and Mayella Ewell as well as Tom Robinson.

Keep in mind that creating and revising identity charts for the central characters in *To Kill a Mockingbird* will help prepare students for a culminating activity, suggested in the Post-Reading section of this guide, that asks students to analyze the moral and ethical growth of a character from the novel.

CHAPTER 16: Connection Questions

1. What "subtle change" does Scout notice in Atticus at the beginning of this chapter? What other evidence in this chapter supports her observation?

2. When Scout asks if the Cunninghams are still their friends, Atticus responds, "Mr. Cunningham's basically a good man, he just has his blind spots like the rest of us." What does Atticus mean by "blind spot"? Do you agree with Atticus's assessment of the Cunninghams?

3. Does the setting in which this story takes place make Mr. Cunningham's "blind spot" understandable? What is the difference between understanding and excusing a point of view?

4. How does Atticus explain the mob? What does he think the children did that changed Mr. Cunningham's mind? Do you think Atticus is right? Is his understanding of a mob realistic or naïve?

5. Based on what you have learned about the history of lynching, do you think Harper Lee's portrayal of the lynch mob in this novel is realistic? Why or why not?

6. What groups of people do Scout, Jem, and Dill watch pass by their house on the way to the courthouse? Which of those groups do you think are part of Maycomb's universe of obligation? Which do you think are not? Why do you think the trial draws so much interest from the people of Maycomb?

7. What do we learn about Mr. Dolphus Raymond in this chapter? Which parts of the story that Jem tells are facts and which are gossip? How can you tell?

8. What is a "mixed child," according to Jem? Why does he think they are "real sad"? Whose universe of obligation do they belong to?

9. According to Jem, how does their society define who is black? How does he answer Scout when she asks how to tell whether or not someone is black? What does Jem's answer suggest about the meaning of race?

10. Scout overhears the members of the "Idlers' Club" discussing Atticus. What does she learn about Atticus and Tom Robinson that she did not know before? What is confusing to her about the revelation? Why, exactly, are so many townsfolk upset at Atticus?

CHAPTER 17: Connection Questions

1. Summarize Heck Tate's testimony. From his point of view, what happened on the night of November 21? Why did he arrest Tom Robinson?

2. Why, according to Tate, did he not call a doctor to examine Mayella Ewell? Why do you think someone would call a doctor in such a situation? For what purpose does Tate imply he would have needed to call a doctor?

3. When he cross-examines Heck Tate, what details about the incident does Atticus seem to think are most important? How does Harper Lee help the reader know?

4. How does Scout feel differently once the trial has started from how she felt earlier in the morning while thinking about the incident at the jailhouse? How do you explain the change?

5. When Bob Ewell is called to the stand, how does Scout describe his appearance? How does Harper Lee use a stereotype related to his appearance to suggest something about Mr. Ewell's character?

6. What does Scout mean when she tells us that the yard around the Ewells' cabin looks "like the playhouse of an insane child"? What details does she provide to further explain this phrase? How is the corner of the yard that Mayella takes care of different from the rest of the property?

7. Compare and contrast the description of the Ewells' home and the black neighborhood nearby. What similarities do you notice? What differences? What conclusions might Harper Lee want the reader to draw about the Ewells and the black families who live nearby based on the descriptions of where and how they live?

8. What does Scout explain about the relationship between Atticus and Mr. Gilmer? What does this suggest about how each views his role in the trial?

9. Why is Judge Taylor upset about the language that Bob Ewell uses to answer the lawyers' questions? Does Mr. Ewell use code-switching? What does his language suggest about how Harper Lee intends the reader to view the Ewells?

10. How does Bob Ewell explain to Atticus why he did not call for a doctor to examine Mayella? What is Atticus implying by asking both Heck Tate and Bob Ewell this question?

11. What other details in Mr. Ewell's description of the incident are most important to Atticus? How does Harper Lee help the reader know?

12. Why does Atticus ask Bob Ewell to write his name? How does this lead Jem to conclude, "We've got him"? Why does Scout think he is jumping to conclusions?

CHAPTER 18: Connection Questions

1. Mayella Ewell's testimony reveals to the reader many new details about the Ewells and their home life. Create identity charts for both Bob and Mayella Ewell. What do they have in common? How are they different?

2. Why does Mayella say that she is afraid of Atticus when she first takes the stand? Why does she think Atticus is mocking her as her testimony proceeds? What does this suggest about the Ewells' status in Maycomb? What does it suggest about how the residents of Maycomb have treated them?

3. Reread Mayella's testimony and record the details of her account of what happened on November 21. Which details in her story change before the end of her testimony?

4. What crucial detail is revealed about Tom Robinson in this chapter? How does it change our understanding of what happened to Mayella on November 21?

5. What alternative account of the events of November 21 is Atticus suggesting took place when he asks Mayella, "What did your father see in the window, the crime of rape* or the best defense of it"? Does he have sufficient evidence for this suggestion? Why might the jury be willing to believe what he is suggesting?

CHAPTER 19: Connection Questions

1. Summarize Tom Robinson's testimony about what happened between him and Mayella on November 21. How does his account differ from Mayella's? Who is telling the truth? How do you know?

2. What new information do we learn about Tom Robinson from his testimony?

---

* We recommend that teachers review "Discussing Sensitive Topics in the Classroom" on page xv before using these questions in class.

---

3. Scout says that Tom seemed to be a "respectable Negro." What does she mean? How might someone from Maycomb describe the difference between a black person who is respectable and one who is not? How might that differ from the characteristics of a "respectable white person"?

4. What examples does this chapter provide of characters practicing empathy? Which characters are able to "climb into the skin" of others and "walk around in it"? How do they respond to others as a result? What are the consequences?

5. What are the unwritten rules about race that Mr. Gilmer attempts to get Tom to break? Does he succeed? What parts of Tom's testimony would have offended jurors who supported the laws and customs of segregated society?

6. When Mr. Gilmer asks Tom if he ran because he was afraid he would have to face up to what he did, Tom replies, "No suh, scared I'd hafta face up to what I didn't do." What does he mean?

7. How does Atticus speak to Tom Robinson differently from the way Mr. Gilmer does? Cite specific examples from the text that show the difference.

8. Do you think Tom Robinson's testimony helps or hurts his chances with the jury? Did you feel more confident that he would be acquitted before or after this chapter? Why?

9. Why does Dill break down crying when Mr. Gilmer questions Tom Robinson? How does Scout try to comfort Dill? Is Dill being "thin-hided"?

CHAPTER 20: Connection Questions

1. What secret does Dolphus Raymond reveal to Scout and Dill outside the courthouse? How does it change the way they think of him? What is his explanation for why he "deliberately perpetuates a fraud against himself"? What does Dill learn from him?

2. Why does Raymond think that children like Scout and Dill can understand his secret better than adults?

3. According to Raymond, how will growing up change Scout and Dill? What will they gain and what will they lose as they get older? Do you think he's right?

4. During Atticus's closing speech to the jury, he states, "This case is as simple as black and white." Explain the double meaning of this statement.

5. During Atticus's speech, Scout sees him do two things she had never seen him do before. What are they, and what do they reveal about how Atticus thinks this speech is different from others he has given in court in the past?

6. What distinction does Atticus make in his speech about the written and unwritten laws of Maycomb? Which does he claim that Mayella Ewell has violated? How does this help explain why she has falsely accused Tom Robinson?

7. Atticus challenges the jury to rise above the "evil assumptions" that Bob and Mayella Ewell are confident that the jury will accept. What are these "evil assumptions"? How do these assumptions prevent the jury from seeing Tom Robinson for who he really is? How do these evil assumptions—or stereotypes—threaten justice?

8. Atticus claims that Mr. Ewell did "what any God-fearing, persevering, respectable white man would do under the circumstances" when he turned in Tom Robinson. Why do you think Atticus makes this claim? Do you think he believes it? Within the "moral universe" of Maycomb, is accusing Tom Robinson of rape* viewed as respectable?

9. Atticus states, "We all know that all men are not created equal in the sense that some people would have us believe." What does he mean? Where are all men created equal and where are they not, according to Atticus? What do you think?

10. What role does Atticus believe the courts play in upholding the ideals of American society?

CHAPTER 21: Connection Questions

1. How do the adults in this chapter respond to Jem's confidence that Atticus has won the case? What do they understand that Jem does not?

2. Scout describes the courthouse as the townsfolk await the verdict this way:

---

* We recommend that teachers review "Discussing Sensitive Topics in the Classroom" on page xv before using these questions in class.

> But I must have been reasonably awake or I would not have received the impression that was creeping into me. It was not unlike one I had last winter, and I shivered, though the night was hot. The feeling grew until the atmosphere in the courtroom was exactly the same as a cold February morning, when the mockingbirds were still, and the carpenters had stopped hammering on Miss Maudie's new house, and every wood door in the neighborhood was shut as tightly as the doors of the Radley place. A deserted, waiting, empty street, and the courtroom was packed with people.

What is she suggesting about the atmosphere in the courtroom as the jury deliberates? What is the mood? What are people doing, thinking, and feeling?

3. Why does this trial draw so much interest from the town? How do you think it is different from other trials that had taken place in Maycomb? How does the book suggest this trial is different even from other cases in which black men have been accused of committing crimes against white people?

4. Reread the last two pages of this chapter and analyze how Harper Lee reveals the verdict and the reactions of Jem, Scout, and the white and black townsfolk. How does she underscore the dramatic intensity of this moment? How does she create the "dreamlike quality" that Scout mentions?

5. At the end of the trial, why does Reverend Sykes tell Scout to "stand up"? What effect does this line have on the reader? Why do you think the author focuses the reader's gaze on Atticus and not on Tom Robinson?

AFTER READING SECTION 5: Connection Questions

1. Many view the verdict in the Tom Robinson trial as the climax in *To Kill a Mockingbird*'s plot. How does Harper Lee signal the importance of this event in her writing and in the way that she has constructed the plot?

2. Sometimes in works of fiction, authors use characters to represent certain perspectives in society. Instead of asking who a character is, we might ask what values and beliefs each character represents. Thinking about the characters who participated in the Tom Robinson trial—Atticus, Judge Taylor, Mr. Gilmer, Heck Tate, Bob Ewell, Mayella Ewell, and Tom

Robinson—what value or belief do you think each represents? How do these characters represent the tensions in the "moral universe" of the American South in the 1930s? Which voices in Maycomb society are not represented?

3. Who or what is the antagonist in *To Kill a Mockingbird*? How do you think Atticus would answer that question? Who or what does he see as his opponent in the Tom Robinson trial?

4. What does the Tom Robinson trial reveal about Maycomb's universe of obligation?

5. Compare and contrast Jem's, Dill's, and Scout's reaction to the trial. What do you think accounts for the different ways each of the children responds to the trial and the verdict?

6. What is a *formative experience*? Are the moments you represented on your memory map at the beginning of your study of *To Kill a Mockingbird* formative experiences? Do you think that the Tom Robinson trial will be a formative experience in the lives of Scout and Jem? If so, how? What lesson do you think they will take away from the trial?

7. Was the law upheld in the Tom Robinson trial? What effect do the "unwritten rules" of a society have on the law and the way that it is upheld? What happens when these unwritten rules are in conflict with the law?

8. What is justice? What factors limit the legal system's ability to deliver justice for Tom Robinson?

9. Atticus and Dolphus Raymond both dissent from the rules of segregation in their society. How do their approaches differ? Which approach do you think is more effective? Which approach offers the best chance at bringing about change? What other approaches might a dissenter take in that society?

Building Historical Context

One of the sources of dramatic tension in the trial of Tom Robinson is Jem's growing expectation that Atticus will win on the strength of the facts he establishes in court. Of course, it does not work out that way, and the jury finds Tom guilty in spite of the evidence to the contrary. This section provides resources to help students understand that the Tom Robinson trial is not an aberration when placed in the historical context of Alabama in the 1930s. In this period, when black men were accused of committing crimes against whites, especially white women, a guilty verdict was often preordained. In such "courtroom lynchings," racial supremacy and the unwritten rules of Jim Crow society trumped the right to a fair trial and impartial jury. Students will learn about perhaps the most infamous example of such trials by exploring the Scottsboro Affair.

There is also considerable dramatic tension in Chapters 16 through 21 in Atticus's cross-examinations of both Bob and Mayella Ewell. This section provides a document that introduces students to the redneck stereotype, often used to describe poor white Southerners, that some critics have suggested is explicitly evoked in Harper Lee's description of the Ewells. By learning about this stereotype, students will better understand how issues of class and social status add to the tension in the exchanges between Atticus and the Ewells. In addition, learning about this particular stereotype will help students explore one prominent criticism of the character of Atticus and the novel in general.

As you explore the resources below with the class, remind students that your goal is to reach a deeper understanding of the plot, characters, and setting of the novel. After analyzing each resource, revisit the following questions:

- How did this resource deepen your understanding of what took place during the trial of Tom Robinson?

- How did this resource help you understand factors that influence the choices and perceptions of characters at the trial (as participants or observers)?

Explore the Scottsboro Affair

The number of lynchings in the South decreased significantly in the 1930s and 1940s from its peak in the 1890s. Many scholars believe one cause of this decrease was the growing prevalence of sham trials in Southern courts, in which guilty verdicts were preordained for blacks accused of crimes against whites, especially white women, and death sentences were far more likely for blacks than whites convicted of the same crimes. Such trials achieved the same results as lynching but in a manner that appeared as if the rule of law was being upheld.

Students will explore in this section the idea of the "courtroom lynching" by learning about one of the most infamous examples, the Scottsboro Affair. In the 1930s the story of the Scottsboro Boys, nine black teenagers accused of raping two white women on a train in Alabama, was reported in newspapers around the world. Many believe the high-profile series of events was an inspiration for the story of Tom Robinson in *To Kill a Mockingbird*. As students explore the events surrounding the Scottsboro Affair, they will consider the nature of justice and the effect that the unwritten rules of a society can have on the way in which the law is carried out.

Handout 5.4 is a summary of the history of the Scottsboro Affair written by Harvard University law professor Michael Klarman. We have divided the summary into five parts. Each part of the story is accompanied by Connection Questions to guide student analysis of the events and help them make connections to *To Kill a Mockingbird*. Part 1 of the document is considerably longer than any of the subsequent parts. You might ask students to read it before class and then share and discuss the next four parts over the course of a class discussion or group activity.

You might structure your class exploration of the Scottsboro Affair as a Fishbowl discussion activity. In this scenario, some students sit in the center of a circle and participate in the discussion while others watch silently from the outside of the circle. As the class turns its attention to each new part of **Handout 5.4**, different students can rotate into the discussion. This structure provides flexibility for the teacher to insert him or herself into the discussion to clarify important ideas, provide additional background information, and move the discussion forward with new questions. See facinghistory.org/mockingbird/strategies for additional details about this strategy.

Another option for exploring the Scottsboro Affair is to show the American Experience documentary *Scottsboro: An American Tragedy* (90 minutes). The DVD is available from the Facing History library at facinghistory.org/library. While **Handout 5.4** focuses most of its detail on the initial Scottsboro Boys trial, the film focuses most of its attention on the retrial that occurred as a result of the US Supreme Court's 1932 decision overturning the initial guilty verdicts. This retrial (the first of three) garnered international attention, and the film provides interesting background information about the political organizations and lawyers that became involved. Many of the Connection Questions from **Handout 5.4** can be adapted to guide a class discussion during or after watching the film.

Finally, three scenes from the film might be especially helpful in bringing this history to life for your students, even if you primarily use **Handout 5.4** to guide your class's exploration of this history:

- **0:00–20:00** – The first 20 minutes of the film provides an overview of the 1931 incident on the train and the initial trial. You might choose to show it along with or in addition to using **Handout 5.4** (Part 1).

- **28:00–54:00** – This segment gives an in-depth, dramatic account of the retrial after the US Supreme Court overturned the first guilty verdicts. You might show this segment instead of or in addition to reading **Handout 5.4** (Part 3). Note that this segment includes detailed testimony about the physical examinations of the two accusers to determine if they had been raped.*

- **57:00–1:01:00** – This segment tells the story of Alabama judge James Horton wrestling with his decision to set aside the guilty verdict of the 1932 retrial at great social and political cost to himself. This aspect of the story is not explored in **Handout 5.4** and would provide an interesting complement to Part 3.

Make Connections through Close Reading

The Appendix includes a set of text-dependent questions, "Close Reading Pairing: Scottsboro and the Tom Robinson Trial," that you can use to guide student analysis of both the history of the Scottsboro Boys and the trial of Tom Robinson. By engaging in the process of close reading to make connections between the informational text about Scottsboro (**Handout 5.4**, "The Scottsboro Affair") and the fictional trial of Tom Robinson, students can reach a deeper understanding of both. This close reading activity is specifically written to align with the Common Core State Standards for English Language Arts. See "Close Reading for Deep Comprehension" in the Appendix for a suggested procedure for implementing this close reading activity. Because of the length of these texts, you might choose to omit the first or second reading of the text from this procedure.

Analyze the Use of the Redneck Stereotype

As Bob Ewell takes the stand in Chapter 17, Scout provides the following description of him: "A little bantam cock of a man rose and strutted to the stand, the back of his neck reddening at the sound of his name. When he turned around to take the

---

* We recommend that teachers review "Discussing Sensitive Topics in the Classroom" on page xv.

oath, we saw that his face was as red as his neck." In this description, Harper Lee is evoking a powerful and prevalent stereotype in American culture, the redneck. **Handout 5.5** provides a description of the redneck stereotype from Joseph Flora and Lucinda MacKethan's *Companion to Southern Literature*.

As Flora and MacKethan point out, the redneck stereotype is not typically applied to all poor Southern whites. You might begin exploring this stereotype by reviewing the introduction of the Cunninghams and Ewells in Chapters 2 and 3 of the novel. Why does Atticus show respect for the Cunninghams and disdain for the Ewells? Students' observations from these early chapters will help them begin to understand the stereotype at play in Scout's description of Bob Ewell and Atticus's cross-examination of him in Chapter 17. After reading **Handout 5.5**, ask students to determine to what extent the character of Bob Ewell fits the redneck stereotype. Ask them to find evidence in the chapter to support their answer.

When analyzing the redneck stereotype with your students, you might introduce the class to one prominent criticism of the novel and the character of Atticus in particular. Writer Malcolm Gladwell maintains that Atticus is not the hero that many readers believe him to be because of the way he uses the redneck stereotype to his advantage in the trial. Atticus highlights several aspects of Bob Ewell's life that fit the stereotype. He also implies that Bob Ewell has an incestuous relationship with his daughter, another characteristic sometimes associated with this stereotype. Gladwell writes:

> Finch wants his white, male jurors to do the right thing. But as a good Jim Crow liberal he dare not challenge the foundations of their privilege. Instead, Finch does what lawyers for black men did in those days. He encourages them to swap one of their prejudices for another.[1]

You might share this quotation with students and ask them whether or not they agree with Gladwell. Does Atticus evoke an unfair stereotype in his defense of Tom Robinson? You might also ask students to evaluate Harper Lee's rendering of Bob Ewell. What purpose does he play as a character in the story? Is his character more than a stereotype?

Reflect on the Role of Poor White Southern Women

Writer Dorothy Allison grew up in the 1960s in South Carolina as a poor white Southern woman who was also, as we are led to believe about Mayella Ewell, a victim

---

1   Malcolm Gladwell, "The Courthouse Ring: Atticus Finch and the Limits of Southern Liberalism," *New Yorker*, August 10, 2009, 26–32.

of incest. Allison has written that poor white Southern women lived particularly powerless and marginalized lives. In fact, scholar Angela Shaw-Thornburg names this powerlessness as a possible motivation for Mayella Ewell's accusation of rape against Tom Robinson: no one in Maycomb cared about her abuse at the hands of her father, so she invoked the one taboo her community would respond to—rape by a black man—in order to draw attention to her victimhood.

Handout 5.6 is an excerpt from Dorothy Allison's National Book Award-nominated memoir *Two or Three Things I Know for Sure* in which she describes the lives of poor white Southern women. Consider sharing this description with your students and asking them to reflect on the following questions:

- Compare and contrast Allison's description with the ideal of the Southern belle that you learned about in the previous section. What does Allison's perspective add to your understanding of the ideals and realities of being a woman in Maycomb?

- How does this brief passage help us better understand the character of Mayella Ewell? What does it add to the information about Mayella that Scout shares with us?

Handout 5.1 Exploring Justice

Read the statement in the left column. Decide if you strongly agree (SA), agree (A), disagree (D), or strongly disagree (SD) with the statement. Circle your response and provide a one- to two-sentence explanation of your opinion.

Statement	Your Opinion			
1. Laws play an important role in shaping who I am.	**SA** Explain:	**A**	**D**	**SD**
2. It is possible to create a fully equal society.	**SA** Explain:	**A**	**D**	**SD**
3. People, not laws, are most responsible for creating a just society.	**SA** Explain:	**A**	**D**	**SD**
4. Culture, custom, and tradition are more powerful than laws.	**SA** Explain:	**A**	**D**	**SD**

Handout 5.2 The Spirit of Liberty

In 1944, federal judge Learned Hand gave a speech on the spirit of liberty, in which he reflected:

I often wonder whether we do not rest our hopes too much upon constitutions, upon laws, and upon courts. These are false hopes; believe me, these are false hopes. Liberty lies in the hearts of men and women; when it dies there, no constitution, no law, no court can save it; no constitution, no law, no court can even do much to help it. While it lies there, it needs no constitution, no law, no court to save it.

Connection Questions

1. Which does Judge Hand believe is a more powerful force in society, the law or the hearts and minds of citizens?

2. To what extent does the Tom Robinson trial and its verdict in *To Kill a Mockingbird* reflect Judge Hand's belief?

3. What do you think?

Handout 5.3 Analyzing the Causes of the Guilty Verdict

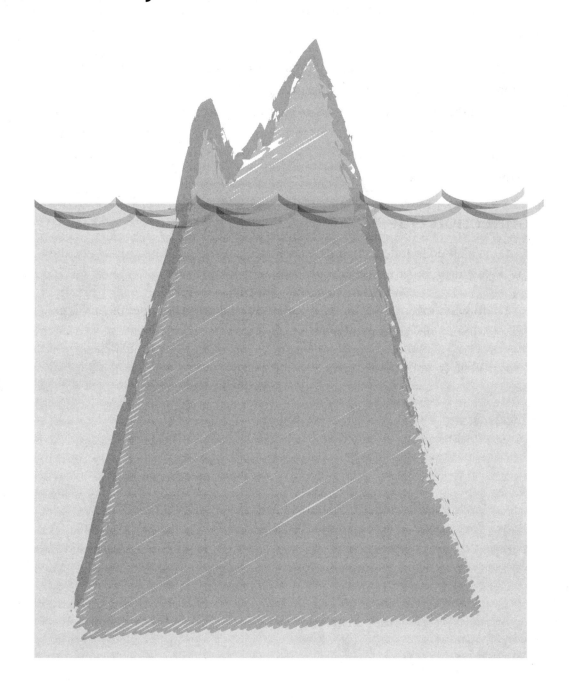

Handout 5.4 The Scottsboro Affair (Part 1)

Note: We have chosen to include certain racial epithets in this reading in order to honestly communicate the bigoted language of the time. We recommend that teachers review the page "Discussing Sensitive Topics in the Classroom" before using this document.

In the 1930s, the story of the Scottsboro Boys, nine black teenagers accused of raping two white women on a train in Alabama, was reported in newspapers around the world. Many believe the high-profile series of events was an inspiration for the story of Tom Robinson in To Kill a Mockingbird: *the Scottsboro Boys story involved similar accusations, and it occurred in the same time and state as the setting of the novel. The legal historian Michael Klarman describes the background and first part of the Scottsboro Affair this way:*

The freight train left Chattanooga for Memphis at 10:20 a.m. on March 25, 1931. Thirty minutes after it had pulled out of Stevenson, Alabama, the stationmaster there saw a group of white hoboes walking along the train tracks back toward the station. They told him that several black youths had thrown them off the train after a fight. The stationmaster telephoned ahead to the next stop, Scottsboro, but the train had already passed through. It was finally stopped at Paint Rock, where a sheriff's posse discovered nine black youngsters and, to everyone's surprise, two young white women dressed in men's overalls.

The nine blacks, known to history as the Scottsboro boys, ranged in age from thirteen to twenty. Five of them were from Georgia, though they claimed not to know one another. The other four did know one another; they were from Chattanooga, Tennessee. All of the nine were vagrants, and most of them were illiterate.

Twenty minutes after the train had been stopped, one of the women, Ruby Bates, called over a posse member and told him that she and her companion, Victoria Price, had been gang-raped by the blacks. The boys were immediately arrested and taken to the Scottsboro jail. As the sheriff sent the women to two local doctors for medical examinations, news of the alleged attacks spread. By day's end, a crowd of several hundred people had gathered outside of the jail, demanding that the "niggers" be turned over for lynching. Sheriff M. L. Wann pleaded with the mob to allow the law to take its course and threatened to shoot anyone who rushed the jail. He also telephoned the governor for assistance, and by 11:00 p.m., twenty-five armed guardsmen were on their way to Scottsboro. To ensure the boys' safety, they were moved to a sturdier jail in nearby Etowah. The local circuit judge, Alfred E. Hawkins, convened a special session of the grand jury to indict them; local citizens complained of the five-day delay. One local newspaper remarked, "It is best for the county that these things be disposed of in a speedy manner as it gives no excuse for people taking the law into their own hands."

A decade or two earlier, black men charged with raping white women under similar circumstances might well have been executed without trial. Lynchings in the South peaked in the late 1880s and early 1890s, when well over a hundred were reported annually and in some years over two hundred. Most lynchings occurred in response to allegations of crime—usually murder or rape—though occasionally the alleged "offense" was as minor as breach of racial etiquette or general uppityness. Prior to World War I, lynchings typically enjoyed the support of local communities; efforts to prosecute even known lynchers were rare, and convictions were virtually nonexistent.

By 1930, however, the number of reported lynchings had declined dramatically—from an average of 187.5 per year in the 1890s to 16.8 in the later years of the 1920s. This decline was attributable to many factors, including the possibility of federal anti-lynching legislation, the diminishing insularity of the South, more professional law enforcement, and better education. But the decline in lynchings probably also depended on their replacement with speedy trials that reliably produced guilty verdicts, death sentences, and rapid executions. Some jurisdictions actually enacted laws designed to prevent lynchings by providing for special terms of court to convene within days of alleged rapes and other incendiary crimes. In many instances, law enforcement officers explicitly promised would-be lynch mobs that black defendants would be quickly tried and executed if the mob desisted, and prosecutors appealed to juries to convict in order to reward mobs for good behavior and thus encourage similar restraint in the future.

In such cases, guilt or innocence usually mattered little. As one white southerner candidly remarked in 1933, "If a white woman is prepared to swear that a Negro either raped or attempted to rape her, we see to it that the Negro is executed." Prevailing racial norms did not permit white jurors to believe a black man's word over that of a white woman; prevailing gender norms did not allow defense counsel to closely interrogate a white woman about allegations involving sex. As one contemporary southern newspaper observed, the honor of a white woman was more important than the life of a black man. And because most southern white men believed that black males secretly lusted after "their" women, they generally found such rape allegations credible . . .

The Scottsboro defendants received precisely the sort of "justice" that often prevailed in trials that substituted for lynchings. Both local newspapers treated the defendants as obviously guilty even before the trial. The hometown newspaper of the alleged victims, the *Huntsville Daily Times*, "described the rapes as the most atrocious ever recorded in this part of the country, a wholesale debauching of society." Judge Hawkins tried to assign all seven members of the Scottsboro bar to represent the defendants, but all but one of them declined. That one was Milo Moody, nearly seventy years old and later described by one investigator as "a doddering, extremely unreliable, senile individual who is losing whatever ability he once had."

The trials began on April 6, just twelve days after the train incident. A crowd estimated at five to ten thousand gathered outside the courthouse, which was protected by national guardsmen wielding machine guns. Hawkins appointed as trial counsel a Tennessee lawyer, Stephen R. Roddy, who had been sent to Scottsboro by the defendants' families to look after their interests. Roddy was an alcoholic, and one observer reported that "he could scarcely walk straight" that morning. When Roddy objected to his appointment on the grounds that he was unprepared and unfamiliar with Alabama law, Hawkins appointed Moody, the local septuagenarian, to assist him. Roddy was permitted less than half an hour with his clients before the trial began. Defense counsel moved for a change of venue based on the inflammatory newspaper coverage and the attempted lynching of the defendants. But Sheriff Wann now denied that the defendants had been threatened, and Judge Hawkins denied the motion.

The state sought the death penalty against eight of the nine defendants—all but the one who was identified as being only thirteen years old. The nine were tried in four groups, beginning with Clarence Norris and Charley Weems. Victoria Price was the main prosecution witness, and she testified that the black youths had thrown the white boys off the train and then gang-raped her and Bates. According to one secondhand account, Price testified "with such gusto, snap and wise-cracks, that the courtroom was often in a roar of laughter."

Judge Hawkins blocked defense counsel's efforts to elicit admissions that the women were prostitutes and that they had had sexual intercourse with their boyfriends the night before the train incident . . . . Testimony provided by the examining doctors raised serious doubts as to whether the girls had been raped . . . . In their testimony, the two women also provided inconsistent accounts of various details of the incident, such as whether they had spoken with the white boys on the train and how long the interracial fracas had lasted. One man present when the train was stopped testified that he had not heard Price make any rape allegations.

However, the admission by Norris on cross-examination that the women had been raped by all of the other eight defendants, though not by him, severely undercut his defense. (It later came out that Sheriff Wann had warned Norris that he would be killed if he did not admit that the girls had been raped.) Defense counsel prodded the illiterate and confused Norris to change his story, but he held firm. The defense called no witnesses and made no closing argument.

While the jury deliberated on the fate of Norris and Weems, the trial of Haywood Patterson began. When the first jury returned to the courtroom to announce guilty verdicts and death sentences, crowds in and out of the courthouse erupted with delight. According to defense lawyer Roddy, "[i]nstantly, a wild and thunderous roar went up from the audience and was heard by those in the Court House yard where thousands took up the demonstration and carried it on for fifteen or twenty minutes." Even though Patterson's jury heard this commotion, Judge Hawkins refused to declare a mistrial.

The prosecution's case grew stronger with each trial, as previously unhelpful witnesses were dropped and the alleged victims improved their stories with each recounting. Within a five-minute span on the witness stand, Patterson contradicted himself as to whether he had seen the girls being raped or indeed had seen them on the train at all. Several of the other defendants also testified inconsistently. After less than twenty-five minutes of deliberation, the jury convicted Patterson and sentenced him to death.

Five of the defendants were prosecuted together in a third trial. The state's case against them was even weaker because these defendants did not incriminate each other on cross-examination, the women were less certain in identifying them as the rapists, and one of the defendants was nearly blind while another had such a severe case of venereal disease that raping a woman would have been very difficult. The jury nonetheless returned five more death sentences. Judge Hawkins declared a mistrial in the case of the last defendant, Roy Wright, when the jury could not agree on whether to sentence the thirteen-year-old to life imprisonment or to death—a sentence the prosecution had not even sought. None of the four trials lasted more than a few hours.[1]

---

1   Michael Klarman, "Scottsboro," *Marquette Law Review* 93, no. 2 (2009): 379–431, http://scholarship.law.marquette.edu/cgi/viewcontent.cgi?article=4943&context=mulr.

Connection Questions

1. Trials such as those of the Scottsboro Boys and Tom Robinson have sometimes been referred to as "courtroom lynchings." What do you think that description means? According to Klarman, what is the relationship between the practice of lynching and these trials? What did many white Southerners believe would happen if black defendants accused of raping white women were found not guilty?

2. What roles did race, gender, and class play in whom juries believed and whom they did not believe in Southern courtrooms in the 1930s?

3. What similarities do you notice between the story of the Scottsboro Boys and the story of Tom Robinson in *To Kill a Mockingbird*? What differences do you notice?

The Scottsboro Affair (Part 2)

In November 1932, the US Supreme Court overturned the convictions, declaring that the defendants were not provided adequate counsel and sufficient time to prepare their case. This violated the "due process" clause of the Fourteenth Amendment. This clause reads:

> No State shall make or enforce any law which shall abridge the privileges or immunities of citizens of the United States; nor shall any State deprive any person of life, liberty, or property, without due process of law; nor deny to any person within its jurisdiction the equal protection of the laws.

Connection Questions

1. What is "due process of law"? How does the failure to provide a defendant with an adequate lawyer and time to prepare a defense violate that person's right to due process?

2. Looking back on Klarman's description of the trial, what details suggest that the Scottsboro Boys' lawyers were not sufficiently competent or prepared for the trial?

3. Did Tom Robinson have adequate representation for his trial?

The Scottsboro Affair (Part 3)

In March 1933, the Scottsboro Boys were given new trials in Decatur, Alabama, one at a time. Haywood Patterson was tried first. High-profile New York lawyer Samuel Leibowitz agreed to be their defense lawyer. The case was reported in newspapers around the world. In his case, Leibowitz challenged Victoria Price's version of events directly, angering many white Alabamians. He also called a physician as a witness, who explained that the physical examination of the girls at the time of the incident suggested that they were not raped. Finally, he surprised everyone by putting Ruby Bates on the stand (she had previously been missing), where she changed her testimony and claimed that the girls made up the charges to avoid being arrested for vagrancy. Patterson was found guilty anyway and sentenced to death. The judge postponed the other eight trials until public tension toward Leibowitz subsided. Then, in June, the judge set aside Patterson's conviction, citing the overwhelming evidence that the charges were false, and he called for yet another new trial. In November and December of that year, Patterson was tried again, along with Clarence Norris, and both were convicted and sentenced to death.[2]

Connection Questions

1. What details does Klarman's report, as summarized above, include that explain why many white Alabamians were angered when Leibowitz challenged Victoria Price on her version of what happened on the train? What unwritten rules of Alabama society in the 1930s did Leibowitz challenge?

2. What effect do you think it might have had on the trial to have so many people around the world following it?

3. How can you explain the fact that despite mounting evidence of their innocence, juries continued to convict the Scottsboro Boys in each new trial? If Jem had known about the Scottsboro Boys, do you think he would have been as optimistic about Tom Robinson's chances?

---

2   Michael Klarman, "Scottsboro," *Marquette Law Review* 93, no. 2 (2009): 379–431, http://scholarship.law.marquette.edu/cgi/viewcontent.cgi?article=4943&context=mulr.

The Scottsboro Affair (Part 4)

On April 1, 1935, the US Supreme Court overturned the new convictions because lawyers for the Scottsboro Boys had proven that Alabama intentionally excluded African Americans from sitting on any juries. This violated the equal protection of the laws guaranteed by the Fourteenth Amendment. This clause reads:

> No State shall make or enforce any law which shall abridge the privileges or immunities of citizens of the United States; nor shall any State deprive any person of life, liberty, or property, without due process of law; nor deny to any person within its jurisdiction the equal protection of the laws.

Connection Questions

1. What does "equal protection of the law" mean? What does it suggest about the universe of obligation of the United States?

2. Would the Supreme Court that ruled on the Scottsboro cases have agreed with Atticus's argument in his closing speech that all people are equal in a courtroom? Use evidence from both *To Kill a Mockingbird* and Michael Klarman's article in Part 1 to support your position.

The Scottsboro Affair (Part 5)

Following the 1935 US Supreme Court ruling, the Scottsboro Boys were each tried again on the charges of raping Victoria Price and Ruby Bates. They were convicted again and served more time in prison.

Scholar Michael Klarman maintains that the Supreme Court rulings in favor of the Scottsboro Boys probably saved their lives, yet he also points out that many white Alabamians responded to the rulings with greater animosity toward the defendants:

> The more the Court intervened on their behalf, the more determined white Alabamians seemed to punish them. Thus, despite two Supreme Court rulings in their favor, the Scottsboro boys each served from five to twenty years in prison for crimes they did not commit.[3]

The following is what happened to each of the nine Scottsboro Boys after 1935:

- Haywood Patterson was convicted of rape for the fourth time in 1936 and sentenced to 75 years in prison. He escaped from prison in Alabama but was convicted of a different crime in Michigan and died in prison there.

- Clarence Norris was convicted again of rape and sentenced to death. In 1938, the Alabama governor reduced his sentence to life in prison. He was paroled and released from prison in 1946 and pardoned by Alabama governor George Wallace in 1976.

- Andrew Wright was convicted of rape and sentenced to 99 years in prison. He was paroled in 1950.

- Charlie Weems was convicted of rape and sentenced to 105 years. He was paroled in 1943.

- Ozie Powell stabbed an officer while being transported between prisons in 1936. The officer shot him in the head in response, causing permanent brain damage. He was sentenced to 20 additional years in prison because of the attack, but his rape charges were eventually dropped. He was released from prison in 1946.

- In 1937, the state of Alabama dropped the charges against Willie Roberson, Olen Montgomery, Eugene Williams, and Roy Wright.[4]

---

3   Michael J. Klarman, "Scottsboro," *Marquette Law Review* 93, no. 2 (2009): 431.

4   Compiled from Douglas Linder, "The Scottsboro Boys Trials: A Chronology," from "Famous Trials," project of University of Missouri-Kansas City School of Law (1999), accessed May 13, 2014, http://law2.umkc.edu/faculty/projects/FTrials/scottsboro/SB_chron.html.

Connection Questions

1. What is justice? Did anyone in the story of the Scottsboro Boys receive justice?

2. Can the legal system force society to change? What does Michael Klarman suggest about the unintended consequences of just court rulings?

3. Which characters in *To Kill a Mockingbird* would believe that justice was served in the repeated convictions of the Scottsboro Boys? Which characters would believe that justice had failed?

4. Why did Alabama courts continue to convict the Scottsboro defendants, even though it became increasingly clear that they were innocent? Why do you think so many of the Scottsboro Boys eventually had their prison time reduced?

5. Why do many people call the story of the Scottsboro Boys a tragedy? What other words might you use to describe the story?

6. Who do you think is responsible for the injustice of the Scottsboro trials? How does that compare to your thoughts about who is responsible for the injustice of the Tom Robinson trial?

Handout 5.5 The Redneck Stereotype

In their book The Companion to Southern Literature, *Joseph Flora and Lucinda MacKethan describe the characteristics of the "redneck," a stereotype of a particular kind of poor white Southerner that dates back to before the Civil War:*

> *Redneck* is a derogatory term currently applied to some lower-class and working-class southerners. The term, which came into common usage in the 1930s, is derived from the redneck's beginnings as a "yeoman farmer" whose neck would burn as he or she toiled in the fields . . .
>
> Rednecks are not necessarily poor and not necessarily farmers, although rednecks can certainly be each of these things. What differentiates rednecks from poor whites is the perception of rednecks as racist, hot-headed, too physical, violent, uncouth, loud, mean, undereducated—and proud of it. The stereotypes follow: Rednecks do not adopt politically correct speech and are proud to be brutally honest about their feelings about nonwhites. Rednecks like to fight to solve their problems, preferring to beat someone at a street dance than to talk about the problem and solve it diplomatically. Rednecks come to the dinner table barefooted not because they have no shoes, but to specifically sneer at rules. Redneck women smoke cigarettes, chew gum, and wear curlers and put on makeup in public. The redneck rebels against education and against standard English, refusing to speak as others would have him or her speak. Rednecks hunt proudly, take baths only occasionally, and work on old cars in their front yard. Rednecks are characterized by excess; they eat too much, drink too much, smoke too much, play too hard, and live too hard. The outsider's perception of all these things differentiates the redneck from the poor white.[1]

1   Joseph M. Flora and Lucinda H. MacKethan, eds., *The Companion to Southern Literature: Themes, Genres, Places, People, Movements, and Motifs* (Baton Rouge: Louisiana State University Press, 2002), 729.

Handout 5.6 Reflections on Poor White Women

In her memoir about growing up poor in South Carolina in the 1960s, Dorothy Allison offers this reflection on the women in her family:

Let me tell you about what I have never been allowed to be. Beautiful and female . . . I was born trash in a land where the people all believe themselves natural aristocrats. Ask any white southerner. They'll take you back two generations, say, "Yeah, we had a plantation." The hell we did.

I have no memories that can be bent so easily. I know where I come from, and it is not that part of the world. My family has a history of death and murder, grief and denial, rage and ugliness—the women of my family most of all.

The women of my family were measured, manlike, sexless, bearers of babies, burdens, and contempt. My family? The women of my family? We are the ones in all those photos taken at mining disasters, floods, fires. We are the ones in the background with our mouths open, in print dresses or drawstring pants and collarless smocks, ugly and old and exhausted. Solid, stolid, wide-hipped baby machines. We were all wide-hipped and predestined. Wide-faced meant stupid. Wide hands marked workhorses with dull hair and tired eyes, thumbing through magazines full of women so different from us they could have been another species.[1]

---

1   Dorothy Allison, *Two or Three Things I Know for Sure* (New York: Dutton, 1995), 32–33.

Connecting to the Central Question

Before beginning Section 6, consider pausing to ask students to review the central question introduced at the beginning of this guide:

What factors influence our moral growth? What kinds of experiences help us learn how to judge right from wrong?

Give students the opportunity to review the response to this question that they wrote and revised in previous sections of this guide. What evidence have they found in this section that confirms their previous response? What evidence have they found that might prompt them to revise their thinking?

Ask students to take a few minutes to reflect on whether or not their thinking has changed, revise their preliminary responses, and record new evidence from Section 5 that can help them answer the question.

Remind students that they will have several opportunities to revise their thinking as they continue to read the novel. Their revised responses and notes will help prepare students for a culminating activity, suggested in the Post-Reading section of this guide, that asks them to analyze the moral growth of a character from the novel.

SECTION 6

It Ain't Right

This section covers Chapters 22 to 31 of the novel.

Introduction

Essential Questions

- What are the responsibilities of citizens in a democracy? What must citizens do to create a just and democratic society?

- How can examining the changes in the characters and setting of a work of fiction help us better understand the relationship between human behavior and social change in our society?

- How can a community seek justice and healing after an act of injustice and violence?

Rationale

In the previous section, students closely examined the events surrounding the trial of Tom Robinson and the resulting guilty verdict. In this section, students will study the aftermath of that verdict, the struggle of Scout and Jem to understand it, and the reflections on democracy and citizenship by the adults who try to help them. They will also examine the subsequent shift in the novel's narrative away from the trial and toward a second climactic event, Bob Ewell's attack on Scout and Jem and their rescue by Boo Radley.

In Chapters 22 through 26, we learn how the town, and the Finches in particular, try to understand the Tom Robinson verdict. As they do so, the characters raise crucial questions about the nature of democracy and the responsibilities of citizenship. Many of the questions and activities in this section are designed to deepen students' reflection about each individual's "share of the bill" (in Atticus's words) in a democracy. To that end, students are prompted here to think about the meaning of democracy itself, beginning with Scout's definition of "equal rights for all, special privileges for none." Students' thinking about democracy and citizenship will deepen as they learn from Atticus's and Miss Maudie's observations that there is a perhaps sizable portion of Maycomb residents that disagrees with the injustices in their society but are unwilling or unable to make their voices heard. This section will prompt students to reflect on the factors that influence individuals to behave as bystanders and what might encourage them to act as upstanders. In other words, they will reflect on how we might help those silent voices for justice make themselves heard. Finally, students will think about how we can both make and measure progress toward creating a more just, democratic society. Does change begin with "baby steps" toward a more just society (as Miss Maudie suggests), or must change come all at once?

In Chapter 27, the story shifts away from the trial, its direct aftermath, and the characters' reflections on justice and democracy. Scout's experiences at home and school once again take precedence in the story, as they did in the first third of the novel. The trial fades into the background, only reappearing as unfinished business and motivation for Bob Ewell's attack in the closing chapters. As Boo Radley is reintroduced to the story and Tom Robinson seems forgotten, it is worth asking students to consider the relationship between these two plotlines and how they might reveal what Harper Lee intends the novel to be about. Is *To Kill a Mockingbird* primarily the story of Atticus taking on the unwritten rules of Jim Crow society by defending Tom Robinson, or is it primarily about Scout's coming of age as she learns to consider others' perspectives?

In considering this question, you might return to the deep analysis of character and setting the class began in Section 2. As they finish the novel, students should be thinking about continuity and change in the world of Maycomb. Has anything changed in Maycomb as a result of the events we experience in the novel? Is Maycomb's "moral universe" significantly different at the end of the book from what it was at the beginning? Students must also consider the characters acting within that moral universe. Who has changed the most, and who has changed the least? What caused the characters to change? Considering these questions will not only help students deepen their analysis of the novel but will also prompt them to reflect on similar questions about human behavior and the possibility for change in society outside of the fictional world of Maycomb.

In this section, it is also crucial to continue to reflect on the effect of point of view in telling the story. In other words, is our narrator, Scout, capable of giving readers a full and accurate view of the changes that have or have not occurred in other people and in her community? Scout's limited point of view leaves readers with a variety of unanswered questions about the impact and legacy in the community of Tom Robinson's trial and subsequent death. In Chapter 27, Scout tells us that "Maycomb was itself again" and that Tom Robinson was largely forgotten. Readers should question in the final four chapters of the novel whether Maycomb's residents truly forgot the injustice Tom Robinson suffered so easily, for examining the history and legacy of Jim Crow-era violence and injustice suggests otherwise. Documents in this section provide historical context to help students understand the powerful legacies such violence and injustice has left in many communities even into the twenty-first century. These documents will also help students explore the approaches many Southern states and towns have taken decades after the end of legal segregation to restore justice and provide healing to their communities. Examining these resources will illustrate for students the powerful ramifications of the choice to remember or to ignore moments of injustice in our history.

Plot Summary

In the days and weeks following the trial, Scout and Jem discuss the verdict with Atticus and try to understand why Tom was found guilty. Bob Ewell confronts Atticus in town, threatening him and spitting in his face. Later in the summer, Tom Robinson tries to escape from prison and is shot dead. Atticus interrupts the missionary circle luncheon that Aunt Alexandra is hosting to share the news. Scout reasons that even though Tom had been given due process of law, he had been condemned from the beginning because he could never win the minds of the people of Maycomb.

That fall, Scout and Jem are attacked while walking home at night from the Halloween pageant at school. In her bulky costume, Scout is knocked over in the commotion and stands up in time to see a man carrying Jem home. Sheriff Tate discovers Mr. Ewell at the scene, stabbed with a knife and killed.

Scout realizes that Boo Radley is the strange man who carried Jem home. It becomes clear that Boo stabbed Mr. Ewell while saving Jem and Scout, and Atticus and Sheriff Tate debate how to proceed. Tate doesn't want to publicize the fact that Boo saved the children because it would bring him unwanted attention. He convinces Atticus to go along with the story that Mr. Ewell fell on his own knife. Scout tells Atticus she understands the lie, because telling the true story of Mr. Ewell's death and bringing so much attention to Boo would be like killing a mockingbird. Scout walks Boo home, and after he goes inside she stands on the Radley porch and imagines how the events of the novel looked from Boo's perspective.

Skills Focus

- Analyzing Continuity and Change in:

  » The moral universe of Maycomb (setting)

  » Characters

- Investigating the Author's Craft: Plot, Pace, Suspense

- Deepening Understanding of the Novel through Analysis of Historical Context from Informational Texts

Academic Vocabulary

CHAPTER 22 *cynical;* CHAPTER 23 *furtive, capital, circumstantial;* CHAPTER 24 *vague, apprehension, impertinence, duress, devout*

Exploring the Text

Before Reading

Before reading Chapters 22 to 31, ask students to respond to the following prompts in their journals:

1. *Identify a time when you went out of your way to help somebody else—a friend, a family member, a neighbor, or a complete stranger. What were the consequences of your actions for you and for others?*

2. *Identify a situation when you knew something was wrong or unfair, but you did not intervene to improve the situation. What were the consequences of your actions for you and for others?*

3. *Compare these two situations. What led you to act in one situation but not to intervene in the other?*

Using Connection Questions

Connection Questions, organized by chapter, are provided below to help guide your class's analysis of the text. A similar set of "After Reading Section 6: Connection Questions" is also provided below to help students synthesize their understanding of Chapters 22 through 31 as a whole.

While these questions are mostly text-based, they are designed to probe important themes in the novel. As you assign chapters for students to read, you might designate all or some of these questions for students to respond to in their journals. These questions can also provide the basis for a class discussion of the text. See facinghistory.org/mockingbird/strategies for suggestions about how to structure effective classroom discussions.

Close Reading

An additional set of text-dependent questions is provided in the Appendix to help facilitate the close reading of a passage from Chapter 26 of the novel. This close reading activity is specifically written to align with the Common Core State Standards for English Language Arts. The passage focuses on the current events lesson Scout experiences at school in the months after the Tom Robinson trial. If you choose to implement this close reading activity, we recommend you do so before engaging the class in other activities related to Chapter 26. See "Close Reading for Deep Comprehension" in the Appendix for a suggested procedure for implementing this close reading activity.

Activities for Deeper Understanding

In addition to the Connection Questions, the following activities can help students reach a deeper understanding of Chapters 22 through 31 of *To Kill a Mockingbird* and its essential themes.

Explore Bystander and Upstander Behavior

Throughout the chapters in this section, Scout, Jem, and Atticus process the Tom Robinson verdict and try to explain why the members of their community collectively participate in an unjust society. In addition, it is revealed that Miss Maudie, and perhaps many more townspeople, would like to see their town change but do not actively challenge the injustices they witness. As students analyze these chapters, it might be helpful to develop a vocabulary to name the behaviors they are discussing: *perpetrator, victim, bystander,* and *upstander*. It is important to note that these terms describe behaviors or roles and not any individual's entire identity. It is likely that all of us will inhabit each of these roles at different points in our lives.

You might begin examining these roles with the students' responses to the pre-reading questions in this section. As students write about times they intervened to help others and times they did not, remember that their stories might be personal; before they begin writing, let them know that they will not be required to publicly share what they write. You can also reassure students that many people choose to act as bystanders, and that there are sometimes very good reasons for choosing not to intervene in a particular situation. Another way to help students feel more comfortable writing honestly is to share your own answer to these journal prompts.

Focus a class discussion on the third question—the reasons why students acted in some situations but not in others. You can record their reasons on a two-column chart, where one column is labeled "Reasons for Bystander Behavior" and the other column is labeled "Reasons for Upstander Behavior."

Finally, you might conclude the activity by asking students to write their own working definitions for the terms *bystander* and *upstander*. You can have them write their definitions individually, in pairs, or as an entire class. These terms will be used in the Connection Questions that appear throughout this section.

Reconsider Plot, Climax, and Themes

In Section 4, students analyzed the trial of Tom Robinson and considered its function as the climax in *To Kill a Mockingbird*. Now that students have finished the novel, it might be worth asking them to think again about the structure of the plot in light of Bob Ewell's attack on Scout and Jem in the final chapters. Some readers might argue that the attack is the true climax of the novel, or at least a second climax in the plot. What do students think? Ask them to write a response in their journals to the following question:

- What do you think is the climax in the plot of *To Kill a Mockingbird*? Explain your answer with evidence from the book and your own analysis.

By answering this question, students will be forced to think about the relationship between the plotlines and themes in the novel. Is the primary plotline Atticus's fight for justice against the unwritten rules of Jim Crow society? Or is it Scout's "coming of age" and the development of her ability to see things from the perspective of others?

Define Democracy

The ideals of democracy are discussed and interpreted in a variety of ways throughout Sections 5 and 6. Atticus reflects on the meaning of the statement "All men are created equal" in his closing argument in the Tom Robinson trial in Chapter 20. In Chapter 26, Miss Gates uses democracy to differentiate between the United States and Nazi Germany. In that chapter, Scout defines democracy as "equal rights for all, special privileges for none."

You might engage students in the process of creating and discussing their own definitions of democracy by sharing the following quotation from Judge William Hastie, the first African American to serve as a federal judge:

> Democracy is a process, not a static condition. It is Becoming, rather than being. It can easily be lost, but never is fully won. Its essence is eternal struggle.

Ask students to reflect on the following questions:

- What does Judge Hastie mean? How would you explain his definition of democracy in your own words?

- In what ways does the story of *To Kill a Mockingbird* reflect the idea of democracy as a process rather than a static condition?

- In what ways has democracy been lost in Maycomb? In what ways has Maycomb come closer to realizing the ideals of democracy?

Write and Reflect in Journals

Any of the Connection Questions in this section might be used as a prompt for journal writing. Also, consider the following questions for a brief reflective writing assignment before, during, or after reading Chapters 22 through 31:

- What are the responsibilities of being a citizen in a democracy? In Maycomb, what factors get in the way of those responsibilities, even for those who wish their community was more just? What factors get in the way in your community?

- What has Scout learned about being a responsible adult and citizen over the course of the novel? What people and experiences were most influential in her growth and development? What people and experiences have had the greatest impact in your life?

Revisit Identity Charts

Students have been working on identity charts for Scout, Jem, Atticus, and other characters throughout their study of *To Kill a Mockingbird*. (See facinghistory.org/mockingbird/strategies for more information about this teaching strategy.) Chapters 22 through 31 provide evidence of how all of these characters have changed over the course of the story. Give students the opportunity to revisit the identity charts. What information might they add? What information might they change or revise? Encourage students to include quotations from the text on their identity charts, as well as their own interpretations of the character or figure based on their reading.

Keep in mind that creating and revising identity charts for the central characters in *To Kill a Mockingbird* will help prepare students for a culminating activity, suggested in the Post-Reading section of this guide, that asks students to analyze the moral and ethical growth of a character from the novel.

CHAPTER 22: Connection Questions

1. This chapter describes the reactions of many of the characters to the Tom Robinson verdict. Choose a quotation from the chapter that sums up the reactions of each of the following characters: Jem, Atticus, the black community of Maycomb, Miss Maudie, Dill, and Bob Ewell. How would you describe this range of responses? How are the characters' responses expressions of their different identities and experiences?

2. How does Miss Maudie define progress in overcoming segregation and discrimination in Maycomb? What do you think of her conclusion? How can we measure progress toward bringing about a more just society? What steps are worth celebrating and what steps are dissatisfying?

CHAPTER 23: Connection Questions

1. Assuming Miss Stephanie's account of Bob Ewell spitting at Atticus in this chapter is true, how do you explain Atticus's decision not to defend himself? How do Scout, Jem, and Dill try to explain it? How does Atticus explain it?

2. What similarities does Atticus see between the men at the jailhouse the night before the trial and the jury the next day? What does he think causes juries to unjustly convict innocent black men? How does Jem propose to fix the problem? How does Atticus propose to fix it? Do you think either of their proposals would guarantee that trials in Maycomb like Tom Robinson's would be fair?

3. What does Atticus mean when he tells Jem, "With people like us—that's our share of the bill. We generally get the juries we deserve"? What responsibilities does Atticus think people like him should live up to? What factors does he think prevent people from doing their civic duty?

4. How does Jem respond to the news that one of the jurors was a Cunningham, and that he had initially moved to acquit Tom? How does Atticus explain why a Cunningham would have such a quick change of heart? How does Atticus suggest that individuals can be persuaded to set aside prejudice to act more justly?

5. After Jem advises Scout, "Don't let Aunty aggravate you," Scout reflects, "It seemed only yesterday that he was telling me not to aggravate Aunty." What disagreement does Scout have with Aunt Alexandra? How does their

disagreement show Scout's growth in how she understands the world? How has the way that Scout and Jem think about Aunt Alexandra changed?

6. Both Atticus and Aunt Alexandra degrade people by referring to them as "trash" in this chapter. How do their definitions of what makes someone "trash" differ?

7. As Scout and Jem try to figure out how they are different from the Cunninghams, how do they understand the word "background"? Which character do you think understands their society better? Which character is more idealistic?

8. Why does Jem conclude that Boo Radley stays inside because he wants to? What does he imagine Boo is trying to avoid?

9. What evidence does this chapter provide that both Scout and Jem have become more mature in their understanding of the world? How has the way that they understand the differences between people changed from the beginning of the novel?

CHAPTER 24: Connection Questions

1. Which of the ladies at the missionary circle luncheon treat Scout with the most respect? How is that respect shown to Scout?

2. Why does Mrs. Merriweather tell Scout that she is "a fortunate girl"? What difference is most important to Mrs. Merriweather between Maycomb and "J. Grimes Everett's land"?

3. According to the ladies in the missionary circle, what are the qualities of a good Christian? What do they think are the qualities of a good citizen?

4. What do we learn about the ladies in the missionary circle from their discussion of the Mruna tribe and the African Americans in Maycomb?

5. To whom is Miss Maudie referring when she asks, "His food doesn't stick going down, does it"? Why does Miss Maudie ask this question? Why is Aunt Alexandra thankful for it?

6. After Miss Maudie interrupts Mrs. Merriweather at the luncheon, Harper Lee describes the two women:

> When Miss Maudie was angry her brevity was icy. Something had made her deeply angry, and her gray eyes were as cold as her voice. Mrs. Merriweather reddened, glanced at me, and looked away.

Analyze how Lee's language creates a contrast between the two women. What does this description suggest about how Mrs. Merriweather feels about the interruption?

7. How does Scout compare and contrast the "ladies' world" and the "world of my father"? In which world is she more comfortable, and why?

8. After hearing about Tom Robinson's death, for what does Alexandra criticize the town? How does Miss Maudie answer her frustration? How does Miss Maudie understand her role in helping Maycomb change?

9. Miss Maudie's comments give Scout "another scrap to add to Jem's definition of background." How is Maudie's definition different from Scout's?

10. Scout concludes the chapter by saying, "If Aunty could be a lady at a time like this, so could I." In what sense are Scout and Alexandra behaving like proper Southern ladies? Is this the appropriate response to all they have heard and learned on this particular afternoon? What has Scout learned about becoming an adult and a lady?

CHAPTER 25: Connection Questions

1. In Chapter 10, Atticus tells Scout and Jem that "it's a sin to kill a mockingbird." Find three examples of that advice being echoed with similar imagery in this chapter. How do these examples help you better understand the meaning of Atticus's advice and the message that Harper Lee intends readers to take away from the story?

2. How does the town of Maycomb respond to news of Tom's death? Who do they blame?

3. Reading Mr. Underwood's editorial about Tom Robinson, Scout concludes, "Tom had been given due process of law to the day of his death . . . but in the secret court of men's hearts Atticus had no case." What does she mean? Could she have reached such a conclusion at the beginning of the novel?

4. Review the quotation from Judge Learned Hand that you read in the previous section. Does Scout agree with Hand? Does she believe that laws or the hearts and minds of citizens play a greater role in creating a just society? What do you think?

CHAPTER 26: Connection Questions

1. Harper Lee reintroduces Boo Radley into the novel in this chapter. What role has he played in the story so far? Is there any connection between the Boo Radley subplot and the story of the Tom Robinson trial so far in the book?

2. How are Scout's fantasies about meeting Boo Radley different now than they were earlier in the novel? How have her feelings about the Radley house changed? How do you explain these changes? What evidence can you find in this chapter to explain them?

3. How do you explain why the townspeople continue to support Atticus and his children while at the same time seeming to approve of the guilty verdict? What does it suggest about the way the people in Maycomb think about justice?

4. How does Miss Gates explain why Hitler is able to treat Jews so poorly in Germany? What irony is exposed in her explanation? What is she forgetting or ignoring? Why do you think Harper Lee chose to include this current events lesson in the novel? What point was she making?

5. How does Scout define democracy? Do you think her definition is satisfactory? Would you add or change anything?

6. Why is Scout confused when Miss Gates explains, "Over here we don't believe in persecuting anybody. Persecution comes from people who are prejudiced"? What is ironic about Miss Gates's explanation?

7. Why does Jem respond so angrily when Scout brings up the courthouse? How does Atticus explain his behavior?

8. How is Jem's forgetting similar to Miss Gates's forgetting? How is it different? What role does forgetting play in allowing us to live our daily lives and be "ourselves"? When is forgetting dangerous?

CHAPTER 27: Connection Questions

1. Why does Aunt Alexandra continue to worry about the threat posed by Bob Ewell? How does Atticus explain Mr. Ewell's behavior around town? Do you think Atticus is being cautious enough? Look through the chapter for signs of foreshadowing of what might happen.

2. What do Atticus's beliefs about the possible threat that Bob Ewell poses to him suggest about Atticus's outlook on the world?

3. Scout declares that "Maycomb was itself again" in this chapter. In what ways is Maycomb the same as it was before the Tom Robinson trial? In what ways is it different? What must happen in order for a community to "become itself again" after a traumatic or divisive event?

CHAPTER 28: Connection Questions

1. Find words and phrases that help create the mood in this chapter. How does the mood of the story change from the Halloween pageant to the walk home? How does the change in mood affect how the reader experiences the attack on Jem and Scout?

2. Why did Bob Ewell attack Scout and Jem? How were they left so vulnerable to being attacked? Why does Atticus misread so badly the signs that Bob Ewell might try to hurt him or his family?

3. Who is the stranger that rescued Jem? What is Scout's first impression of him?

CHAPTER 29: Connection Questions

1. How does Atticus view human nature? Does he think people are fundamentally good or fundamentally bad? What evidence from the book, especially Chapters 28 and 29, supports your interpretation of Atticus's view of human nature? Does Heck Tate agree or disagree? Whose view is closest to yours?

2. What makes Scout realize that the man who rescued her and Jem is Boo Radley? Summarize her description of him. How is his actual appearance similar to what the children imagined him to look like? How is it different?

CHAPTER 30: Connection Questions

1. On the front porch with Atticus, Heck Tate, and Boo Radley, Scout reports, "A curious contest, the nature of which eluded me, was developing between my father and the sheriff." What did Atticus and Heck argue about? From their argument, what do we learn about Bob Ewell's death? Who killed him? How do we know?

2. Is following the law always the right thing to do? How would Atticus answer the question? How would Heck Tate? Does either of their positions change over the course of their discussion? Who do you think is right?

3. The motif of shooting mockingbirds recurs in this chapter. Who, according to Scout, is the mockingbird in this chapter? Who else does the mockingbird symbolize in this novel?

4. When Atticus begins to explain to Scout why they must go along with Heck Tate's lie, she quickly understands, saying that telling the truth about who killed Bob Ewell would be "sort of like shootin' a mockingbird." Who is the mockingbird in her comparison?

5. Why do you think this situation is so challenging for Atticus? Does going along with the lie force him to "live one way in town and another way in my home"? If he goes along with the lie, will he be consistent in the way he lives according to the law? Will he be consistent in the way he lives according to what is right and what is wrong?

6. What will Scout, Jem, Atticus, and Heck Tate need to forget in order to move forward from this incident? Is forgetting a form of lying? Is forgetting helpful or necessary in this situation?

CHAPTER 31: Connection Questions

1. How does Scout demonstrate that she has taken to heart Atticus's advice about seeing things from others' perspectives?

2. How does Scout feel when she reflects on her relationship with Boo Radley? How would she define the responsibilities of being a neighbor?

3. After bringing Boo home, Scout observes that she feels old. She says, "I thought Jem and I would get grown but there wasn't much left for us to learn. . . ." What have Scout and Jem learned over the course of the novel? How do those lessons differ from what she will learn in school?

AFTER READING SECTION 6: Connection Questions

1. Who is most responsible for the injustices that Tom Robinson and his family endure in *To Kill a Mockingbird*? Use evidence from the book to support your position.

2. Which characters behave as bystanders in the novel? In what circumstances did they behave that way? What choices did they make that made them bystanders? What other options were available to them? What factors encouraged them to behave as bystanders?

3. Which characters behave as upstanders in the novel? In what circumstances did they behave that way? What choices did they make that made them upstanders? What other options were available to them? What factors encouraged them to stand up to injustice?

4. Do you think there is a hero in *To Kill a Mockingbird*? If so, who is it? Explain your thinking.

5. What role does the "secret court of men's hearts" play in changing a society? Is changing the hearts of citizens necessary in order for society to change? Is it enough?

6. Scout says that shortly after the Tom Robinson verdict, Maycomb "became itself" again. What does it mean for Maycomb to "become itself" again? What role does forgetting play in the community's response? Who wants to forget? Who cannot? When is forgetting helpful, and when is it destructive?

7. Has Maycomb society become more just? How do you measure progress toward bringing about a more just society? Should "baby steps" be celebrated as progress or lamented for not going far enough?

8. What is the relationship between the trial of Tom Robinson and the Boo Radley subplot in the novel? How does Harper Lee weave the two stories together to reinforce common themes?

9. How do the resolutions of the stories of Tom Robinson and Boo Radley complicate the relationship between the law and justice?

10. By the end of the novel, how does Scout reconcile the pressure on her to be a "Southern lady" with the fact that she prefers her "father's world"?

Building Historical Context

In the closing chapters of *To Kill a Mockingbird*, Scout tells readers that "Maycomb was itself again" shortly after the Tom Robinson trial. Atticus tells Scout in Chapter 26 that "after enough time passed people would forget that Tom Robinson's existence was ever brought to their attention." In the next chapter, Scout reports that "Tom Robinson was as forgotten as Boo Radley," and Tom is not mentioned in the last four chapters of the novel.

Readers may call into question Scout's description of Maycomb becoming "itself" again after the trial and death of Tom Robinson for at least two reasons. First, we must again consider the limitations of Scout's perspective, for she likely does not know the effects these incidents have on Maycomb's black community, and Tom Robinson's family and friends in particular. Second, history tells us that the legacy of racial violence and injustice that occurred under Jim Crow persisted, and in many cases continues to persist, in the lives and memories of communities decades after the end of legal segregation.

The resources below have been included here to help students consider the legacy of racial violence and injustice in Southern communities and learn about the ways that some communities have attempted to come to grips with their histories in order to seek justice and healing. As students explore each resource, they might consider the following questions:

- How does this resource help us understand what must happen in order for a community to move forward after a traumatic or divisive event?

- How does this resource help us understand the requirements for justice in response to violence and injustice that occurred many years ago?

- What does this resource suggest to us about the possibility of healing, both for individuals and communities, after episodes of injustice and violence?

Watch "The Trouble I've Seen"

This 17-minute video describes the work of the Northeastern University School of Law's Civil Rights and Restorative Justice Project. Law students participating in this program research cases of violence and injustice that occurred during the Jim Crow era, attempt to set the historical record straight, and help communities and families search for reconciliation and remediation decades after the end of legal segregation.

This video raises profound questions about the persistent effects of racial violence and injustice. It explores the powerful effects of both trying to forget or ignore past injustices and attempting to remember them and establish them as part of the community's shared history.

The video is available to stream from the Northeastern University website (see facinghistory.org/mockingbird/links to watch the video). Consider showing the video as the class discusses Chapters 21 through 27. As students watch the video, have them take notes on the viewing guide included below (**Handout 6.1**).

Explore Approaches to Justice and Healing

Handouts 6.1 to **6.6** describe a variety of ways that communities, states, and nations have sought justice and healing after episodes of injustice and violence. These approaches seek a type of justice often called *restorative justice*. Sometimes restorative justice methods are employed in a matter of years after the event, but more often they are put in place decades later. These documents introduce students to examples of five such methods of restorative justice: truth and reconciliation commissions, pardons, apologies, reparations, and memorials.

One way to have students explore these approaches to restorative justice is to create a gallery walk with **Handouts 6.1** to **6.6**. (For information on this teaching strategy, visit facinghistory.org/mockingbird/strategies.) Post the documents around the classroom, and then give students time to visit each document. You might have students travel in small groups. As they view each document, students should record in their journals a definition of the approach to restorative justice each document describes and then discuss the Connection Questions that follow the text.

Follow up the gallery walk by discussing with the class which of these approaches to healing or justice, or which combination of approaches, would be appropriate for Maycomb to take today to remember Tom Robinson. You might have students work individually or in the small groups to develop a detailed proposal for a restorative justice program in Maycomb.

Design Memorials to Tom Robinson

In addition to, or instead of, having students develop proposals for a restorative justice program in Maycomb (see above), you might ask students to design a memorial for Tom Robinson. You might also provide clay or other art materials so that students can create a model of their memorial.

As they design their memorials, students should consider the following questions:

- What is the purpose of the memorial?

- Where will the memorial be placed?

- What is the memorial's audience? Who will visit it and why?

- Who or what will be remembered, and for what reasons?

You might require students to accompany their designs with a written proposal that answers these questions.

Handout 6.1 "The Trouble I've Seen"

Use the following questions to guide your note-taking and reflection on the video "The Trouble I've Seen":

1. Summarize the story of Della McDuffie. How was justice denied in her case? How was the history of her murder erased?

2. What does the film suggest about how people in Wilcox County, Alabama, remember Sheriff Lummie Jenkins, the perpetrator of McDuffie's murder?

3. What did the work of Bayliss Fiddiman, the law student, reveal about the truth of the McDuffie murder?

4. Summarize the story of Malcolm Wright. How was justice denied in his case? How was the history of his murder erased?

5. How did Robert Sanderman, the law student, help correct the history of Malcolm Wright's murder? Where did he go to get information and firsthand accounts?

6. What did Margaret Burnham mean when she said that the Malcolm Wright case had "the appearance but not the reality of justice"?

7. Why does Chickasaw County resist attempts to acknowledge the injustice that occurred at the expense of Malcolm Wright and his family?

8. The film quotes the Mayor of Houston, Mississippi, as saying: "If we've already closed it, you start the healing process of a wound. You have another wound that you want to reopen. Reopening a wound, it takes longer to heal." Do you agree with him? Does correcting the historical record of past violence and injustice reopen old wounds? Does it help or hinder the chance for a community to heal?

9. Summarize the story of John Earl Reese. How was justice denied in his case? How was the history of his murder erased?

10. What did Kaylie Simon, the law student, do to try to correct the injustice done to Reese? Did she succeed?

11. What effect did Simon's work have on the community? What effect did it have on John Earl Reese's family, friends, and descendants?

12. Which part of Simon's work in Mayflower, Texas, do you think had the greatest positive impact?

13. How has this film helped you think about the consequences of forgetting or ignoring past violence and injustice? What about the consequences of remembering?

14. How does Maycomb respond to Tom Robinson's conviction and death? How does it affect individuals in the town, and which individuals? Does the town remember or forget?

Handout 6.2 Truth and Reconciliation Commissions

Over the last three decades, truth commissions have been integral to the attempts of many communities and nations to support reconciliation and healing after episodes of mass violence. One of the most significant examples is the Truth and Reconciliation Commission formed in South Africa after the end of apartheid. Truth commissions come in many forms. Some, such as South Africa's, have heard testimony from both perpetrators and victims of violence. Others have heard only from victims. Truth commissions are usually established for only a specific length of time, and they investigate a particular period or event in a community's or nation's past. Most seek to gather testimony and documentation to detail what happened to victims of violence and abuse. They also attempt to establish who was responsible for the events: individuals, communities, and/or the government. Commissions have sometimes, but not always, been complemented by other efforts to restore justice, such as prosecutions, institutional reforms, or reparations.

The first truth commission established in the United States was in Greensboro, North Carolina. In 1979, local white supremacists clashed with African Americans who were holding a rally against the Ku Klux Klan. Even though videotape captured white supremacists firing guns at the black and white protesters, killing five and wounding ten, the men who fired the guns were acquitted by all-white juries in both state and federal criminal trials. In later civil trials, several of the white supremacists were held liable for some of the deaths, but the city agreed to pay the damages awarded to the victims' families. Twenty years later, the Greensboro Truth and Community Reconciliation Project was created, modeled after the commission in South Africa.[1] The following is an excerpt from the commission's mandate:

> There comes a time in the life of every community when it must look humbly and seriously into its past in order to provide the best possible foundation for moving into a future based on healing and hope. Many residents of Greensboro believe that for this city, the time is now.
>
> In light of the shooting death of 5 people and the wounding of 10 others in Greensboro, North Carolina, on November 3, 1979, and

1 "Truth Commissions," Civil Rights and Restorative Justice Project, Northeastern University School of Law (2014), accessed May 21, 2014, http://nuweb9.neu.edu/civilrights/truth-commissions/.

In light of the subsequent acquittal of defendants in both state and federal criminal trials, despite the fact that the shootings were videotaped and widely viewed, and

In light of the further investigations, passage of time and other factors which allowed a jury in a later civil trial to find certain parties liable for damages in the death of one of the victims, and

In light of the confusion, pain, and fear experienced by residents of the city and the damage to the fabric of relationships in the community caused by these incidents and their aftermath,

The Greensboro Truth and Community Reconciliation Project, including the signers of its Declaration, calls for the examination of the context, causes, sequence and consequence of the events of November 3, 1979.

We affirm that the intention of this examination shall be:

a) Healing and reconciliation of the community through discovering and disseminating the truth of what happened and its consequences in the lives of individuals and institutions, both locally and beyond Greensboro.

b) Clarifying the confusion and reconciling the fragmentation that has been caused by these events and their aftermath, in part by educating the public through its findings.

c) Acknowledging and recognizing people's feelings, including feelings of loss, guilt, shame, anger and fear.

d) Helping facilitate changes in social consciousness and in the institutions that were consciously or unconsciously complicit in these events, thus aiding in the prevention of similar events in the future.

This examination is not for the purpose of exacting revenge or recrimination. Indeed, the Commission will have no such power. Rather, the Commission will attempt to learn how persons and groups came to be directly or indirectly involved in these events; it will assess the impact of these events on the life and development of this community. It will seek all possibilities for healing transformation . . . .[2]

---

2 "The Mandate and Guiding Principles" (Greensboro, NC: Greensboro Truth and Reconciliation Commission, 2006), accessed May 21, 2014, http://www.greensborotrc.org/mandate.php.

Connection Questions

1. According to the Greensboro project's mandate, what actions can help provide healing and hope to their community? What actions might impede healing and hope? Do you agree?

Handout 6.3 Pardons

Pardons, issued by state or national government, acknowledge that the past arrests and prosecutions of particular individuals were unjustified. Pardons correct the official record, declaring that an individual was falsely accused and convicted of a crime he or she did not commit.

In the United States, pardons have been issued by nearly every Southern state to exonerate individuals who were unjustly arrested and punished for crimes they did not commit during the Jim Crow era and the civil rights movement. Sometimes pardons are issued many years after victims were prosecuted and punished. For example, in 2013, the Alabama legislature voted to issue pardons for all nine of the Scottsboro Boys, falsely accused and convicted of raping two girls on a train in Alabama in 1931.[1] Upon signing the pardon, Alabama governor Robert Bentley made the following statement:

> While we could not take back what happened to the Scottsboro Boys 80 years ago, we found a way to make it right moving forward. The pardons granted to the Scottsboro Boys today are long overdue. The legislation that led to today's pardons was the result of a bipartisan, cooperative effort. I appreciate the Pardons and Parole Board for continuing our progress today and officially granting these pardons. Today, the Scottsboro Boys have finally received justice.[2]

Connection Questions

1. Governor Bentley states that the Scottsboro Boys have finally received justice. Do you agree?

2. Under what circumstances do you think pardons can provide justice and healing for individuals and communities?

---

1 "Pardons – United States," Civil Rights and Restorative Justice Project, Northeastern University School of Law (2014), accessed May 21, 2014, http://nuweb9.neu.edu/civilrights/pardons-in-the-united-states/.

2 "Governor Bentley's Statement on the Pardoning of the Scottsboro Boys," Office of Alabama Governor Robert J. Bentley (2014), accessed May 21, 2014, http://governor.alabama.gov/newsroom/2013/11/governor-bentleys-statement-pardoning-scottsboro-boys/.

Handout 6.4 Apologies

Note: We recommend that teachers review the page "Discussing Sensitive Topics in the Classroom" before using this document.

Local, state, or national governments sometimes issue apologies, acknowledging past injustices. Such apologies admit that moral or ethical wrongs have been committed, leading to injustice or violence against individuals or entire groups.[1]

Both houses of the US Congress and several individual states have issued apologies for slavery and Jim Crow segregation. Sometimes state governments have apologized for what the state failed to do. In 2011, the state of Alabama issued an apology to Recy Taylor, an African American woman who was raped by several white men. The all-white grand jury failed to charge any of the men with a crime. The following is the text of the state's apology:

EXPRESSING REGRET FOR THE STATE OF ALABAMA'S INVOLVEMENT IN THE FAILURE TO PROSECUTE CRIMES COMMITTED AGAINST RECY TAYLOR.

WHEREAS, on September 3, 1944, in the small Town of Abbeville, Alabama, Recy Taylor, a young Black mother was walking home from church with her companions when she was confronted by a car of seven white men; the men forced Ms. Taylor into the car at knife and gunpoint, drove off, and six of the seven men brutally raped her in a deserted grove of pine trees; and

WHEREAS, Taylor's younger brother, Robert Corbitt, of Abbeville, said he remembers the day his sister was raped 67 years ago like it was yesterday, saying the police tried to blame his sister, and the family was harassed so that he was not allowed to play in the front yard; and

WHEREAS, an all white, all male grand jury failed to bring any charges for indictment; and then Governor Chauncey Sparks ordered a second investigation, and the grand jury again failed to indict; and

WHEREAS, the case got the attention of NAACP activist Rosa Parks, who interviewed Taylor in 1944 in Abbeville and later recruited other activists to create the "Alabama Committee for Equal Justice for Mrs. Recy Taylor"; and

---

1   "Apologies," Civil Rights and Restorative Justice Project, Northeastern University School of Law (2014), accessed May 21, 2014, http://nuweb9.neu.edu/civilrights/apologies/.

WHEREAS, in an interview last year with the AP, Recy Taylor, who now resides in Florida, said she eventually gave up trying to bring charges against the men; and

WHEREAS, this deplorable lack of justice remains a source of shame for all Alabamians; now therefore,

BE IT RESOLVED BY THE LEGISLATURE OF ALABAMA, BOTH HOUSES THEREOF CONCURRING, That we acknowledge the lack of prosecution for crimes committed against Recy Taylor by the government of the State of Alabama, that we declare such failure to act was, and is, morally abhorrent and repugnant, and that we do hereby express profound regret for the role played by the government of the State of Alabama in failing to prosecute the crimes.

BE IT FURTHER RESOLVED, That we express our deepest sympathies and solemn regrets to Recy Taylor and her family and friends.

BE IT FURTHER RESOLVED, That it is the specific intent of the Legislature that reparations shall not be considered or made regarding past actions of the government of the State of Alabama concerning the lack of prosecution of the crimes committed against Recy Taylor, and that this resolution shall not be used or construed in any manner whatsoever as support for such reparations.[2]

Connection Questions

1. Recy Taylor was 91 when Alabama issued this apology. Her brother, speaking on her behalf, said the apology provided their family closure.[3] What is closure? How is it different from justice?

2. Under what circumstances do you think pardons can provide justice and healing for individuals and communities? In what ways do both the perpetrator and the victim benefit from apologies?

2   "Expressing Regret for the State of Alabama's Involvement in the Failure to Prosecute Crimes Committed Against Recy Taylor," H.R.J. Res. HJR194, 2011 Leg. (Ala.), accessed May 21, 2014, http://alisondb.legislature.state.al.us/acas/searchableinstruments/2011RS/Printfiles/HJR194-enr.pdf.

3   Cynthia Gordy, "Recy Taylor's Brother: Rape Apology to Give 'Closure,'" *The Root*, March 30, 2011, accessed May 22, 2014, http://www.theroot.com/blogs/blogging_the_beltway/2011/03/alabama_house_apologizes_to_recy_taylor_brother_says_it_will_give_some_closure.html.

Handout 6.5 Reparations

Reparations go beyond apologies and offer tangible, usually financial, compensation for past injustices either to the victims themselves or to their descendants. The financial compensation might simultaneously be a symbolic acknowledgment of the effects of injustice and a very real attempt to repair, to some extent, the negative effects that the past injustice caused for the opportunities and wealth of the victims and their descendants.

In 1994, the state of Florida offered reparations to the victims and their descendants of the Rosewood Massacre, a 1923 episode of racial violence that began with the false accusation that a black man raped a white woman and led to the complete destruction of an all-black town by a mob of white Floridians. In 1994, the Sun Sentinel *newspaper described the debate in the Florida legislature and the terms of the reparations they passed as follows:*

"Our system of justice failed the citizens of Rosewood," said Sen. Daryl Jones, D-Miami. "This is your chance to right an atrocious wrong."

Jones and Reps. Al Lawson, D-Tallahassee, and Miguel De Grandy, R-Miami, overcame heavy odds to persuade their colleagues to support reparations. The House earlier passed the bill 71-40.

"It's time for us to send an example, a shining example, that we're going to do what's right—for once," said Sen. Matthew Meadows, D-Fort Lauderdale.

The package includes $1.5 million to be divided among the 11 or so survivors of the massacre, $500,000 to compensate Rosewood families who were run out of town for the property they lost and $100,000 in college scholarships for Rosewood descendants and other minorities.

Sen. Charles Williams, D-Tallahassee, whose district includes the area that used to be Rosewood, said the state should spend the $2.1 million on more pressing matters. "How long do we have to pay for the sins of our forefathers?" he said.[1]

---

1   Jerry Fallstrom, "Senate Oks $2.1 Million for Rosewood Reparations," *Sun Sentinel* (Fort Lauderdale, FL), April 9, 1994, accessed May 21, 2014, http://articles.sun-sentinel.com/1994-04-09/news/9404080701_1_rosewood-descendants-rosewood-bill-reparations.

Connection Questions

1. What do you think reparations can accomplish? What do they fail to accomplish?

2. How might you calculate the damage done by acts of racial violence and injustice? How might you estimate the damage done by the legacy of those acts?

3. How would you answer Charles Williams's question at the end of the article?

Handout 6.6 Memorials and Monuments

Establishing memorials is often a crucial part of a community's process of coming to grips with difficult past events. Memorials and monuments create a visual, often symbolic, marker of a past event or important person in a community's history. They might honor a community's heroes or commemorate its tragedies.

Memorials and monuments—whether they take the form of grand, elaborate structures or simple roadside markers—often provoke strong feelings from the members of a community about what parts of their history must be remembered and what parts are better off forgotten. That debate is taking place in Montgomery, Alabama, as the community grapples with a history that includes traumatic events such as slavery and segregation, as well as more inspiring periods such as the Civil War and the civil rights movement. In 2013, one group began to address the city's lack of memorials to some of the challenging parts of its history. For instance, until December of that year, Montgomery had only one marker commemorating its role in the history of slavery. The New York Times *reported:*

> On Tuesday, the Equal Justice Initiative, an organization that since 1989 has provided legal representation to poor defendants and prisoners, will be unveiling three new markers describing in greater detail the city's role in the domestic slave trade . . . . That role was substantial: in 1860, there were more than 20,000 slaves in Montgomery . . . and Dexter Avenue was a busy corridor of slave pens and depots . . .

> "We're constantly inviting people to the city to think and reflect on civil rights to think and reflect on the Civil War," said Bryan Stevenson, the director of the Equal Justice Initiative.

> "If you don't understand slavery, you can't possibly understand the civil rights movement and you certainly can't understand the Civil War."

> But Southern history is a custody battle still in litigation . . .

> The installation of the markers . . . could possibly be the least controversial part of what Mr. Stevenson sees as a multiyear campaign to develop a "deeper, more meaningful historical context" for the country's racial history.

His group has already been discreetly sending researchers to scores of lynching sites around the South, with a plan to put up memorials in the next year.

For the next phases, Mr. Stevenson is considering ways to explore publicly the psychological consequences of life in the Jim Crow South, especially among those who experienced it, and then to focus on what he sees as an extension of this long history: the high incarceration rates of the present day.

Southern cities and states, including Alabama, have embraced commemorations of the civil rights era, but facing some of the less inspirational parts of the past has been tougher going.[1]

Connection Questions

1. How do memorials and monuments help us remember our history? What dangers might they pose in relation to the way that history is remembered?

2. Should memorials and monuments always commemorate parts of history of which we are proud? Why is it important to commemorate parts of history that make us ashamed?

1   Campbell Robertson, "Before the Battles and the Protests, the Chains," *New York Times*, December 9, 2013, accessed May 21, 2014, http://www.nytimes.com/2013/12/10/us/before-the-battles-and-the-protests-the-chains.html?_r=0.

Connecting to the Central Question

Before beginning the Post-Reading section, consider pausing to ask students to review the central question introduced at the beginning of this guide:

What factors influence our moral growth? What kinds of experiences help us learn how to judge right from wrong?

Give students the opportunity to review the response to this question that they wrote and revised in previous sections of this guide. What evidence have they found in this section that confirms their previous response? What evidence have they found that might prompt them to revise their thinking?

Ask students to take a few minutes to reflect on whether or not their thinking has changed, revise their preliminary responses, and record new evidence from Section 6 that can help them answer the question.

Their revised responses and notes will help prepare students for a culminating activity, suggested in the Post-Reading section of this guide, that asks them to analyze the moral growth of a character from the novel.

SECTION 7

Post-Reading: Empathy to Action

Introduction

Essential Questions

- How can literature help us reach a deeper understanding of ourselves and our growth as moral and ethical people? How can it help shape the way we think and act?

- How can we cultivate in each other and ourselves the values, experiences, and skills we need to build a stronger democracy?

Rationale

If, as literary critic Wayne C. Booth contends, when we read literature we "stretch our own capacities for thinking about how life should be lived,"[1] then the study of a novel such as *To Kill a Mockingbird* ought to conclude with reflection on what we can learn by reading it and then put into practice in our own lives. Yet, while Harper Lee's novel wrestles with profound moral and ethical questions, students should not expect to find simple lessons or morals waiting to be discovered in the text. The themes in *To Kill a Mockingbird* about caring, growth, justice, and democracy represent ongoing cultural conversations that are never truly resolved; Lee does not provide the answers. Our task, then, is to reflect with our students on the process of engaging in those ongoing conversations. In doing so, we can learn together about the shared experience of growing as moral and ethical people and about our shared responsibility for strengthening democracy and bringing about a more just society.

---

1   Wayne C. Booth, *The Company We Keep: An Ethics of Fiction* (Berkeley: University of California Press, 1988), 187.

The resources in this section were chosen to help the class conclude its study of *To Kill a Mockingbird* through this sort of reflection. First, students should have the opportunity to reflect more generally on their experience reading the novel. To help them, this section provides four responses to the novel written by reviewers and literary critics. These responses reflect a variety of responses to the book, including praise for the way it confronts issues of race and justice, admiration for its craft, and reverence for its place in American culture, as well as criticism for its depiction of its African American characters as passive victims. We believe it is helpful for students to be exposed to both the reverence and criticism reviewers have given *To Kill a Mockingbird* during the 50 years since its publication because such a range can inform their own evaluation of the novel. For instance, if they are only exposed to praise of the book as a classic of literature, students may feel silenced if their reaction to the book is a negative one. By being exposed to thoughtful criticism, they may be able to better formulate their own critical response.

Once students have reflected on and articulated their experience of reading *To Kill a Mockingbird*, they can begin to make deeper and broader connections between the novel and their own moral and ethical lives. To help them make these connections, this section introduces students to the model of moral development created by psychologist Lawrence Kohlberg in the 1950s. His six-stage model, describing motivations for moral behavior that progress from the goal of simply avoiding physical punishment to the desire to live according universal principles of justice, offers students a framework for conducting a deep analysis of the main characters in *To Kill a Mockingbird*. By analyzing the factors that influenced the moral growth of one character, students can then reflect on the influences that contribute to the development of their own sense of right and wrong. This analysis and reflection can provide the basis for a culminating assignment or assessment for a unit based on the novel. The central question, introduced at the beginning of this guide and revisited throughout, might also serve as the basis for a final assessment.

Finally, after students have considered how their own moral values have developed—and continue to develop—they might reflect on how those values can translate into action. While reading *To Kill a Mockingbird* might help them recognize the importance of "walking around in someone else's skin," it is crucial to ask whether or not developing the skill of empathy is enough, or if more is required to fulfill our moral and civic responsibilities. To guide students' reflection on the connection between identity, values, and action, this section includes a speech by Bryan Stevenson, a lawyer who founded the nonprofit Equal Justice Initiative in Montgomery, Alabama, to create a fairer criminal justice system. Stevenson discusses the deep roots of his family and how he puts the values he learned from his grandmother into action through his work. In a previous section of this guide, students reflected on the difference between bystander and upstander behavior; in this section, Bryan Stevenson will deepen that reflection and hopefully inspire students to seek ways to make their voices heard and put their values into action.

Activities for Deeper Understanding

Respond to To Kill a Mockingbird

As is the case with any classic work of literature, *To Kill a Mockingbird* can prompt a variety of responses from readers, including both praise and criticism. While Harper Lee's novel is one of the most beloved books in American literature, even those who love the book sometimes offer critical views of some aspects of the work. Any work of fiction that provides as complex and nuanced a look at society and its flaws as *To Kill a Mockingbird* provides of the Depression-era South is bound to be the subject of much debate. Therefore, after students reach the end of their study of the novel, it is important not only to give them an opportunity to formulate their own individual responses but also to allow room in class discussion for a range of responses. For some students, encouraging thoughtful, substantive criticisms of the novel may even open the door to a deeper level of engagement with the novel.

Handout 7.1 provides a range of responses to *To Kill a Mockingbird* that can help students reflect on their own experiences reading the novel and form their own assessments of it. Two responses are excerpted from reviews when the book was initially published in 1960, and two are excerpted from reflections 50 years later. These excerpts were not chosen to represent all points of view. Rather, they provide a variety of opinions, including both praise and criticism, that may help students think about their own responses to the book.

You might post these four responses around the classroom to create a gallery walk and give students time to circulate around the room to read and briefly reflect on each one (see facinghistory.org/mockingbird/strategies for more information). Consider asking students to record a headline in their journals for each excerpt, summarizing the perspective the author takes on the book. Finally, ask students to choose one of the excerpts and write a response to its author. In their writing, students should include answers to the following questions:

- What about this assessment of *To Kill a Mockingbird* strikes a chord with you? What made you choose this review for your response?

- What do you agree with? What do you disagree with?

- What else did you experience while reading *To Kill a Mockingbird* that this assessment leaves out?

Connect to the Film

Many teachers show the classic 1962 film adaptation of *To Kill a Mockingbird* once the class has finished reading the novel and then ask students to compare and contrast the two versions of the story. This exercise can help students better understand the craft of storytelling in different media and recognize that Harper Lee's construction of the story of *To Kill a Mockingbird* involved a series of choices about character, setting, and plot that all authors face.

When presenting the film to students, it is crucial to help them understand that the novel and the film are truly two different texts. Film versions of novels are often adaptations, made sometimes by the author of the original work and other times by a different screenwriter. In the case of *To Kill a Mockingbird*, screenwriter Horton Foote made changes to the characters, setting, and plot of Harper Lee's novel. As a result, the film tells a story that is similar to but distinct from the novel. By comparing and contrasting these two versions of *To Kill a Mockingbird*, students can reach a deeper appreciation of the choices writers make and the impact these choices have on the way the story impacts the audience and engages them in considering its essential themes.

After showing the film, you might use any of the following questions to guide student reflection in their journals or a class discussion:

1. Which scenes in the film are most memorable to you? Are they the same scenes that are most memorable to you from the book? Compare and contrast your responses to these two different versions of *To Kill a Mockingbird*.

2. What are the most noticeable changes that Horton Foote (the screenwriter) made in his film adaptation of Harper Lee's novel? What differences in characters, setting, and plot are most obvious? How do those changes impact the way you experience and respond to the story?

3. How does the film present the world of Maycomb differently from the way the book does? Which scenes in the film are pivotal in helping the viewer understand "Maycomb's ways"? What important details about Maycomb from the book are left out in the film?

4. How is the way the story is told in the film different from the way it is told in the book? Compare and contrast the point of view of the book and the film. How do the differences impact what the story is about?

5. Who is the protagonist of *To Kill a Mockingbird*? Would you have answered this question differently before viewing the film version? Why or why not?

6. How do the differences in characters, setting, and plot in the film affect its thematic focus? Which "ongoing cultural conversations" from the book are emphasized most strongly in the film? Which ones are diminished or missing?

Analyze Character Growth and Moral Development

In order to extend students' thinking about moral development, it is helpful to introduce students to the ways in which some psychologists have thought about the process. In this activity, students will learn about a well-known model of moral development developed by psychologist Lawrence Kohlberg in the 1950s, and they will use it to analyze the growth of characters in *To Kill a Mockingbird*. Consider the following suggestions and adapt them to best fit the needs of your classroom:

1. Before introducing Kohlberg's model, you might first ask students to review their reflections so far on the central question: *What factors influence our moral growth? What kinds of experiences help us learn how to judge the difference between right and wrong?* Explain that this activity will extend both their analysis of the characters in the novel and their exploration of how we develop our sense of right and wrong.

2. Introduce Kohlberg's stages of moral development (See **Handout 7.2**). Explain that these stages are one of a variety of models of moral development that psychologists have developed. Kohlberg focuses on how people think about issues of fairness and justice, and his theory asserts that moral reasoning progresses linearly through each of six stages involving different ways of thinking about moral issues. Students should understand that Kohlberg's stages are a useful way to think about moral growth, but they have been critiqued and modified by other experts. For instance, some have questioned Kohlberg's belief that we move linearly through the stages of moral development, positing instead that we proceed indirectly, sometimes taking backward steps as part of an overall pattern of growth. Psychologist Carol Gilligan has offered another

critique of Kohlberg's model. Seeking to better represent the moral growth of women, she developed a different model that explores the roles of caring and compassion in addition to fairness and justice.

After introducing and discussing Kohlberg's model with students, give them the opportunity to offer their own critiques. You might ask students to reflect on the six stages in their journals and respond to the following questions:

- Which parts of Kohlberg's thinking about moral development do you agree with? Which parts do you disagree with?

- Are there any parts of Kohlberg's model that you would modify or remove? Is there anything you would add to the model to make it better reflect your ideas about how we grow as moral and ethical people?

Follow up this reflection with a brief class discussion of the strengths and weaknesses of Kohlberg's stages. To deepen this discussion, you might have students research Gilligan's ideas about the "ethics of care."

3. Ask students to think about which character has changed the most over the course of the book, using Kohlberg's stages (or their modified version) as a measure. For instance, you might ask students to think about Scout in the first seven chapters of the book. Which of Kolhberg's stages does her thinking seem to reflect the most? (Students should find evidence in the book to support their answers.) Then ask students to think about Scout in the final chapters of the book. Which of Kohlberg's stages does her thinking seem to reflect the most? By following a similar process for Jem and Atticus, students can begin to draw some conclusions about which character they believe has changed the most.

4. After students have chosen the character that they think has changed the most, have them create a memory map for that character. Students may have created memory maps for themselves in the Pre-Reading section of this guide. They should follow a similar process for creating their character memory maps. (See the Pre-Reading section for detailed instructions.) This time, however, the map should help answer the following question: What pivotal moments from the novel most influenced the character's moral growth? Students should choose at least three and represent those three moments on their character memory maps. The identity charts that students created for characters while

reading the novel can help them brainstorm and select these pivotal moments. Students might also review their ongoing reflection about the central question for help identifying pivotal moments for their chosen character.

5. After they complete the memory map for a character, you might then ask students to write a short reflection or essay stating their conclusions about the moral growth of the character. Their analysis should answer the following questions:

   - How did this character's understanding of right and wrong change over the course of the novel?

   - Using Kohlberg's stages of moral development as a guide, how would you describe how the character thinks about fairness and justice at the end of the novel? Which of Kohlberg's stages does he or she reach?

   - What experiences did you choose for your memory map to represent this character's moral growth? How do these experiences show the development of the character's judgment about right and wrong?

6. Finally, you might give students the opportunity to review the memory maps they made about their own lives in the Pre-Reading section. Since making these maps, students have learned and thought deeply about moral growth. How might they revise their own memory maps to better reflect how their judgment about right and wrong has developed?

Respond to the Central Question

Throughout their study of *To Kill a Mockingbird*, students have been exploring and gathering evidence to support their thinking about a central question concerning the factors that influence our moral growth.

Before concluding your study of the novel, consider having students respond to the central question in a formal assignment or activity in order to demonstrate what they have learned. This might take the form of a structured class discussion, such as a Socratic Seminar, or an essay assignment. (See facinghistory.org/mockingbird/strategies for more information on this strategy.) You can use the following prompt to guide students' responses to the central question, regardless of the format you choose for the activity:

What factors influence our moral growth? What kinds of experiences help us learn how to judge the difference between right and wrong? Use evidence from To Kill a

Mockingbird *and the other resources you have explored while studying the book to support your thinking.*

Reflect on the Connection between Identity and Action

Students began their study of *To Kill a Mockingbird* by reflecting on the relationship between the individual and society and the complexity of identity. In this section, students used their analysis of characters from the novel to draw conclusions about the ways in which individuals develop in society as moral and ethical people. As students finish their study of the novel, it is important to ask them to reflect not only on how society impacts the individual but also on how the individual impacts society. To that end, we might ask how one can cultivate the identity of an upstander. What values, experiences, and skills are necessary?

Bryan Stevenson, a lawyer who founded the Equal Justice Initiative to bring about a fairer criminal justice system in the United States, reflects on this question in the presentation he made at a TED conference in 2012.* We recommend showing the video of his presentation, titled "We Need to Talk About an Injustice," which is available to stream at facinghistory.org/mockingbird/links. If the video is unavailable to you, an excerpt is provided in **Handout 7.3**. Regardless of how you share Stevenson's presentation with the class, follow it with a class discussion based on the Connection Questions that accompany **Handout 7.3**.

---

* The nonprofit organization TED (the name stands for "Technology, Entertainment, Design") sponsors conferences comprised of short talks by leaders and thinkers from a variety of disciplines.

Handout 7.1 Responses to *To Kill a Mockingbird*

1. From the *Washington Post*, July 3, 1960:

A hundred pounds of sermons on tolerance, or an equal measure of invective deploring the lack of it, will weigh far less in the scale of enlightenment than a mere 18 ounces of new fiction bearing the title *To Kill a Mockingbird*.

Harper Lee, the talented 34-year-old expatriate Southerner who makes her literary debut with this engrossing novel, carefully eschews preaching, from either side of the Mason-Dixon line, about the grave issues which confront her native South. What she does, more adroitly than any recent novelist, is present in dramatic terms just how it feels to be a Southerner, with all that it entails of pride, pleasure, anxiety and shame . . .

The result is an unusually accurate rendering of attitudes that must be reckoned with in any solution to the South's contemporary problems. And yet, though so pertinent, the novel is not itself contemporary. There were no sit-in strikes during the depression years when Jean Louise (alias Scout) Finch and her brother, Jem, began to observe the human landscape of Maycomb County, Ala. No protests at all—but the seeds for them were being planted.

Her street is the world to Scout, a restless and ingratiating 6 at the outset. This world is bounded by grouchy Mrs. Dubose on the north, by the haunted Radley house on the south, and in winter, by the school yard just around the corner. Within these narrow limits occur the important small dramas of childhood, which as interpreted by Atticus Finch, the children's admirable father, become lessons in fair play, courage, and love.

"You never really understand a person until you climb into his skin and walk around in it," is his patient, oft-repeated advice, which really sums up the purpose and achievement of this novel.[1]

2. From the *Atlantic Monthly*, August 1, 1960:

The book's setting is a small town in Alabama, and the action behind Scout's tale is her father's determination, as a lawyer, liberal, and honest man, to

---

1 Glendy Culligan, "Listen to That Mockingbird," *Washington Post*, July 3, 1960, E6.

defend a Negro accused of raping a white girl. What happens is, naturally, never seen directly by the narrator. The surface of the story is an Alcottish filigree of games, mischief, squabbles with an older brother, troubles at school, and the like. None of it is painful, for Scout and Jem are happy children, brought up with angelic cleverness by their father and his old Negro housekeeper. Nothing fazes them much or long. Even the new first-grade teacher, a devotee of the "Dewey decimal system" who is outraged to discover that Scout can already read and write, proves endurable in the long run.

A variety of adults, mostly eccentric in Scout's judgment, and a continual bubble of incident make *To Kill a Mockingbird* pleasant, undemanding reading.[2]

3. **From "On Reading *To Kill A Mockingbird* Fifty Years Later" by professor of English Angela Shaw-Thornburg:**

It is one thing to teach a novel that students might be resistant to reading, and quite another to teach a novel that I find *myself* deeply resistant to reading, much less teaching. Unfortunately for me (African American *and* an Americanist), I often find myself in this position when I am preparing to teach a novel or work that represents African Americans as peripheral, incapable of self-representation, monumentally passive, and positively grateful for the small compensation of white guilt over injustices done to African Americans. It is not that I naïvely expect the black citizens of 1935 Maycomb to endorse strategies that would not begin to gain traction in Alabama or other southern states for many decades after that. It is not that I expect Atticus Finch to suddenly acknowledge the degree to which he is complicit in the racism that undergirds the legal system in Alabama. That is not the root of my resistance at all.

What gets me are those moments of struggle or, even worse, dreadful silence when we read *Huckleberry Finn* or even a novel like *To Kill a Mockingbird*, which was certainly seen as progressive in its day, when students who are people of color try to figure out why they feel unvoiced by the literature they are reading, or ask why we are reading *this* stuff . . . .

When I begin my course prep for *To Kill a Mockingbird* by reading the novel, I finish up with a profound sense of alienation, a sense of bewilderment that Lee decentered the story of Tom Robinson so utterly. Because of that aftertaste, I only read such works because I am expected to teach them . . . .[3]

---

2   Phoebe Lou Adams, "*To Kill a Mockingbird*, by Harper Lee" (review), *Atlantic Monthly*, August 1960, available at http://www.theatlantic.com/magazine/archive/1960/08/to-kill-a-mockingbird-by-harper-lee/306456/.

3   Angela Shaw-Thornburg, "On Reading *To Kill a Mockingbird*: Fifty Years Later," in *Harper Lee's* To Kill a Mockingbird: *New Essays*, ed. Michael J. Meyer (Lanham, UK: Scarecrow Press, 2010), 114–115.

4. From Attorney General Eric Holder's speech commemorating the 50th anniversary of *To Kill a Mockingbird*:

This story—of Scout's painful education, of Tom Robinson's shameful trial, of Boo Radley's unexpected heroism, and of the prejudices, passions and values that can split apart communities—became our story. It became America's story. With the new issues and fears that now confront us, it remains our story. And it remains an essential teaching tool for students and educators, for advocates and policymakers, for law enforcement officers and judges, for the American people and—of course—for the countless attorneys whose professional paths were first inspired by a small-town Alabama lawyer named Atticus Finch.

So many of us will never forget the goose bumps we felt when Atticus decided to represent Tom; or the image of him—in a chair outside Tom's jail cell—keeping watch against the mob he's sure will soon come clamoring for blood, and keeping faith with his belief that every person—regardless of race or creed or the crime he committed—deserves what Atticus called a "square deal . . . in a courtroom."

For the last five decades, *To Kill a Mockingbird* has reminded us that, in the work of ensuring justice, one person can make a difference. Individual actions count. And those who are willing to stand up for a principle, to take even one step toward progress, or, simply, to take a seat—be it outside a jailhouse, in a courthouse or a classroom, at a lunch counter or the front of a bus—can help to change the world.[4]

---

4   Eric Holder, "Remarks as Prepared for Delivery by Attorney General Eric Holder at the University of Alabama: *To Kill a Mockingbird* Anniversary Event," speech presented at University of Alabama, September 21, 2010, available at http://www. mainjustice.com/2010/09/21/holder-echoes-atticus-finch-at-to-kill-a-mockingbird-commemoration/.

Handout 7.2 Kohlberg's Stages of Moral Development

LEVEL ONE: We make decisions based on how the consequences will affect us personally.

STAGE 1: We obey authority figures in order to avoid punishment.

STAGE 2: We trade or cooperate with others in order to get what we want or need. "You scratch my back, and I'll scratch yours."

LEVEL TWO: We strive to meet the expectations of our peers, families, and/or nation.

STAGE 3: We are "good" by doing what is approved by others. Approval can come from individuals or the expectations of peers, groups, or society. Meaning well counts, even if the outcome isn't what we intended.

STAGE 4: We are "good" by following the law and obeying authority. We do our duty and avoid challenging the social order.

LEVEL THREE: We strive to live up to "higher" laws of morality and ethics even when they conflict with the law, authority, and social order.

STAGE 5: We look beyond laws and decisions by authority members to the rights and principles that our society is based on (i.e., "All men are created equal" is a principle we might try to live by even if it is contradicted by a particular set of laws or customs).

STAGE 6: We strive to live according to our own consciences and universal principles of justice and human dignity.[1]

---

1 Lawrence Kohlberg, "The Development of Children's Orientations Toward a Moral Order: Sequence in the Development of Moral Thought," *Vita Humana* 6 (1963), 11–33.

Handout 7.3 "We Need to Talk About an Injustice"

In 2012, Bryan Stevenson, a lawyer who founded the Equal Justice Initiative to seek fairness in the criminal justice system, spoke about identity and action at a TED conference. TED is a nonprofit organization that sponsors conferences comprised of short talks by leaders and thinkers from a variety of disciplines. Explaining why he thinks identity is important, Stevenson said: "If you're a teacher your words can be meaningful, but if you're a compassionate teacher, they can be especially meaningful. If you're a doctor you can do some good things, but if you're a caring doctor you can do some other things. And so I want to talk about the power of identity." The following is excerpted from his speech:

I grew up in a house that was the traditional African American home that was dominated by a matriarch, and that matriarch was my grandmother. She was tough, she was strong, she was powerful. She was the end of every argument in our family. She was the beginning of a lot of arguments in our family. She was the daughter of people who were actually enslaved. Her parents were born in slavery in Virginia in the 1840s. She was born in the 1880s and the experience of slavery very much shaped the way she saw the world.

And my grandmother was tough, but she was also loving. When I would see her as a little boy, she'd come up to me and she'd give me these hugs. And she'd squeeze me so tight I could barely breathe and then she'd let me go. And an hour or two later, if I saw her, she'd come over to me and she'd say, "Bryan, do you still feel me hugging you?" And if I said, "No," she'd assault me again, and if I said, "Yes," she'd leave me alone. And she just had this quality that you always wanted to be near her. And the only challenge was that she had 10 children. My mom was the youngest of her 10 kids. And sometimes when I would go and spend time with her, it would be difficult to get her time and attention. My cousins would be running around everywhere.

And I remember, when I was about eight or nine years old, waking up one morning, going into the living room, and all of my cousins were running around. And my grandmother was sitting across the room staring at me. And at first I thought we were playing a game. And I would look at her and I'd smile, but she was very serious. And after about 15 or 20 minutes of this, she got up and she came across the room and she took me by the hand and she said, "Come on, Bryan. You and I are going to have a talk." And I remember this just like it happened yesterday. I never will forget it.

She took me out back and she said, "Bryan, I'm going to tell you something, but you don't tell anybody what I tell you." I said, "Okay, Mama." She said, "Now you make sure you don't do that." I said, "Sure." Then she sat me down and she looked at me and she said, "I want you to know I've been watching you." And she said, "I think you're special." She said, "I think you can do anything you want to do." I will never forget it.

And then she said, "I just need you to promise me three things, Bryan." I said, "Okay, Mama." She said, "The first thing I want you to promise me is that you'll always love your mom." She said, "That's my baby girl, and you have to promise me now you'll always take care of her." Well I adored my mom, so I said, "Yes, Mama. I'll do that." Then she said, "The second thing I want you to promise me is that you'll always do the right thing even when the right thing is the hard thing." And I thought about it and I said, "Yes, Mama. I'll do that." Then finally she said, "The third thing I want you to promise me is that you'll never drink alcohol." (Laughter.) Well I was nine years old, so I said, "Yes, Mama. I'll do that."

. . . And I'm going to admit something to you . . . I'm 52 years old, and I'm going to admit to you that I've never had a drop of alcohol. (Applause.) I don't say that because I think that's virtuous; I say that because there is power in identity. When we create the right kind of identity, we can say things to the world around us that they don't actually believe makes sense. We can get them to do things that they don't think they can do. When I thought about my grandmother, of course she would think all her grandkids were special. My grandfather was in prison during prohibition. My male uncles died of alcohol-related diseases. And these were the things she thought we needed to commit to.

. . . And it's interesting, when I teach my students about African American history, I tell them about slavery. I tell them about terrorism, the era that began at the end of Reconstruction that went on to World War II. We don't really know very much about it. But for African Americans in this country, that was an era defined by terror. In many communities, people had to worry about being lynched. They had to worry about being bombed. It was the threat of terror that shaped their lives. And these older people come up to me now and they say, "Mr. Stevenson, you give talks, you make speeches, you tell people to stop saying we're dealing with terrorism for the first time in our nation's history after 9/11." They tell me to say, "No, tell them that we grew up with that." And that era of terrorism, of course, was followed by segregation and decades of racial subordination . . . .

And yet, we have in this country this dynamic where we really don't like to talk about our problems. We don't like to talk about our history. And because of that, we really haven't understood what it's meant to do the things we've done historically. We're constantly running into each other. We're constantly creating tensions and conflicts. We have a hard time talking about race, and I believe it's because we are unwilling to commit ourselves to a process of truth and reconciliation. In South Africa, people understood that we couldn't overcome apartheid without a commitment to truth and reconciliation . . . .

. . . Well I believe that our identity is at risk. That when we actually don't care about these difficult things, the positive and wonderful things are nonetheless implicated. We love innovation. We love technology. We love creativity. We love entertainment. But ultimately, those realities are shadowed by suffering, abuse, degradation, marginalization. And for me, it becomes necessary to integrate the two. Because ultimately we are talking about a need to be more hopeful, more committed, more dedicated to the basic challenges of living in a complex world. And for me that means spending time thinking and talking about the poor, the disadvantaged . . . . But thinking about them in a way that is integrated in our own lives.

You know ultimately, we all have to believe things we haven't seen. We do. As rational as we are, as committed to intellect as we are. Innovation, creativity, development comes not from the ideas in our mind alone. They come from the ideas in our mind that are also fueled by some conviction in our heart. And it's that mind-heart connection that I believe compels us to not just be attentive to all the bright and dazzly things, but also the dark and difficult things. Vaclav Havel, the great Czech leader, talked about this. He said, "When we were in Eastern Europe and dealing with oppression, we wanted all kinds of things, but mostly what we needed was hope, an orientation of the spirit, a willingness to sometimes be in hopeless places and be a witness."

Well that orientation of the spirit is very much at the core of what I believe even TED communities have to be engaged in. There is no disconnect around technology and design that will allow us to be fully human until we pay attention to suffering, to poverty, to exclusion, to unfairness, to injustice. Now I will warn you that this kind of identity is a much more challenging identity than ones that don't pay attention to this. It will get to you.

I had the great privilege, when I was a young lawyer, of meeting Rosa Parks. And Ms. Parks used to come back to Montgomery every now and then, and she would get together with two of her dearest friends, these older women, Johnnie Carr who was the organizer of the Montgomery bus boycott—amazing African American woman—and Virginia Durr, a white woman, whose husband, Clifford Durr, represented Dr. King. And these women would get together and just talk.

And every now and then Ms. Carr would call me, and she'd say, "Bryan, Ms. Parks is coming to town. We're going to get together and talk. Do you want to come over and listen?" And I'd say, "Yes, ma'am, I do." And she'd say, "Well what are you going to do when you get here?" I said, "I'm going to listen." And I'd go over there and I would, I would just listen. It would be so energizing and so empowering.

And one time I was over there listening to these women talk, and after a couple of hours Ms. Parks turned to me and she said, "Now Bryan, tell me what the Equal Justice Initiative is. Tell me what you're trying to do." And I began giving her my rap. I said, "Well we're trying to challenge injustice. We're trying to help people who have been wrongly convicted. We're trying to confront bias and discrimination in the administration of criminal justice. We're trying to end life without parole sentences for children. We're trying to do something about the death penalty. We're trying to reduce the prison population. We're trying to end mass incarceration."

I gave her my whole rap, and when I finished she looked at me and she said, "Mmm mmm mmm." She said, "That's going to make you tired, tired, tired." (Laughter.) And that's when Ms. Carr leaned forward, she put her finger in my face, she said, "That's why you've got to be brave, brave, brave."

. . . We need to find ways to embrace these challenges, these problems, the suffering. Because ultimately, our humanity depends on everyone's humanity. I've learned very simple things doing the work that I do. It's just taught me very simple things. I've come to understand and to believe that each of us is more than the worst thing we've ever done. I believe that for every person on the planet. I think if somebody tells a lie, they're not just a liar. I think if somebody takes something that doesn't belong to them, they're not just a thief. I think even if you kill someone, you're not just a killer. And because of that there's this basic human dignity that must be respected by law. I also believe that in many parts of this country, and certainly in many parts of this globe, that the opposite of poverty is not wealth. I don't believe that. I actually think, in too many places, the opposite of poverty is justice.

And finally, I believe that, despite the fact that it is so dramatic and so beautiful and so inspiring and so stimulating, we will ultimately not be judged by our technology, we won't be judged by our design, we won't be judged by our intellect and reason. Ultimately, you judge the character of a society, not by how they treat their rich and the powerful and the privileged, but by how they treat the poor, the condemned, the incarcerated. Because it's in that nexus that we actually begin to understand truly profound things about who we are.[1]

1 Bryan Stevenson, "We Need to Talk About an Injustice," speech presented at TED conference, March 2012, TED.com, accessed May 28, 2014, https://www.ted.com/talks/bryan_stevenson_we_need_to_talk_about_an_injustice/transcript.

Connection Questions

1. What themes from *To Kill a Mockingbird* are echoed in Bryan Stevenson's speech? What themes are echoed in his work?

2. What was Stevenson's grandmother's legacy to him? How does his work build on her legacy? What values did he learn from her that he continues to display in his adult life?

3. What legacies, from your family, your community, or from literature and history, would you like to build on? What values are you willing to commit to?

4. What does Stevenson suggest American society values most? What does he think American society should value more? What does he think the universe of obligation of the United States should look like? What does he think it actually looks like?

5. According to Stevenson, how do we sometimes misunderstand each other's identities? How do we confuse one's behavior with his or her entire identity? What parts of other people's stories do we sometimes ignore?

6. According to Stevenson, whose stories are neglected in the identity of the United States? What does he think might happen if more Americans knew those stories?

7. How do you measure social change? What evidence would you look for? How is social change similar to an individual's moral growth? How is it different? Are the two linked?

Appendix

Fostering a Reflective Classroom

We believe that a Facing History and Ourselves classroom is in many ways a microcosm of democracy—a place where explicit rules and implicit norms protect everyone's right to speak; where different perspectives can be heard and valued; where members take responsibility for themselves, each other, and the group as a whole; and where each member has a stake and a voice in collective decisions. You may have already established rules and guidelines with your students to help bring about these characteristics in your classroom. If not, it is essential at the beginning of your Facing History course of study to facilitate the beginning of a supportive, reflective classroom community. Once established, both you and your students will need to continue to nurture the reflective community on an ongoing basis through the ways that you participate and respond to each other.

We believe that a reflective, supportive classroom community is fostered by:

- Creating a sense of trust and openness

- Encouraging participants to speak and listen to each other

- Making space and time for silent reflection

- Offering multiple avenues for participation and learning

- Helping students appreciate the points of view, talents, and contributions of less vocal members

Creating Classroom Contracts

One way to help classroom communities establish shared norms is by discussing them openly through a process called "contracting." Some teachers already customarily create classroom contracts with their students at the start of each course. If you do not typically do so, we recommend that before beginning your class's journey through this Facing History unit, you engage the students in the process of creating one. Contracts typically include several clearly defined rules or expectations for participation and consequences for those who do not fulfill their obligations as members of the learning community. Any contract created collaboratively by students and the teacher together should be consistent with the classroom rules already established by the teacher. Many Facing History teachers differentiate their own classroom rules, which are non-negotiable, from the guidelines set forth in the classroom contract, which are negotiated by the students with the teacher's guidance. Some sample guidelines that might be included in a class contract are provided below.

We have also found that the classroom environment is enhanced by emphasizing journal writing and employing multiple formats for facilitating large and small group discussions. Throughout this unit, we suggest specific teaching strategies designed to develop students' critical thinking and encourage each of them to share their ideas. Detailed descriptions and additional examples of these strategies can be found at facinghistory.org/mockingbird/strategies.

We encourage you to frequently remind your students that, regardless of the classroom strategy you are using or the topic you are addressing, it is essential that their participation honors the contract they helped create and follows your own classroom rules. In addition, we strongly recommend that you post the contract in a prominent location in your classroom and that when students stray from the guidelines set forth in the contract, you refer to the specific language in the contract when you redirect them. You might find that when one student strays from the guidelines of the contract, other students will respond by citing the specific expectations listed in the contract.

Consider the following list of guidelines for your classroom contract. As you work together to create your own, we encourage you to include (or modify) any or all of the items on this list:

- Listen with respect. Try to understand what someone is saying before rushing to judgment.

- Make comments using "I" statements. ("I disagree with what you said. Here's what I think . . .")

- If you do not feel safe making a comment or asking a question, write the thought down. You can ask the teacher after class to help you find a safe way to share the idea.

- If someone says an idea or question that helps your own learning, say "thank you."

- If someone says something that hurts or offends you, do not attack the person. Acknowledge that the comment—not the person—hurt your feelings and explain why.

- Put-downs are never okay.

- If you don't understand something, ask a question.

- Think with your head and your heart.

- Share talking time—provide room for others to speak.

- Do not interrupt others while they are speaking.

- Write down thoughts, in a journal or notebook, if you don't have time to say them during our time together.

Journals in a Facing History Classroom

Facing History and Ourselves is committed to helping students develop their ability to critically examine their surroundings from multiple perspectives and to make informed judgments about what they see and hear. Keeping a journal is one tool that Facing History has found to be instrumental in helping students develop these skills. A journal might be defined as any place where thoughts are recorded and stored. Loose-leaf and bound notebooks both make excellent journals. Many students find that writing or drawing in a journal helps them process ideas, formulate questions, and retain information. Journals make learning visible by providing a safe, accessible space for students to share thoughts, feelings, and uncertainties. In this way, journals are also an assessment tool—something teachers can review to better understand what their students know, what they are struggling to understand, and how their thinking has changed over time. In addition to strengthening students' critical thinking skills, journal writing serves other purposes. Journals help nurture classroom community. Through reading and commenting on journals, teachers build relationships with students. Frequent journal writing also helps students become more fluent in expressing their ideas in writing or speaking.

Students use their journals in different ways. Some students may record ideas throughout class, while others may use it only when there is a particular teacher-driven assignment. Some students need prompts to support their writing, while other students feel more comfortable expressing their ideas without any external structure. Just as students vary in how they use their journals, teachers also vary in their approach to journal writing. While there are many effective ways to use a journal as a learning tool in the classroom, below are six questions, based on decades of experience working with teachers and students, that we suggest you consider:

1. **What is the teacher's relationship with students' journals?** Students are entitled to know how you plan on reading their journals. Will you read everything they write? If they want to keep something private, is this possible? If so, how do students indicate that they do not want you to read something? Will their journals be graded? If so, by what criteria? (See more on grading journals below.) For teachers at most schools, it can be impossible to read everything students write in their journals; there is just not enough time in the day. For this reason, some teachers decide to collect students' journals once a week and only read a page or two—sometimes a page the student selects and sometimes a page selected by the teacher. Other teachers may never collect students'

journals but might glance at them during class time or might ask students to incorporate quotations and ideas from their journals into collected assignments. You can set limits on the degree to which you have access to students' journals. Many teachers establish a rule that if students wish to keep information in their journals private, they should fold the page over or remove the page entirely.

2. **What is appropriate content for journals?** It is easy for students to confuse a class journal with a diary (or blog) because both of these formats allow for open-ended writing. Teachers should clarify how the audience and purpose for this writing is distinct from the audience and purpose for writing in a personal diary. In most classrooms, the audience for journal writing is the author, the teacher, and, at times, peers. Facing History believes that the purpose of journal writing is to provide a space where students can connect their personal experiences and opinions to the concepts and events they are studying in the classroom. Therefore, some material that is appropriate to include in their personal diaries may not be appropriate to include in their class journals. To avoid uncomfortable situations, many teachers find it helpful to clarify topics that are not suitable material for journal entries. Also, as mandatory reporters in most school districts, teachers should explain that they are required to take certain steps, such as informing a school official, if students reveal information about possible harm to themselves or another student. Students should be made aware of these rules as well as other guidelines you might have about appropriate journal writing content.

3. **How will journals be evaluated?** Many students admit that they are less likely to share their true thoughts or express questions when they are worried about a grade based on getting the "right" answer or using proper grammar or spelling. Therefore, we suggest that if you choose to grade students' journals, which many teachers decide to do, you base these grades on criteria such as effort, thoughtfulness, completion, creativity, curiosity, and making connections between the past and the present. Moreover, there are many ways to provide students with feedback on their journals besides traditional grading, such as by writing comments or asking questions. Students can even evaluate their own journals for evidence of intellectual and moral growth. For example, you might have students look through their journals to find evidence of their ability to ask questions or to make connections between what was happening during Reconstruction and an event from their own lives.

4. **What forms of expression can be included in a journal?** Students learn and communicate best in different ways. The journal is an appropriate space to respect different learning styles. Some students may wish to draw their ideas rather than record thoughts in words. Other students may feel most comfortable responding in concept webs and lists instead of prose. When you introduce the journal to students, you might brainstorm different ways that they might express their thoughts.

5. **How can journals be used to help students build vocabulary?** Throughout this unit, students will be encountering new vocabulary while they develop a more sophisticated understanding of concepts that might already be familiar to them. From the earliest days of Facing History, the journal was used as a place to help students build their vocabulary through construction of *working definitions*, a phrase that implies that our understanding of concepts evolves as we are confronted with new information and experiences. Students' definitions of words such as *identity* or *freedom* should be richer at the end of the unit than they are on day one. We suggest you use perhaps a special section of the journal as a space where students can record, review, and refine their definitions of important terms referred to in this unit.

6. **How should journal content be publicly shared?** Most Facing History teachers have found that students are best able to express themselves when they believe that their journal is a private space. Therefore, we suggest that information in students' journals never be publicly shared without the consent of the writer. At the same time, we encourage you to provide multiple opportunities for students to voluntarily share ideas and questions they have recorded in their journals. Some students may feel more comfortable reading directly from their journals than speaking "off the cuff" in class discussions.

Once you settle on the norms and expectations for journal writing in your class, there are many possible ways that you can have students record ideas in their journals. Here are some examples:

Teacher-selected prompts: One of the most common ways that teachers use journals is by asking students to respond to a particular prompt. This writing often prepares students to participate in a class activity, helps students make connections between the themes of a lesson and their own lives, or provides an opportunity for students to make meaning of ideas in a reading or film.

Dual-entry format: Students draw a line down the center of the journal page or fold the page in half. They write the factual notes ("What the text says" or "What the historians say") on one side and on the other side their feelings about the notes ("Reactions").

"Lifted line" responses: One way to have students respond to what they have read is to ask them to "lift a line"—select a particular quotation that strikes them—and then answer questions such as, "What is interesting about this quotation? What ideas does it make you think about? What questions does this line raise for you?"

Brainstorming: The journal is an appropriate place for students to freely list ideas related to a specific word or question. To activate prior knowledge before students learn new material, you might ask students to brainstorm everything they know about a concept or an event. As a strategy for reviewing material, you might ask students to brainstorm ideas they remember about a topic. Moreover, as a pre-writing exercise, students can brainstorm ways of responding to an essay prompt.

Freewriting: Freewriting is open, no-format writing. Freewriting can be an especially effective strategy when you want to help students process particularly sensitive or provocative material. Some students respond extremely well to freewriting, while other students benefit from more structure, even if that means a loosely framed prompt such as, "What are you thinking about after watching/reading/hearing this material? What does this text remind you of?"

Creative writing: Many students enjoy writing poems or short stories that incorporate the themes addressed in a particular lesson. To stimulate their work, some students benefit from ideas that structure their writing, such as a specific poem format or an opening line for a story (for example, "I could not believe my eyes when my friend came running down the street, yelling . . . ").

Drawings, charts, and webs: Students do not have to express their ideas in words. At appropriate times, encourage students to draw their feelings or thoughts. They can also use symbols, concept maps, Venn diagrams, and other charts to record information.

Note-taking: To help students retain new information, they can record notes in their journals. Notes could be taken in various formats, such as lists, concept maps, or graphic organizers.

Vocabulary: Students can use their journals as a place to keep their working definitions of terms, noting how those definitions change as they go deeper into the resources. The back section of their journals could be used as a glossary—the place where students record definitions and where they can turn to review and revise their definitions as these terms come up throughout the unit.

Close Reading for Deep Comprehension

One way to help students of all abilities enhance their comprehension of *To Kill a Mockingbird* and engage deeply in the complex themes at its core is through the practice of close reading. As the term is used in the Common Core State Standards, close reading is carefully and purposefully *rereading* a text to deepen comprehension. During this encounter with the text, students focus exclusively on the words, structure, tone, and other elements in order to reach a deeper understanding of its meaning.

One way this guide facilitates students' deeper exploration of the novel is through the Connection Questions provided for each chapter. Many of these questions require students to return to the text to find evidence for their answers. Instead of asking students to simply retrieve answers from the book, most of these questions also prompt students to use the details they find in the text to make inferences about the meaning and implications of what they have read. Students are then prompted to make connections with important themes in the novel.

In addition to these chapter-based questions, this guide also identifies key passages from the book (and in two instances, passages that connect to supplementary informational text) that are worthy of additional consideration via close reading.

Close reading is the methodical investigation of a complex text through answering text-dependent questions geared toward unpacking the text's meaning. Close reading directs students to examine and analyze the text through a series of questions that focus on the meanings of individual words and sentences as well as the overall development of events and ideas. It calls on students to extract evidence from the text as well as draw meaningful inferences that logically follow from what they have read.

This sort of careful attention to how the text unfolds allows students to assemble an overarching picture of the text as a whole as well as to grasp the fine details on which that understanding rests. It prepares students for the kinds of detailed reading tasks they will encounter in college and careers. It motivates students by rewarding them for reading inquisitively and discovering the meaning and insight within the text that makes it worthy of attention. This process also helps students sharpen their analysis and deepen their reflection on the themes of justice and moral growth explored in *To Kill a Mockingbird* and throughout this guide.

To facilitate this process, this section includes a set of text-dependent questions for each key passage we have highlighted for close reading. Two different versions of each set of questions are included: a teacher guide and a student handout. While the teacher guide for each set of questions suggests specific answers to help guide the discussion, students might respond to many of the questions with a variety of possible correct answers.

These questions and their suggested answers were created by Dr. David Pook, chair of the history department at the Derryfield School and an educational consultant. Pook was a contributing writer for the Common Core State Standards for English Language Arts, and he consults with several organizations, districts, and schools on work aligned with those standards.

Guidelines for Close Reading Activities

For the close reading activities developed for this guide, the passages were chosen because they represent pivotal scenes in the development of the themes of growth, caring, justice, and democracy that emerge from the book. These passages, along with additional materials to guide close reading of them, are highlighted in the sections of this guide in which they appear.

The following steps can be used to facilitate the close reading of the highlighted passages from the novel. Adapt this procedure to best meet your goals and the needs of your students while keeping the focus on the text itself.

FIRST READ: Read aloud. Either the teacher or an extremely fluent student can read the text aloud. Ask students to circle unfamiliar words as they listen. After the read-aloud, as students share these words with the class, decide which words to define immediately to limit confusion and which definitions you want students to uncover through careful reading.

SECOND READ: Individual read. Ask students to read the passage silently to get a feel for the text. They can note specific words or phrases that jump out at them for any number of reasons: because they are interesting, familiar, strange, confusing, funny, troubling, difficult, and so on. Share some of these as a class.

THIRD READ: Text-dependent questions. Through discussions facilitated by the teacher (or through small groups), have students answer a set of sequenced text-dependent questions provided specifically for the close reading. Teachers can ask the questions (and logical follow-up questions depending on the answers students give) to lead the class in a close reading of the text. Alternatively, teachers can ask groups to answer the questions themselves while circulating around the room helping individual groups as they pursue a deeper understanding of the passage in question.

Transition to Facing History themes and discussion. We recommend concluding a close reading by organizing a class discussion so that students can make connections beyond the text, especially to this guide's central question: *What factors influence our moral growth? What kinds of experiences help us learn how to judge right from wrong?*

This discussion can be informal or can use the format of the Socratic Seminar or Final Word teaching strategy (see facinghistory.org/mockingbird/strategies for more details).

Close Reading A for Chapter 3 | Teacher Guide

Questions and suggested answers created by David Pook.

PASSAGE BEGINS: "After supper, Atticus sat down with the paper. . . ."

PASSAGE ENDS: "So to school you must go."

1. Why does Scout go to the front porch?

As she says, she "was weary from the day's crimes" and felt that they were more than she "could bear." Implicitly, it is to draw Atticus to her and convey the seriousness with which she makes her otherwise unwittingly humorous request to withdraw from school.

For most of the following questions, teachers ought to consider asking a follow-up question that asks students to explain how the differences between Scout and Atticus reveal how these two characters see the world. *Brief answers to those questions will follow the explanation for the initial question and appear in italics.*

2. What news does Scout deliver on the porch? How does Atticus initially react? How do their reactions to the news differ?

Scout says she doesn't feel well, and then she connects that feeling to never wanting to go to school again. Instead of immediately responding, Atticus thoughtfully waits for Scout to reveal more information. *This reveals an underlying difference between Scout's impatience compared to the "endurance" of Atticus.*

3. What reasons does Scout initially give for why she doesn't need to go to school? Is Atticus convinced by them?

Scout points out that despite not going to school himself, Atticus does just fine, so she'll stay home and let him teach her. Atticus is unpersuaded, and he notes that he has a job and he'd be breaking the law if he kept her home. Unconvinced that illness is the source of her unease with school, he suggests she take some medicine to cure her of her aforementioned illness so she can return to school.

His reaction shows how he thinks in terms of rules and responsibilities instead of Scout's vague generalities. It's also revealing that Atticus doesn't settle for Scout's explanation but gently probes to see if the initial explanation is in fact the true one.

4. Scout eventually tells Atticus what happened at school, and Atticus takes a patient stroll before responding. What is his advice to Scout, and how does he apply that advice to the situation Scout found herself in at school?

His advice is that "You never really understand a person until you consider things from his point of view," and he applies that to Miss Caroline to show Scout that her teacher's missteps during the day were an "honest mistake" and that she should not be held responsible for not grasping all of Maycomb's ways "in one day." Atticus's observations show how he takes the long view of things and also demonstrate how an understanding adult would be forgiving of Miss Caroline's errors.

5. How does Scout's reaction show that she disagrees with Atticus?

Her exclamation, "I'll be dogged" shows that she flat-out disagrees with Atticus, and Scout follows up her remark by (unconsciously) switching tactics and refocusing her resolve not to go to school on the fact that Burris Ewell only "goes to school the first day." This reaction also illustrates Scout's childlike stubbornness in her unwillingness to accept Atticus's reasoned and deeply ethical reply about the proverbial walking of a mile in another's shoes.

6. Why does Atticus interrupt her response this time? What does his response tell the reader about his view of the law and of rules generally?

He somewhat forcefully says that Scout cannot bring the law in on her side in this instance, and he elaborates on his point by saying that Scout is not like Burris Ewell, and in some instances it's acceptable to "bend the law a little." Atticus's reply shows a sophisticated view of rules, revealing that there are shades of gray when "special cases" arise instead of the black and white certainties that Scout wants to operate within.

Close Reading A for Chapter 3 | Student Handout

Questions created by David Pook.

PASSAGE BEGINS: "After supper, Atticus sat down with the paper. . . ."

PASSAGE ENDS: "So to school you must go."

1. Why does Scout go to the front porch?

2. What news does Scout deliver on the porch? How does Atticus initially react? How do their reactions to the news differ?

3. What reasons does Scout initially give for why she doesn't need to go to school? Is Atticus convinced by them?

4. Scout eventually tells Atticus what happened at school, and Atticus takes a patient stroll before responding. What is his advice to Scout, and how does he apply that advice to the situation Scout found herself in at school?

5. How does Scout's reaction show that she disagrees with Atticus?

6. Why does Atticus interrupt her response this time? What does his response tell the reader about his view of the law and of rules generally?

Close Reading B for Chapter 9 | Teacher Guide

Questions and suggested answers created by David Pook.

PASSAGE BEGINS: "Well, if you don't want me to grow up talkin' that way. . . ."

PASSAGE ENDS: "Simply because we were licked a hundred years before we started is no reason for us not to try to win," Atticus said.

1. **Scout's "campaign" to quit going to school has not relented, but in this scene she brings up a new concern. What is that worry?**

Scout has heard in school the accusation that her father defends "negroes"—couched in derogatory terms—and this was said in a tone that made Atticus's actions sound like the moral equivalent of brewing illegal moonshine.

2. **What explanation does Atticus initially give for defending Tom Robinson? What elaboration of his reasons does he offer in response to Scout's question about why he's defending him if others think he shouldn't?**

The sigh Atticus offers up initially—and his bald statement that he is "simply" defending him—signals both his disappointment and his patience with those who would say that he should not defend Tom Robinson. He goes on to defend Tom's character by way of Calpurnia's recommendation. Scout presses him further, and Atticus states his reasons, which all reflect the fact that his strong sense of personal integrity compels him to defend a black man.

3. **Scout is intrigued by the reasons Atticus gives for defending Tom, especially the final one: "I couldn't even tell you or Jem not to do something again." What can be inferred about why Atticus would say such a thing?**

The reply he offers in response to her question—"Because I could never ask you to mind me again"—offers subtle clues as to why he cannot refuse to take the case. The emphasis in that statement is on the notion of minding *him*, leading one to infer that if he were not to defend Tom, he would no longer have any moral authority to command others to follow his instructions.

4. What does Atticus say in response to her question asking for elaboration of that point, and how does his answer show what it means to have integrity?

Atticus says that this particular case is one that "affects him personally" and that his reasons for taking it go beyond the prospect of winning or losing. Indeed, he is convinced that he will lose the case, but in his eyes that is "no reason for us not to try to win." Instead, he instructs Scout that regardless of what she hears at school, she should "hold her head high and keep those fists down"— signaling that acting with integrity is about following one's own moral compass with quiet conviction, regardless of whether it leads to a favorable or unfavorable outcome.

Close Reading **B** for Chapter 9 | Student Handout

Questions created by David Pook.

PASSAGE BEGINS: "Well, if you don't want me to grow up talkin' that way. . . ."

PASSAGE ENDS: "Simply because we were licked a hundred years before we started is no reason for us not to try to win," Atticus said.

1. Scout's "campaign" to quit going to school has not relented, but in this scene she brings up a new concern. What is that worry?

2. What explanation does Atticus initially give for defending Tom Robinson? What elaboration of his reasons does he offer in response to Scout's question about why he's defending him if others think he shouldn't?

3. Scout is intrigued by the reasons Atticus gives for defending Tom, especially the final one: "I couldn't even tell you or Jem not to do something again." What can be inferred about why Atticus would say such a thing?

4. What does Atticus say in response to her question asking for elaboration of that point, and how does his answer show what it means to have integrity?

Close Reading Pairing: Virginia Durr and Scout | Teacher Guide

Questions and suggested answers created by David Pook.

Note: We have chosen to include certain racial epithets in this reading in order to honestly communicate the bigoted language of the time. We recommend that teachers review the section "Discussing Sensitive Topics in the Classroom" before using this document.

Paired Texts:

"The Birthday Party" by Virginia Durr (Handout 3.4)

To Kill a Mockingbird, Chapter 9

PASSAGE BEGINS: Beginning of Chapter 9

PASSAGE ENDS: "Simply because we were licked a hundred years before we started is no reason for us not to try to win," Atticus said.

Scout in Chapter 9 and Virginia Durr in her memoir excerpt "The Birthday Party" are both thrown into situations that reveal social tensions around race and prompt a recognition of and reaction to these tensions. The questions that follow explore these issues.

1. **What incident sparks Scout's questions regarding whom Atticus chooses to defend as a lawyer? What do her questions reveal about her understanding of the situation?**

   After hearing what Cecil Jacobs tells everyone at school—that Scout's father "defends niggers"—Scout asks Atticus if what Cecil said was true and then follows up by asking if all lawyers do. Her inquiry into Atticus's defense of Tom Robinson shows that she is trying to understand whether what Atticus is doing is right or wrong, signaling that she does not fully understand why defending a black man would cause such problems.

2. **What event does Virginia describe as "the great trauma of [her] early life"? How does this event highlight racial tensions, and what does her reaction indicate about her understanding of her family's decision?**

For Virginia, the planning of her seventh birthday party is troubled when her family tells her that she cannot have black children at the party as she had in the past. She reacts by having a temper tantrum, and as a result her family compromises and allows her to have two parties—one for the black children and one for the whites. Her reaction shows that, like Scout, she does not understand how others might react to the idea of whites and blacks together.

3. **In these excerpts, both Scout and Virginia are provoked by other children's racially charged words. How do Scout and Virginia's reactions differ?**

After hearing Cecil Jacobs in the schoolyard, Scout waits before confronting him, asking questions of Atticus to better understand the situation. On the other hand, Virginia immediately tells Elizabeth to "go to hell" after she is rude to Sarah, the daughter of Nursie and a friend with whom Virginia grew up.

4. **Both not only react in different ways but react in defense of different people. Who is Scout prepared to defend, and who does Virginia defend?**

Scout is prepared to fight Cecil in defense of Atticus, but she ultimately decides not to because she doesn't want to "let Atticus down."
In Virginia's case, she stands up for someone who is black and does not weigh the consequences of her actions.

5. Language and word choice play a role in both Scout and Virginia's coming-of-age experiences and early understandings of the unequal racial customs in the South. How does Atticus respond to Scout's use of the word "nigger"? How does Josephine, Virginia's sister, respond to Aunt May's order that the black children must start calling her "Miss Josephine" instead of "Sis"? How does each response signal recognition of racial tensions without fully addressing them?

In the excerpt from *To Kill a Mockingbird*, Atticus asks Scout not to use the derogatory word that she copied from Cecil Jacobs; however, his only explanation of his request is that the word is "common" rather than a further reason for why Scout should not use it. In the connecting text, Josephine tells the black children that they can call her "Miss Sis" instead of "Miss Josephine." Much like Atticus's response of simply telling Scout not to use the word "nigger," Josephine's "solution" does not address why Aunt May's request might be hurtful and instead just offers a response that placates both her aunt and the black children.

6. How do the reactions of the adults in each text (Atticus and Aunt May) differ in response to the racial tensions that surface? What explanation can you give for their different reactions?

Atticus and Aunt May react in different ways when confronted with racial tensions. Atticus tries to defuse the immediate situation with Cecil Jacobs while recognizing that his actions will cause friction among friends and in Maycomb. Aunt May creates the initial tension in her response to the black children calling Josephine "Sis" and exacerbates matters further with her support of segregating Virginia's birthday party—culminating in her postmortem over supper of the underlying cause of Virginia's supposed disagreeableness.

Atticus offers several reasons to Scout for why he is defending a negro, which all come back to his moral sensibilities and unwavering integrity—despite the fact that he knows he will lose the case because of his community's racial prejudices. Aunt May, on the other hand, appears motivated not by moral concerns but rather by excessive pride and blatant racism.

Close Reading Pairing: Virginia Durr and Scout | Student Handout

Questions created by David Pook.

Note: We have chosen to include certain racial epithets in this reading in order to honestly communicate the bigoted language of the time.

Paired Texts:

"The Birthday Party" by Virginia Durr (Handout 3.4)

To Kill a Mockingbird, Chapter 9

PASSAGE BEGINS: Beginning of Chapter 9

PASSAGE ENDS: "Simply because we were licked a hundred years before we started is no reason for us not to try to win," Atticus said.

Scout in Chapter 9 and Virginia Durr in her memoir excerpt "The Birthday Party" are both thrown into situations that reveal social tensions around race and prompt a recognition of and reaction to these tensions. The questions that follow explore these issues.

1. **What incident sparks Scout's questions regarding whom Atticus chooses to defend as a lawyer? What do her questions reveal about her understanding of the situation?**

2. What event does Virginia describe as "the great trauma of [her] early life"? How does this event highlight racial tensions, and what does her reaction indicate about her understanding of her family's decision?

3. In these excerpts, both Scout and Virginia are provoked by other children's racially charged words. How do Scout and Virginia's reactions differ?

4. Both not only react in different ways but react in defense of different people. Who is Scout prepared to defend and who does Virginia defend?

5. Language and word choice play a role in both Scout and Virginia's coming-of-age experiences and early understandings of the unequal racial customs in the South. How does Atticus respond to Scout's use of the word "nigger"? How does Josephine, Virginia's sister, respond to Aunt May's order that the black children must start calling her "Miss Josephine" instead of "Sis"? How does each response signal recognition of racial tensions without fully addressing them?

6. How do the reactions of the adults in each text (Atticus and Aunt May) differ in response to the racial tensions that surface? What explanation can you give for their different reactions?

Close Reading C for Chapter 12 | Teacher Guide

Questions and suggested answers created by David Pook.

PASSAGE BEGINS: "That Calpurnia had led a modest double life . . . ."

PASSAGE ENDS: "We'd be glad to have you."

1. **In Chapter 12, Scout experiences the "modest double life" Calpurnia lives by going to church with her, and this spurs her on to question Calpurnia about her "command of two languages." Summarize the reasons Calpurnia gives in response to Scout's question about why she continues to use different language with other African Americans when she knows "it's not right."**

   An accurate summary would note the different reasons Calpurnia offers for why she speaks the way she does: because she is black, because different registers of language would be out of place in certain settings, and because it would "aggravate" those individuals who "don't want to learn" to use the "language" of Blackstone's Commentaries when speaking with them.

2. **What clues are there to indicate that Calpurnia's own thinking regarding whether or not it's right to use two languages when speaking to different audiences is at odds with Jem's blanket declaration that she knows better?**

   Tellingly, Calpurnia uses the logical diction of the courtroom when listing her reasons ("in the first place . . . in the second place . . ."), indicating what language she thinks is appropriate for the particular setting she is in. She goes on to inform the children that "It's not necessary to tell all you know," perhaps hinting at the fact that even in this instance she might not be telling Jem and Scout all of her reasons. She scratches her head and says that "It's right hard to say" why she speaks the way she does, but then she revealingly places her hat carefully over her ears, signaling that what she is about to say next has been thoughtfully considered.

3. **How is Calpurnia's reply to Jem similar to the advice Atticus gave to Scout earlier regarding Miss Caroline (Chapter 3)? How does Calpurnia's response reveal her view of Scout and Jem's condemnation of speaking in two languages?**

What Calpurnia says next is a variation of Atticus's earlier advice (in Chapter 3) that you have to walk a mile in another's shoes in order to understand that person. She asks the children to imagine themselves using "colored-folks' talk at home" (a telling revision of the derogatory and ironically unrefined language whites sometimes use) and states that it would be out of place there; hence, speaking "white-folks' talk" at church and with her neighbors would make her appear prideful and vain. By attempting to engage their moral imagination in this way, Calpurnia signals that she does not in fact agree with Scout and Jem that her decision to employ two languages is wrong—it is instead the polite ("lady-like") thing to do.

Close Reading C for Chapter 12 | Student Handout

Questions created by David Pook.

PASSAGE BEGINS: "That Calpurnia had led a modest double life . . . . ."

PASSAGE ENDS: "We'd be glad to have you."

1. In Chapter 12, Scout experiences the "modest double life" Calpurnia lives by going to church with her, and this spurs her on to question Calpurnia about her "command of two languages." Summarize the reasons Calpurnia gives in response to Scout's question about why she continues to use different language with other African Americans when she knows "it's not right."

2. What clues are there to indicate that Calpurnia's own thinking regarding whether or not it's right to use two languages when speaking to different audiences is at odds with Jem's blanket declaration that she knows better?

3. How is Calpurnia's reply to Jem similar to the advice Atticus gave to Scout earlier regarding Miss Caroline (Chapter 3)? How does Calpurnia's response reveal her view of Scout and Jem's condemnation of speaking in two languages?

Close Reading D for Chapter 15 | Teacher Guide

Questions and suggested answers created by David Pook.

PASSAGE BEGINS: "All right, Mr. Finch, get 'em outa here . . . ."

PASSAGE ENDS: "Doors slammed, engines coughed, and they were gone."

1. **Create a chronicle of Scout's efforts to make a connection with Mr. Cunningham. What do these efforts reveal about her character?**

Scout's cheerful ignorance of the reasons why Mr. Cunningham is at the jail reveals her to be an innocent person who tries to do the right thing (as she understands it) regardless of the context. In this instance, she thinks that the right thing is to be polite and "talk to people about what they were interested in, not about what you were interested in."

Scout first tries to reach out to Mr. Cunningham through mention of his entailment, which she is familiar with. When that doesn't work, she changes her approach and tries to trigger in him a positive memory of her by evoking the time when he brought Scout's family hickory nuts. When that still doesn't register, rather than getting frustrated, she pivots and tries again by speaking about his son Walter, which does elicit the barest of acknowledgments from Mr. Cunningham. As a result, Scout then persists in that line of inquiry, revealing her good-natured determination to be on good terms with Mr. Cunningham—only to discover that Mr. Cunningham is not interested in talking about his child. Less resolute children would have given up long ago, but not Scout; her dogged insistence evokes astonishment and wonderment from her father, who is awed and "fascinated" by his daughter's actions to the point where his mouth hangs open in an atypically "uncouth" manner.

In a last-ditch effort to bond with the only person she recognizes in a crowd of strangers, Scout returns to the topic of Mr. Cunningham's entailment, but she gets nowhere once again and begins to feel embarrassed—only to be saved by Mr. Cunningham's kind gesture of grasping her shoulders and telling Scout that he'll tell Walter she said hello. Her lack of guile and unyielding determination to reach out to those she knows shines through in this passage.

2. **Now reread the passage a second time. What clues are revealed about Mr. Cunningham that might explain his eventual decision to leave the jail and take the rest of the men with him?**

The passage opens with Scout revealing that she's well aware of the tangled state of Mr. Cunningham's affairs; as the only lawyer in town, Atticus would be the person Mr. Cunningham would have sought out for advice. He is therefore in debt to Atticus for his services—a debt that could have only partially been met through the gesture of giving Scout's family hickory nuts, which signals his impoverished state. Scout also reveals that Cunningham's son Walter has shared the midday meal with her family in the past, revealing that the kindness Atticus has shown to the father through his encouraging advice ("not to worry . . . . You all'd ride it out together") has also been extended to his son. Ultimately the cumulative weight of recollecting these small acts of kindness by Atticus and Scout moves Mr. Cunningham to relent and disperse the crowd of vigilantes with him.

Close Reading D for Chapter 15 | Student Handout

Questions created by David Pook.

PASSAGE BEGINS: "All right, Mr. Finch, get 'em outa here . . . ."

PASSAGE ENDS: "Doors slammed, engines coughed, and they were gone."

1. Create a chronicle of Scout's efforts to make a connection with Mr. Cunningham. What do these efforts reveal about her character?

2. Now reread the passage a second time. What clues are revealed about Mr. Cunningham that might explain his eventual decision to leave the jail and take the rest of the men with him?

Close Reading **E** for Chapter 20 | Teacher Guide

Questions and suggested answers created by David Pook.

PASSAGE BEGINS: "Gentlemen," he was saying, "I shall be brief . . ."

PASSAGE ENDS: "In the name of God, do your duty."

1. **What does *detachment* mean? What clues are there to its meaning in the paragraph in which it appears? How does it convey the tone of Atticus's final speech to the jury?**

   Detachment in the context of the paragraph means that Atticus's speech is no longer formal and dry ("aridity") but rather friendly and intimate—as if the jurors were "folks on the post office corner."

2. **Atticus tells the jury that the case is not a difficult one. Why does he think that way? What words does he use to argue his point?**

   Atticus states that the case requires "no minute sifting of complicated facts" because there is not "one iota of medical evidence." His use of the terms "not one iota" and "minute" signals that the case is a simple one—as simple as "black and white"—because the jury does not have to sort through tiny ("minute") differences of fact to determine the truth. That is because there are no facts on the side of the prosecution, as Atticus conveys though his folksy assertion that there is not even a shred ("one iota") of evidence—and not just any evidence, but medical evidence, indicating that other experts agree with his assertions.

3. **If the facts are not at issue, what question does Atticus think the jury is left to decide?**

   The jury is left to decide whether or not the guilt of the defendant has been proven "beyond a reasonable doubt" based on the testimony of the witnesses.

4. **Besides the lack of evidence, what other doubts does Atticus raise about the case against Tom Robinson?**

The state's entire case rests on "the testimony of two witnesses" whose credibility has been severely damaged by the cross-examination Atticus conducted earlier.

Atticus declares that Tom Robinson is not guilty, but that someone else is. Summarize in your own words Atticus's explanation of what drove Mayella to accuse Tom Robinson of a crime he did not commit.

Atticus offers a powerful and searing examination of Mayella's motives, focusing on her guilty feelings for breaking "a rigid and time-honored code of our society"—lusting after a black man. She was driven to do so out of ignorance and indigent circumstances, but her desires drove her to act against the rules of her society. As a result of her guilt, she compounded her error of judgment by acting as a child does when caught doing something wrong—by refocusing her remorseful feelings on someone else and creating a scapegoat (not unlike the actions of Scout in Chapter 3 when she changed tactics in trying to get out of going to school by focusing her attention on Burris Ewell).

5. **Does Atticus approve of the actions of Mayella's father after seeing her kiss Tom Robinson?**

Atticus appears to signal his approval by stating that "any God-fearing, persevering, respectable white man" would have done exactly what Mr. Ewell did in turning in Tom Robinson. But in making that statement, he alludes to another fact that came up at trial that casts doubt on the testimony and therefore on the character of Mr. Ewell—that he likely signed the warrant with his left hand (whereas Tom took his oath with his right hand), and that Mayella was likely beaten by someone who was left-handed, not right-handed.

6. **What does the word cynical mean in the context of this passage? What is Atticus's response to what he sees as a cynical ploy by the Ewells?**

Atticus accuses the Ewells of acting cynically—of contemptuously assuming that the jurors will not do their duty to discover the truth and will merely accept the Ewells' testimony unquestioningly, agreeing with them that all black men are liars, untrustworthy, and immoral. Atticus calls such an assumption "evil" and "a lie" and calls on the jurors to recognize the truth: that some humans, regardless of their race, are rightly described as liars, untrustworthy, and immoral, but that this is not true of all black men—that indeed everyone in the courtroom has at some point in their life told a lie, lusted after a woman they have seen, and even committed immoral acts. In Atticus's view, to claim, as the Ewells have done, that white people (by virtue solely of their skin color) always tell the truth and black men (again, solely because of their skin color) do not is cynical.

7. **Does Atticus believe that all men are created equal?**

Atticus is keen to point out to his audience that he does not believe in equality in the way that some use that term, particularly in the context of public education, where the "stupid and idle" are promoted with the "industrious." He freely acknowledges that "some people are born gifted beyond the normal scope of most men," and that makes them unequal to others. But—and teachers should point out Atticus's use of that transitional word—he does believe in equality before the law and equality in the courtroom, regardless of whether you are intelligent or unwise, wealthy or poor, white or black.

8. **What assurances does Atticus give that all men will be treated equally before the law? How do his views reflect his earlier discussion with Scout and Jem about why he even took the case in the first place?**

Atticus can give no such assurances—indeed, as indicated earlier in Chapter 9, Atticus believes that he will lose the case even though there is a wealth of evidence not just of a reasonable doubt as to Tom Robinson's guilt but also of his complete innocence of all the charges brought against him. Atticus is "no idealist" with respect to the "integrity" of the jury system—to him it is a "living, working reality" that manifests itself in the actions of each man sitting before him on the jury. This links closely to his prior discussion of integrity in Chapter 9, where he insists that he was compelled to act and take the case to preserve his integrity. In explaining that he could not stand on the sidelines and retain his moral authority, Atticus foreshadowed his argument here to the jurors that they had to "do your duty" to "review without passion" the evidence that they have heard and render the just decision: to "restore his defendant to his family."

Close Reading E for Chapter 20 | Student Handout

Questions created by David Pook.

PASSAGE BEGINS: "Gentlemen," he was saying, "I shall be brief . . ."

PASSAGE ENDS: "In the name of God, do your duty."

1. What does *detachment* mean? What clues are there to its meaning in the paragraph in which it appears? How does it convey the tone of Atticus's final speech to the jury?

2. Atticus tells the jury that the case is not a difficult one. Why does he think that way? What words does he use to argue his point?

3. If the facts are not at issue, what question does Atticus think the jury is left to decide?

4. Besides the lack of evidence, what other doubts does Atticus raise about the case against Tom Robinson?

5. Does Atticus approve of the actions of Mayella's father after seeing her kiss Tom Robinson?

6. What does the word *cynical* mean in the context of this passage? What is Atticus's response to what he sees as a cynical ploy by the Ewells?

7. Does Atticus believe that all men are created equal?

8. What assurances does Atticus give that all men will be treated equally before the law? How do his views reflect his earlier discussion with Scout and Jem about why he even took the case in the first place?

Close Reading Pairing: Scottsboro and the Tom Robinson Trial | Teacher Guide

Questions and suggested answers created by David Pook.

Note: We recommend that teachers review the page "Discussing Sensitive Topics in the Classroom" before using this document.

Paired Texts:

"The Scottsboro Affair" (Handout 5.4)

To Kill a Mockingbird, testimonies of Heck Tate, Bob Ewell, and Mayella Ewell from Chapters 17 and 18

1. **How is Mr. Gilmer's questioning of the witnesses different from Atticus's questioning? What does it reveal about both men?**

   Mr. Gilmer's questions are direct and straight to the point, and he rarely asks a follow-up question. Atticus's questions are smaller and "bite sized," revealing them to be piecemeal but ultimately exhaustively thorough.

2. **How do Mr. Tate and Mr. Ewell respond to Atticus's questioning about whether or not they thought to call a doctor on the night of the incident? How does their course of action differ from what happened in the real-life example in the Scottsboro Affair text?**

   Mr. Tate and Mr. Ewell both tell Atticus that a doctor was not called because they didn't even think to call a doctor to examine Mayella's injuries after the incident; they took her at her word. In the Scottsboro case, on the other hand, a doctor was called by the sheriff to examine the women, and he later provided evidence that called into question the rape accusations—evidence similar to the kind that in the novel Atticus himself (and not a doctor) elicits through his careful questions.

3. **Based on the information in the Scottsboro Affair text, what could one infer might have happened to Tom Robinson if he had been accused of the crime from *To Kill a Mockingbird* in the 1880s or 1890s?**

The connecting text explains that in the 1880s and 1890s, it was common for black men who were accused of raping white women to be lynched. Given that Tom Robinson faced the same accusation, one could expect that in previous decades he might have been executed without a trial. (Tellingly, earlier, in Chapter 15, Atticus confronted an angry mob determined to do exactly that.)

4. **Given the information on the Scottsboro Affair and Mayella Ewell's testimony from the novel, why might one believe that Tom Robinson had little chance of being acquitted?**

The information within the Scottsboro Affair text explains that in the South, racial norms did not allow jurors to believe the word of a black man over a white woman, and therefore Mayella's testimony could have been enough to convict Tom Robinson of rape regardless of his testimony and other evidence found and presented at his trial.

5. **How did the tone of Mayella Ewell's testimony differ from that of Victoria Price (one of the alleged victims in the Scottsboro Affair text)?**

In the excerpt from *To Kill a Mockingbird*, Mayella is clearly scared to testify, given her sobbing before Atticus when it is his turn to question her, as well as her wringing of her handkerchief. Victoria Price, however, is reported to have treated her testimony as if she was on stage rather than in a courtroom—a witness explained that she spoke "with such gusto, snap and wise-cracks, that the courtroom was often in a roar of laughter."

6. **After reading the two selections, explain how Atticus Finch's defense of Tom Robinson differed from the kind of counsel that the Scottsboro defendants received.**

The excerpt from *To Kill a Mockingbird* shows how Atticus asked questions of the witnesses that ultimately formed a persuasive case in defense of Tom Robinson—for example, by asking why neither the sheriff nor Mr. Ewell called a doctor. On the other hand, the connected text explains how the Scottsboro defendants were appointed lawyers who were described as "alcoholic" or an "extremely unreliable, senile individual" rather than attorneys who were competent and willing to defend them.

7. **What differences can you detect in the way both judges acted?**

Judge Taylor allowed Atticus to proceed with his questions and even made offhand remarks that, with an impartial jury, would have helped the defense (e.g., his observation that Mr. Ewell is left-handed). He also tried to maintain a civil courtroom and chastised observers who audibly reacted to testimony. Tellingly, the judge in the Scottsboro Affair—Judge Hawkins—blocked certain lines of questioning and failed to declare a mistrial when Patterson's jury heard the crowd's lengthy and quite vociferous reaction to the Norris and Weems verdict announcement. Judge Hawkins expedited the trials, whereas Judge Taylor had earlier given Atticus a continuance. That said, Judge Hawkins did try to assign the defendants competent local counsel but was unsuccessful; interestingly, the novel calls into question the ultimate effectiveness of that approach, as illustrated in the outcome of Tom Robinson's defense by Atticus.

Close Reading Pairing: Scottsboro and the Tom Robinson Trial |

Student Handout

Questions created by David Pook.

Paired Texts:

"The Scottsboro Affair" (Handout 5.4)

To Kill a Mockingbird, testimonies of Heck Tate, Bob Ewell, and Mayella Ewell from Chapters 17 and 18

1. How is Mr. Gilmer's questioning of the witnesses different from Atticus's questioning? What does it reveal about both men?

2. How do Mr. Tate and Mr. Ewell respond to Atticus's questioning about whether or not they thought to call a doctor on the night of the incident? How does their course of action differ from what happened in the real-life example in the Scottsboro Affair text?

3. Based on the information in the Scottsboro Affair text, what could one infer might have happened to Tom Robinson if he had been accused of the crime from *To Kill a Mockingbird* in the 1880s or 1890s?

4. Given the information on the Scottsboro Affair and Mayella Ewell's testimony from the novel, why might one believe that Tom Robinson had little chance of being acquitted?

5. How did the tone of Mayella Ewell's testimony differ from that of Victoria Price (one of the alleged victims in the Scottsboro Affair text)?

6. After reading the two selections, explain how Atticus Finch's defense of Tom Robinson differed from the kind of counsel that the Scottsboro defendants received.

7. What differences can you detect in the way both judges acted?

Close Reading F for Chapter 26 | Teacher Guide

Questions and suggested answers created by David Pook.

PASSAGE BEGINS: "Cecil Jacobs knew what one was, though . . . ."

PASSAGE ENDS: "Time for arithmetic, children."

1. **In Chapter 26, Miss Gates defends America through an analysis of the meaning of democracy. What clues are there in the text that her analysis may be faulty? More generally, how does the story of Tom Robinson challenge her claim that America is fully democratic?**

This passage offers an excellent forum for summing up some of the themes regarding prejudice and discrimination in the novel and viewing their application in several different contexts. After a student offers a clunky presentation on current events in Nazi Germany, Scout offers a definition of democracy she learned from Atticus: "Equal rights for all, special privileges for none." Miss Gates approvingly declares that America is a democracy because, unlike in Nazi Germany, "over here we don't believe in persecuting anybody"—because persecution stems from people who are prejudiced, and Americans are not prejudiced. She herself declares that she is not prejudiced against the Jews and is mystified as to why the Nazis are, and she finally offers up the possible explanation that their hatred of the Jews may be due to the fact that Jews are religious, and the Nazis are trying to do away with religion. *Note: Miss Gates is a person of her time, and her perspective does not square with contemporary understanding of Nazi antisemitism. She fails to acknowledge the role religious prejudice played in creating a climate for antisemitism, and she does not mention (or she is not aware of) the support the Nazis received from certain religious groups within Germany.*

Yet despite America most definitely not being a "dictatorship," there are clues in the passage that point to problems with Miss Gates's analysis that all is well in America. The first crops up even before she articulates her defense of the Jews. In the beginning of the scene she hovers over a struggling student who is presenting his "current event" on the persecution of the Jews in Germany, correcting every grammatical error he makes but passing over the chance to discuss the horrific actions he is describing. It is only through the inquisitiveness of another student that she seizes the opportunity to "make education dynamic" and launches into her disquisition on democracy. Even then, however, she misses an opportunity to correct a student who vaguely recalls that Jews have been identified as money changers (a traditional antisemitic stereotype) when the student concludes, "but that ain't no cause to persecute 'em," because in the end analysis, Jews are "white."

Miss Gates's moral blindness to the students' antisemitic prejudices reflects the culture's deeper blindness to the fact that—as the story of Tom Robinson so powerfully demonstrates—there is prejudice and therefore persecution in America, and that prejudice distorts democracy.

Close Reading F for Chapter 26 | Student Handout

Questions created by David Pook.

PASSAGE BEGINS: "Cecil Jacobs knew what one one was, though . . . ."

PASSAGE ENDS: "Time for arithmetic, children."

1. In Chapter 26, Miss Gates defends America through an analysis of the meaning of democracy. What clues are there in the text that her analysis may be faulty? More generally, how does the story of Tom Robinson challenge her claim that America is fully democratic?

Credits

Grateful acknowledgment is made for permission to reproduce the following: